# FAITH FINDING A VOICE

# FAITH FINDING A VOICE

*Cardinal Vincent Nichols*

Archbishop of Westminster

BLOOMSBURY CONTINUUM
LONDON • NEW YORK • OXFORD • NEW DELHI • SYDNEY

BLOOMSBURY CONTINUUM
Bloomsbury Publishing Plc
50 Bedford Square, London, WC1B 3DP, UK

BLOOMSBURY, BLOOMSBURY CONTINUUM and the Diana logo are
trademarks of Bloomsbury Publishing Plc

First published in Great Britain 2018

Copyright © Vincent Nichols, 2018

Vincent Nichols has asserted his right under the Copyright,
Designs and Patents Act, 1988, to be identified as Author of this work.

All rights reserved. No part of this publication may be reproduced or transmitted
in any form or by any means, electronic or mechanical, including photocopying,
recording, or any information storage or retrieval system, without prior permission
in writing from the publishers.

Bloomsbury Publishing Plc does not have any control over, or responsibility for, any
third-party websites referred to or in this book. All internet addresses given in this
book were correct at the time of going to press. The author and publisher regret any
inconvenience caused if addresses have changed or sites have ceased to exist, but can
accept no responsibility for any such changes.

A catalogue record for this book is available from the British Library.

Library of Congress Cataloguing-in-Publication data has been applied for.

ISBN: HB: 978-1-4729-5042-0; TPB: 978-1-4729-5044-4; EPDF: 978-1-4729-5045-1;
EPUB: 978-1-4729-5046-8

2 4 6 8 10 9 7 5 3 1

Typeset by Newgen KnowledgeWorks Pvt. Ltd., Chennai, India
Printed and bound in Great Britain by CPI Group (UK) Ltd, Croydon CR0 4YY

To find out more about our authors and books visit www.bloomsbury.com
and sign up for our newsletters.

To my brothers, Peter and John,
who in very different ways lived life to the full
with faithfulness and joy

# Contents

List of Illustrations — x

Introduction — 1

## PART ONE GOD REVEALED

1 The Lure of God — 13

2 The Mystery of Christ — 27
   *The Nativity with Saints* Altarpiece, by
     Pietro Orioli — 30
   The Nativity of Christ — 30
   The Passion of Christ — 36
   The Resurrection of Christ — 46
     The Altarpiece: A Lay Perspective –
     Elaine Parsons — 53
     The Altarpiece: A Priest's Perspective –
     Fr Richard Parsons — 59
     Ite, Missa Est — 65

3 The Holy Spirit: Community and Creation — 73
   Community — 76
   Creation — 80

## CONTENTS

### PART TWO  EDUCATION FOR LIFE

4  Faith in Education ... 91

5  Faith Finding a Voice: Looking to Bede ... 109

6  The Voice of Faith in Schools and Universities: Looking to Newman ... 131

### PART THREE  RELIGIOUS DIALOGUE AND THE HOPE FOR HUMANITY

7  The Journey to God and Faith Today ... 153
   Sacredness and Our Religious Heritage ... 154
   Catholicism and Inter-Religious Dialogue ... 157
   Religious Faith and Public Policy ... 165
   Our Spiritual Quest ... 169

8  Inter-Religious Dialogue: People and Places ... 183
   Singers Hill Synagogue, Birmingham ... 184
   Yad Vashem Memorial, Jerusalem ... 190
   Gaza: The Catholic Community as a Source of Hope ... 193

9  Speaking in the Name of the Church and Manifesting *Caritas* ... 199

10  The Hope for Humanity ... 213

### PART FOUR  MINISTRY: TREASURE IN EARTHENWARE VESSELS

11  The Papacy ... 231
    Pope St John Paul II ... 231
    Pope Benedict XVI ... 235
    Pope Francis ... 240

## CONTENTS

| | | |
|---|---|---|
| 12 | The Episcopate | 251 |
| 13 | The Presbyterate | 259 |
| 14 | The Diaconate | 267 |
| 15 | The Consecrated Life | 277 |
| 16 | The People of God | 287 |

| | |
|---|---|
| *References and Abbreviations* | 297 |
| *Acknowledgements* | 305 |
| *Further Reading* | 307 |
| *Index of Biblical References* | 311 |
| *Index of Proper Names and Subjects* | 320 |

*List of Illustrations*

1. The Church of the Holy Sepulchre, Jerusalem: Stone of Unction. Pilgrims are lured by God to pray with loving devotion at the place where Jesus was anointed and clothed for burial. (© Cardinal Vincent Nichols)

2. In Rome with Pope Francis and Bishop Peter Doyle, here representing the collegiality of the episcopal office symbolising the unity and the faith of the Church. (© Marcin Mazur)

3. The wilderness of Judaea where the devil tempted Jesus to deny his divine vocation. Through faithfulness to his heavenly Father, Jesus emerged victorious and opened the path to eternal salvation for us. (© Cardinal Vincent Nichols)

4. We are called by God to create a desert in the heart so that in our lives we may concentrate solely on him.

5. Map illustrating the strategic position of Gaza within the Middle East. I pray daily for peace and stability within this region, especially for

## LIST OF ILLUSTRATIONS

the wellbeing of every member of the community. (From *Gaza: A History* by Jean-Pierre Filiu [London: Hurst, 2014]. Cartography by Sebastian Ballard. Reproduced by kind permission of the publishers.)

6. *The Nativity with Saints Altarpiece*, Pietro Orioli, reveals the panorama of the history of God's salvation through his Beloved Son, Jesus Christ our Lord. The voice of the everlasting Gospel is proclaimed here by the messages which Orioli is giving through the beauty and solemnity of his artistry. (© The National Gallery, London)

# Introduction

Theophany is not a word in everyday use. Yet it refers to an experience that is not at all uncommon. Theophany means a manifestation of God. The word is normally used to indicate a direct and awesome manifestation of the divine, but it can also refer to those many different ways in which our attention is drawn, often compellingly, to the horizon beyond our normal attention, to the horizon of the infinite: the horizon that opens on to God's presence in our lives.

This book is an exploration of that dimension of our lives: our openness to the presence of God. It is also an exploration of how that sense of God's presence finds a voice both in our history and in our lives. It is, not surprisingly, an exploration arising from and shaped by my Christian faith and the definitive theophany given to us in the person of Jesus Christ. I hope it also carries clear signs of much friendship and dialogue with members of the other great world faiths, for that too is very much part of my journey.

At the heart of the Christian faith is the relationship that a person has with Jesus Christ. In many ways, that relationship is summed up in a single phrase: missionary disciple. This is what we seek to be: disciples, or companions of Jesus, treasuring the joy that he brings into our lives; and missionary, sharing in the task he receives from his heavenly Father, the reason for his coming into our history in the incarnation.

This faith entails believing that Jesus Christ offers salvation for humanity through his incarnation, ministry, suffering, resurrection and glorification. St Paul understood the totality of Christ's mission in terms of 'the first fruits' (1 Cor 15.23). By this proclamation he means the offering to all people of the divine harvest of love, a harvest gained by Christ's offering of himself, which every person is able to enjoy. Pope Francis speaks of this harvest at the beginning of his Apostolic Exhortation *Evangelii Gaudium: The Joy of the Gospel*, when he writes of our being liberated from 'sin, sorrow, inner emptiness and loneliness' (*EG*, 1). I should like to think that *Faith Finding a Voice* is a way of understanding and reflecting upon this document.

There is much within the contemporary world which is preventing us from receiving the fullness of this divine harvest. We can so easily be preoccupied with excessive self-interest, needless gratification and pleasure. This attitude is a type of 'consumerism' which ensures that 'there is no longer room for others, no place for the poor' (*EG*, 2). Not only may our personal lives be marked in this way, but so too may our community and civic lives, leaving many people with a strong sense that they are outside the circle of benefit and security, and unable to find a point of entry. The challenge facing the Christian is that of bringing the light of Christ: a light throws into sharp relief the truths of our human nature, to bear on the darkest places in our hearts and in our world. This light, and the joys it brings, are found in the Gospel of Jesus Christ, in whom all darkness is destroyed (Col 1.11–14).

Fundamental to this task is our discipleship. By our attentive dedication to the teaching and activity of Jesus as the bringer of God's reign (Mk 1.14–15), we grow to understand the positive response required from us in terms of *metanoia*, radical change and renewed belief in the saving power of the Gospel (Mk 1.15). In return we are able to receive from God the challenges, gifts and blessings which the dawning of his reign offers (e.g., Mt 5.3). The Gospel is concerned both now and in the future with the effects of God's kingdom, which 'is about loving God who reigns in our world' (*EG*, 180). As his disciples we seek his reign above all else (Mt 6.33). The extent to which we do so will be the extent to which society will be able to provide a suitable environment where 'universal fraternity, justice, peace and dignity' (*EG*, 180) will flourish.

As missionary disciples we also have the task of finding the 'voice' that will communicate this faith. In one sense, this is the voice of direct proclamation (Rom 10.17–18), the preaching of the message of the Gospel as found in the homily, lecture, address or catechetical instruction. Such means of presenting Catholic life and teaching always seek to share and deepen our understanding of the message and truth of our faith. They are also given in order that we might create dialogue and partnership with those around us, so that the common good of society might be enhanced and renewed. The contemporary world, of course, is full of diverse voices. There are voices which offer immediate satisfaction of needs and desires; those which promote a vision of the person as a self-sufficient individual, striving always for autonomy and 'freedom'; those caring for the distant consequences of a course of action and offering no substantial moral framework; those extolling violence as a virtue; those extolling apathy as the solution for human fulfilment. The task of the missionary disciple is to understand how to enable the voice of Christ to be heard in this context by surfacing the deeper and lasting questions which echo in our hearts. Through our ministry we must always proclaim the voice of God and his saving power, which is given to humanity through the redeeming work of Christ.

We might ask, however, how this authentic voice is to be acquired. Here, I suggest that we return to the voice of the Father spoken to the Son, Jesus, at his Baptism (Mk 1.11; Mt 3.17; Lk 3.22; see also Jn 12.28) and Transfiguration (Mk 9.7; Mt 17.5; Lk 9.35): 'You are my Son, the Beloved; with you I am well pleased' (Mk 1.11 [NRSV]). The voice of the Father at the Baptism of Jesus is the voice of affirmation. It declares the unique royal (Ps 2.7) and prophetic role (Is 42.1) of the Son, who identifies wholly with humanity and, as a result of his absolute fidelity to his vocation, also offers salvation to the world, exchanging sin and darkness for grace and light. The voice of Jesus the Good Shepherd is all-embracing. It is addressed to the believing community (Jn 10.4); at the same time he is calling individuals 'by name' (Jn 10.3), given our status as unique and precious sons and daughters of God; even the dead hear the voice of the Son in order that they may be granted eternal life by the Father (Jn 5.25–6). At every celebration of Baptism this divine voice is repeated, bringing sinful humanity into the divine life of God, through which we are affirmed and renewed by the power of the Holy Spirit. For us, then, to respond positively to the voice of God in the ways I suggest is to reaffirm our Baptismal calling through Jesus as his royal, prophetic and priestly sons and daughters.

The divine voice at the Transfiguration is also important because it points to the future, to the hope of heavenly glory offered by Jesus at his resurrection (e.g., Lk 24.25–6) and ascension (Acts 1.8). Here, the Risen Lord commands his disciples to witness to his glory in the power of the Holy Spirit 'to the ends of the earth' (Acts 1.8); in this context we shall be asking about the purpose of mission and how this purpose is advanced in relation to the suggestions contained in this book. Despite the evil and suffering in the world, we are offering here the divine voice of hope, the opportunity to follow the way of God in order that humanity might return to the things of God. At the same time we must also be aware that the voice of God is liable to be drowned by the use of too many words spoken too loudly. The voice of God came to Elijah, for example, not in wind, earthquake or fire but in 'a still small voice' (1 Kings 19.12). It is often in silent prayer, through meditation, that we hear God's voice, showing how, through the Holy Spirit, we are able to exercise the prophetic ministry in our age, which we know is needed in order that the world might radiate justice, peace, compassion and kindness.

There are numerous ways in which we are able to hear God's voice, especially in the time we give to both prayer and *caritas*. Here we are able to give voice to our faith. Indeed, our listening to God's voice and our giving voice in word and deed in the ways in which we are touched deeply are intertwined closely. I have, therefore, attempted to present the material in such a way that the reader is able to be challenged by two main questions. First, as we receive and ponder the traditional material – Scripture, Church teaching, the Fathers and teachers of the faith (e.g., Bede) – what understanding and courses of action in contemporary life are we to consider? Second, how are we to analyse, interpret and understand more deeply what we are receiving in order that we might discover new areas for thought and action? St Catherine of Siena (*c.*1347–80) uses the metaphor of the ocean in the prayer 'Eternal Trinity, you are like a deep sea, in which the more I seek, the more I find; and the more I find, the more I seek you.'[1] This is exactly my purpose for the rationale and objectives of this book: that together, through dialogue and partnerships, we might create a deeper faith with the hope that a more informed and compassionate Church and society will emerge. We are asked to be both creative and imaginative in order that faith may find in our time its true voice: the voice of love.

*Faith Finding a Voice* has four main parts. Part I is entitled 'God Revealed' and deals with personal theological reflections on the revelation of God through the persons of the Blessed Trinity. In the first chapter I have used the idea of 'the lure of God', by which I believe that, because God has planted his divine image in each of us (Gen 1.26), we are, therefore, all capable of loving him and loving each other. We are all seekers, not necessarily according to our own will, but because, even if we fail to recognize the fact, God is working within us for the establishment of virtue (1 Tim 4.7–8) in order that we might become like him. Being drawn into a relationship with the Trinitarian God has repercussions:

how do we live in solidarity with all God's creation in the world? The second chapter deals with the mystery of Jesus Christ. At the heart of this chapter is a reader-response approach to *The Nativity with Saints* altarpiece, by Pietro Orioli. Here the reader is invited to enter into a sustained reflection on the birth, life, passion and resurrection of Christ, from which all else flows both in terms of salvation and hope. The third chapter concerns the work of the Holy Spirit, the continuation of the divine wisdom in the world. I have divided this presentation into two parts: the work of the Spirit in empowering mission and consolidating community, and the presence of the Spirit in the preservation of creation. Both themes have been addressed by Pope Francis: 'I wrote to all members of the Church [in *Evangelii Gaudium*] with the aim of encouraging ongoing missionary renewal [...] I would like to enter into dialogue with all people about our common home' (*LS*, 3). The fulfilment of these vital aims is made possible through the work of the Holy Spirit.

Part II is entitled 'Education for Life' and affirms my belief in lifelong learning in that, in all areas of our human pilgrimage, we are confronted and challenged by new ideas, new ways for entering into the continuing dynamic of spirituality and of being renewed in the practice of virtue. In both schools and universities I am aware of the importance of theological and religious literacy to be exercised in dialogue with all members of a diverse global society. I offer a series of educational maxims in order that we might all be open to the creation of a more compassionate society and to the increasing acknowledgement of the spiritual dimension within us for human growth and educational awareness.

I affirm the importance of faith schools within the totality of the educational provision, and one that offers parents a choice for their children. Catholic schools form a vital element within this framework, providing Catholic teaching, worship, spirituality and the Catholic way of life. In order to discuss these elements within the modern context I have engaged with a range of thinkers from the Venerable Bede to the Blessed John Henry Newman.

Part III is entitled 'Religious Dialogue and the Hope for Humanity' and is placed within the framework of St Paul's exposition in Romans 8. My intention is to open for discussion areas of thought in order that we may affirm our journey to God and faith today within the global context. Under God's care we are able to be the builders of a better world through our efforts to mobilize great causes in the service of humanity. In this work the Catholic Church demonstrates charity towards other faith traditions. I express solidarity with those powerful voices of faith in God who live amid the darkest depths of intolerance and oppression. I also relate my personal experiences and I pray that hope for humanity will be nourished under God's eternal providence in, for example, Jerusalem and Gaza.

Part IV is entitled 'Ministry: Treasure in Earthenware Vessels' and forms an interpretation of how St Paul's idea of the ministry is to be understood and practised in terms of being a partner with Christ in the work of the Gospel. Paul is clear that as slaves of Jesus we proclaim not ourselves 'but Jesus Christ as Lord' (2 Cor 4.5), his glory, the one 'who is the likeness of God' (2 Cor 4.4). We know that this God-given likeness (Gen 1.26, 5.1) has been disfigured within us through sin.

INTRODUCTION

Origen expressed this truth when he said that 'the son of God is the painter of this [divine] image' within us, which 'can be obscured by negligence; [but] cannot be destroyed by malice.'[2] Here, then, we see the reason why we are able to preach and live the priceless treasure of the Gospel of Christ: through our human 'earthenware vessels' which God is using for the advancement of his power and love. I maintain that God's people possess a diversity of gifts and talents to spread the message of divine love, hope and mercy to the world (1 Cor 12.4–13; Eph 4.4–6, 11–13; *EG*, 114), yet from this community God chooses priests and deacons, bishops and popes: men and women of the Consecrated Life who are called to guide and inspire but, above all, to live and act in conformity to the life and ministry of Jesus. I understand the ministry as a vast, interrelated, integrated whole, the task of which is to communicate Jesus Christ with joy (*EG*, 30).

During a recent break I read the novel *Stoner*, by John Williams. One scene, in particular, inspired and challenged me. William Stoner is retiring from his post as an assistant professor in the department of English at the University of Missouri. He has endured many years of academic isolation and has now entered his final illness, which renders him barely able to sustain attention to all the somewhat hollow words being spoken at the dinner held in his honour. When asked to speak, he struggles to find his voice; he struggles to formulate his thoughts. Finally, he gives voice to the most profound truth of his life, the conviction that has carried him through every obstacle, hostility and darkness. Thus, he sums up his whole life, his entire endeavour, with these words: 'I have taught at this University for nearly forty years. I do not know what I would have done if I had not been a teacher [...] I want to thank you all for letting me teach.'³ It is in this spirit that I wish to thank God for letting me be his priest and teach the faith in his name. *Faith Finding a Voice* is offered to the reader in this spirit, and my prayer is that the divine voice may be heard in the mind and the heart of humanity so that we may all respond to this voice with a more fervent love for each other but, above all, for God who is our creator, redeemer, consoler and shepherd (Ps 23 [Vg 22].1).

## Notes

1. St Catherine of Siena, *The Dialogue on Divine Revelation*, Chapter 167, *DO*, II, 124★.
2. Origen, *Genesis Homily XIII*. Heine, Ronald E. (trans.) (1981), *Origen, Homilies on Genesis and Exodus*. Washington, DC, The Catholic University of America Press, p. 193.
3. Williams, John (2012), *Stoner*. London, Vintage Books (first published in Great Britain, 1973), p. 276.

# PART ONE

## *God Revealed*

Through the concept of 'God Revealed' I am attempting to illustrate how God encourages us to enter more deeply into his revelation and life. I believe that we can only understand the purpose of the journey of faith if we have first appreciated the ground for faith: God himself. Even at a subconscious level the divine is moving within the human heart, and this pathway demands from us a loving response, so that God's glory might be manifested in the world. The basis for this affirmation is the statement found in the first creation story recorded in the book of Genesis that God created the world and humanity in his own 'image' and after his 'likeness' (Gen 1.26; 5.1–2). The prerequisite for religious faith is our empathic response to God's invitation. This approach could be called 'proto-mission' as it enables the seed of God's word to be sown in our lives (Ps 33 [Vg 32].4) and prepares us for a deeper commitment to our faith.

For Christianity the revelation of God is Trinitarian: one God, three persons: Father, Son and Holy Spirit. This truth 'is the central mystery of

Christian faith and life' (*CCC*, 234) and the way in which God's saving actions towards humanity might be entered. When we begin the day in the name of the Triune God, this action also ensures that our Baptismal promises are being renewed (*CCC*, 233).

Baptism is also 'the gateway to life' (*CCC*, 1213) in the Holy Spirit. This Spirit bestows the gifts of wisdom and the knowledge of God (*CCC*, 1831). The Spirit offers constant consolation and renewal of life and faith: each new day sees the return of the Pentecostal Spirit (Acts 2.1–4).

In the sections that follow I shall be attempting to explore the mystery of this Trinitarian understanding of God's revelation and exposing ways in which we are able to respond lovingly to this gift of life and hope.

I believe that we should reflect upon the lives of the saints and also of holy men and women through the ages. They are both a constant source of encouragement and inspiration to me in my ministry, and through them 'proto-mission' may be discerned. Such mission enables us to move towards a greater understanding of the being and activity of the Trinitarian God.

# I
## *The Lure of God*

*There's him* [Lord Marchmain] *gone and Sebastian gone and Julia gone. But God won't let them go for long, you know. I wonder if you remember the story mummy read us the evening Sebastian first got drunk – I mean the bad evening. 'Father Brown' said something like 'I caught him' (the thief) 'with an unseen hook and an invisible line which is long enough to let him wander to the ends of the world and still to bring him back with a twitch upon the thread.'*

EVELYN WAUGH, *Brideshead Revisited*,
BOOK TWO, CHAPTER 3

Many years ago, as a young lad, I was on holiday in southern Ireland. A local boy of my age took my brothers and me mackerel fishing. I had never done this before. We rowed out into the bay – in fact, we went too far and had some difficult moments on our return journey – he prepared the lines and over they went into the sea. Almost immediately there were characteristic pulls on the lines, as the array of hooks caught the mackerel. We hauled them in, six or seven at a time, and soon had enough for a healthy supper for everyone in the hotel. At the end of each line, on each of the many hooks, was a spinner – a rotating, highly coloured piece of metal with sharp hooks attached. The mackerel could not resist the flash of light reflecting off the spinners and, once we hit a shoal, they were caught quickly.

This image came back to me as I was thinking about the title of this chapter – *The Lure of God* – for I should like to touch on some ways in which God can reel us in, if we are prepared to allow him. This is an address about our spiritual striving in how we seek God, to feel the pull of God, to sense our desire for God and about how to turn all these ideas into action.

I feel, therefore, very diffident about talking of these things, of even discussing the lure of God, because, in regard to myself, I have little to say. Indeed, I have to search hard for encouragement to continue and for guidance as to why I should even attempt such an exercise. I find encouragement, however, in the words of St Francis of Assisi. We are told that, as he was dying, St Francis asked his brethren to take him from his hard bed and place him on the floor. There, lying on the earth, he looked round at them and said: 'I have done *what is mine; may Christ teach you what is yours!*'[1] May Christ teach us what we are to do as he only can truly lead us, so these words of St Francis are heartening for me and enable me to continue with this address. It is in the Franciscan context that you must understand everything I say. So far in my ministry I have made little progress in seeking God. There is a second, more contemporary, occurrence, however, that offers me reassurance. It is to be found in Fr Cyprian Smith's publication *The Way of Paradox*.[2] This book is a wonderful exploration of the thought and teaching of Meister Eckhart, the fourteenth-century

German mystic. I read it quite recently, and it rang bells in my mind and heart. Here, I thought, is an expression of my poor striving. The strange thing is that the book had been sitting untouched on my shelf (travelling with me!) from 1987, when I was given it by Cardinal Hume.[3] It was only this year that I picked it up; and it was the right time to do so!

So where do I begin?

Reading this text revealed that there is clarity of purpose within our spiritual lives. This clarity may be expressed in this way: what we seek is that Christ be born in us, day by day, so that he can do his work through us. That's all. I like the simplicity of this message. Eckhart was fully aware of the power of this idea. Utilizing St Augustine, who asks, 'What does it avail me that this birth [the birth of Christ, the Son of God, in eternity] is always happening if it does not happen in me?', Eckhart argues that 'We shall therefore speak of this birth, of how it may take place in us and be consummated in the virtuous soul.'[4] Here in its simple form is our hope: that our union with the Lord is such that his birth takes place within us and that, somehow, we give him our actions, our flesh, in order that his saving presence may continue in our world through us. Mary, after all, is the first of the disciples, and what she does is what we also may endeavour to do in our lives. Or rather, with her, we may strive to say, 'Let it be to me according to your word' (Lk 1.38). Like Mary, we should open ourselves to receive the power and grace of God, who makes himself known to us by revelation. In return, by seeking to act upon his will, we strive to come into harmony with him. God then becomes a reality whom we are able to know. This is the first step of our quest.

Indeed, we can begin to trace out something of a pathway in our spiritual life: our route is to come to know something of God, to seek to know something about ourselves and thereby to see the place so uniquely filled by Christ, the one in whom God is fully incarnate. Primarily, we need to think a little about how we come to know God and what it is that opens up ourselves to God. Here I take my cues from Meister Eckhart, only because they resonate in me, only because in these assertions I find a clear statement of what I experience tentatively or strive to reach. On this pathway the aspect of God on which we have to focus is God's transcendence. This perception may sound strange at first, but it is very important. We have to concentrate on the otherness of God. We have to do so in order to free ourselves of a most fundamental error: that of idolatry. God is not of any of the finite things of creation. The otherness of God lies in the fact that we cannot identify, contain and possess God in any way. Of course, God is so close to us that he is the reality in which we live and move and have our being. Yet at the same time, in this way of paradox, we must assert and strive to experience God as totally other, totally different, totally beyond all for which we stand. To worship God as transcendence is a kind of leap into the dark. It means abandoning so much that is familiar to us. But this is the way to understand the lure of God.

There is the lure of mystery – the unfathomable, the intangible. To say 'God' is to say that at the heart of the world in which we live, the world of people and things, there lies an unfathomable mystery, something in the end which is unsayable. To assert this truth is to affirm that, in the end, there is the possibility that all creation may have some ultimate meaning, that life may, after all, be worthwhile. Then we can say that the lure of God is the call to an adventure. We cannot pin down or control a transcendent God. Any religion – whatever it may be – which in practice supposes that it has God tied down is failing to fathom this mystery. In our faith it is important to remember that, even though the sacraments, for example, offer us great security, as has been attributed to St Thomas Aquinas: 'he [God] himself is not bound by his sacraments' (*CCC*, 1257). To seek God is to embark on an adventure which is far from secure and domestic.

Then there is the lure of God as truth. By this I mean the kind of truth in which I slowly learn the truth about God and the truth about myself. I suppose this is the truth that only slowly emerges in a lifelong relationship or marriage. Only gradually are the various surface levels stripped away, until there is no pretence left. Only as that happens does something else emerge which is purer, stronger and more truthful. Yet, as in any relationship, this slow search for what is really true can lead to disaster. The process of self-revelation may be too much for some, who move off into another relationship, which may well end in the same way, either in another break-up or in an accommodation at a level of mutual comfort.

The same can happen in our search for God. Many will tell us that the very idea of God is no more than a fantasy or a projection. If we are tempted to accept that there may be some truth in this view, we run the risk of losing the impetus for our search for God and consequently end up barren. Indeed, the challenge of atheism and rationalism in stripping away projection can leave us with precisely nothing. In contrast, this pathway of seeking the transcendent God, which asks us to get beyond all the names and attributes of God, leads to the slow revelation of the hidden depth and truth of the fact and mystery of God himself. Thus we get beyond the external pointers to God in the material world, in a particular form of liturgy or music, or even a particular way of devotion. On this pathway we strive to practise a detachment from these material approaches to the ultimate mystery of God. This is not easy!

We also need to step back from our mental and emotional religious imagery, seeing that the symbols offered to us, for example, by the Church are pointers and not ultimate substance. They are given to us so that we may know which way to look. But we always need to see beyond them to search for the ultimate mystery which will be found only in a profound stillness. Indeed, this is Eckhart's way to what he calls the Silent Desert, the inner truth of God, which is beyond all names and all forms.[5]

This idea I only barely understand and sense. Perhaps we can only ever do so. It is what is meant, I think, in the phrase 'unknowing knowing'. It is found not particularly at the heart of our prayer but at the heart of our whole being, especially of our inner life, which goes on, often without our being fully aware of it, in the depth of ourselves. Only occasionally do we take a step closer to this reality. Only occasionally do we sense a clearing away of so much clutter that we can glimpse and be filled with a perception of the simple truth, love and beauty of God. If this slow dawning sense of the silent truth of God, the Silent Desert, is the first dimension of our journey, the second is similar. It is indicated to us in the phrase of the Psalm: 'Deep calls to deep' (Ps 42.7 [Vg 41.8]).

The second part of our quest runs alongside and is intermingled with the first and is, of course, the struggle to find the inner depth of ourselves. In Eckhart's terminology we seek to establish contact with the 'Ground of my Being', or the 'Ground of the Soul'. In many ways this perception is a mirror image of the first. There exists a kind of kinship between this Silent Desert which is God and this personal Ground of the Soul. Indeed, here lies the truth of the doctrine that we are made in the image and likeness of God (Gen 1.26). As there is a kinship, then there is attractiveness, an impulse of love. Yet there is much debris to clear away if we are ever to get even so much as a glimpse of this deeper reality of ourselves.

Perhaps we first have to move beyond the functions, the work and the task which often constitute our sense of self. This deeper selfhood which we seek is not always related to our actions. Yet many aspects of our culture assert the opposite: that we are what we do. Thus, we struggle to step back from activity and the esteem, the rewards, the sense of failure that it might bring, and thereby enter into a deeper sense of self. In addition to this perception, we also have to move beyond our inner world, our private world of emotions and thoughts, if we are to penetrate our true depth. This search does not consist of ignoring these powerful inner realities. They are there whether we spend time reflecting upon them or not. Rather, we have simply to try to move beyond them, find the space behind them, in order to go more deeply into the mystery of life. Perhaps the simile of the deep lake may help us here. On its surface there is activity and movement, creating ripples. Occasionally there is a deeper movement of the water, perhaps caused by a rock crashing into the lake. Yet beneath the surface there is a still, silent depth which we can only glimpse infrequently. This is the Ground of the Soul, that still, silent centre of ourselves.

Ideally, we act from this centre. When we do so we operate with a certain freedom, expressing our deepest selves and yet not aiming at any particular effect or being anxious to calculate the reaction to what we have said and done. We know that we have spoken in the truth of ourselves, and that, in itself, is its own gentle yet profound justification. In this way we retain stillness beyond all other things. This ground of self, the Ground of the Soul, is where the image of God resides in us in numerous ways. This space, this place, is where we meet God and where we find the possibility of union with him. This place is the inner sanctuary. This place of meeting, this moment of encounter, is where the mystery happens and something actual is born in us.

At this point I should like to add that one of the paradoxes of the mystery of God is that of his going out and coming in, revealed, for example, in the doctrine of the Trinity, the theology of the tri-personal God (see, for example, *CCC*, 234–7). The mystery of the Trinity is this: that God is movement, yet also stillness; that God moves out of himself without ever leaving; that God returns to himself without ever leaving the place which he has created. There is to be found a similar truth in us. We go out and express ourselves, yet never truly leave ourselves. We remain within yet also reach out. We encounter others yet always experience a certain existential aloneness. Indeed Fr Cyprian, in *The Way of Paradox*, through reflecting on the Trinity as that

'Communion of Persons', explains the true mystery of 'Person' (and, therefore, by extension each of us) as:

> To be a Person, then, means to have learned the secret and paradoxical art: to go out, yet remain within; to exert power, yet exercise restraint; to transcend, yet remain oneself; to be in movement, yet be in total repose. This is a deeper concept of personhood than is to be found in most thinkers, either ancient or modern. But it is the truest, being based on the reality of God and of the Human Self.[6]

Let me come to my third step. What opens for us the mystery of God, and what opens for us the mystery of our inner selves? Are these mysteries one and the same thing? From all eternity the Word has been spoken (Jn 1.1). It is the Christ, the Eternal Word. This is the key to the revelation of the Father's glory (Jn 1.14) and to the revelation of our true depth, our true capacity to receive the mystery of God (Jn 1.12–13). In this context it is important to understand the difference between chatter and speech. Chatter fills a silence. Speech, the speaking of the Word, enhances silence by pointing to its depth through the truth of the Word that is spoken. The Eternal Word, spoken everlastingly in the mystery of God, is the very nature of the Holy Trinity; it is the source of life itself, of every living thing in the universe and of the universe, the ordered cosmos. The Eternal Word is also the realization of the ultimate human capacity: to receive that Word and to allow it to echo within the created world.

Eckhart would have said that the difference between the human person and the created world is this: the created world is the echo of the Eternal Word. The human person, however, on the basis of our spiritual nature, is uniquely capable not only of receiving the Word but also of allowing the Word to echo in our created words and actions. Human beings only are capable of true salvation, for we alone have that inner space in which the birth of the Eternal Word can reside each day. Only in the person is there such an inner sanctuary which is capable of receiving that Word, and here in this sanctuary a space is provided in which the echo of that Word will give rise to grace-filled action.

Thus, my programme unfolds – much more in theory than in practice. Each day I am able to be with God in that Silent Desert which is God's deepest, inner nature. Each day I am to set aside not only cares but also inner emotions and desires, no matter how worthy or religious, and try to enter that Ground of my Soul. There, according to the will of God, the Eternal Word may be born again in me, and from that birth a new pathway of action in the Holy Spirit may stream. What does this vision look like? Perhaps when we stand in that place, no matter how fleetingly, we might see and act as God sees and acts. Such true vision would be like standing within the heart of God and looking out – seeing the world and each other from the heart of God. What a great gift of grace! What a sight of constant beauty that would be! What a joy, mingled with great sorrow that would bring! This is not something I know. It is something to which I aspire.

What is definitive in this endeavour is that this Word of God has been made fully flesh in the person of Jesus of Nazareth. This is the Word spoken (Ps 33 [Vg 32].6), received and expressed at a particular historical moment. This Word is utterly transcendent yet has become incarnate in human form, God made man entering into the world at a point in the past (Jn 1.1 and 1.14). This entry changes all history. Perhaps we can say that until Jesus came, the historical world was like a prison – beginning, ending, incomplete, unsatisfying. With his breaking into time the world is now the antechamber of heaven and our pathway to an ultimate fulfilment through the ministry of Jesus – the Word, the Son and the Christ (Heb 1.1–2). Therefore, all history takes on a new meaning and every action is filled with eternal significance, taking us nearer or further away from our true destiny. This approach to theology and spirituality urges us to return to its foundations in order that we can be in silence before the mystery of God. As a result, we are able to still all restlessness and reach out towards the deepest soul of our being, in order that there the birth of the Word may again occur and its ripple echo in our words and actions.

I believe that in the life and writings of St Thérèse of Lisieux we are led through her experience and teaching to a deeper appreciation of this spirituality.[7] Certainly she is an attractive and loving tutor. Hundreds of thousands of souls bear witness to this fact. She was as vulnerable as a child, and it is in the combination of her vulnerability and her strength that her secret is to be found. No one, therefore, is too weak to approach her. She understands our brokenness and knows it is the highway in which God can approach us. Brokenness lays open our deepest, empty self. Paradoxically, it brings us nearer to the Ground of our Being for so much else has been stripped away, enabling the Word to find a welcome at his coming. In her strength St Thérèse is an inspiration – seen, for example, by her testimony to the spiritual dimension of human living. This dimension takes us beyond that which can be measured and lifts human reasonableness to a higher level until it flowers in heroism and perseverance when in great difficulties. For St Thérèse love is the key to how we should understand human living. She expresses the idea as: 'I understood that LOVE COMPRISED ALL VOCATIONS, THAT LOVE WAS EVERYTHING, THAT IT EMBRACED ALL TIMES AND PLACES [...] IN A WORD, THAT IT WAS ETERNAL! [...] MY VOCATION IS LOVE! [...] Yes, I have found my place in the Church [...] in the heart of the Church, my Mother, I shall be *Love*.'[8] These words were written in October 1896, when Thérèse was experiencing anguished pain and suffering through illness. Such sentiments are not the words of a young romantic, daydreaming of an ideal future. Born of abandonment to God in darkness and desolation, they are a powerful testimony to the grace of God at work in our weakness, and not to the power of a self-centred romantic imagination. Our mission today is shaped by the power of the witness offered by St Thérèse, which constitutes an aspect of how the lure of God is moving within individuals and humanity. This movement is found not in pride or self-sufficiency but in humility and boundless trust in God, which St Thérèse demonstrated by steadfastness. As a result she focused on the little things: doing all things well, out of love, especially for those whom she found to be the most difficult. Thus, every day there is an opportunity to follow her 'Little Way of Spiritual Childhood'. All our actions, when accompanied with humility and love, are steps which lure us closer to God. Here we see his Word, born in us, echoing out into action. Thérèse indeed is our tutor on this pathway of prayerful silence in the city. She helps us to surrender our selfish desires, even the fascination we have with our own spiritual experiences: they are of no matter in our journey to God through life.

Similarly, to paraphrase Eckhart, we must not let our love of the things of God become an obstacle to the love of God himself. Rather, we strive not for an experiential knowledge of God for its own sake, not for a love of the things of God for their sake, but so that we may be filled with his Word and be changed.[9] This is the purpose of our spiritual lives and of the silence we seek each day.

## Notes

1. St Francis of Assisi (1181/2–1226) was the founder of the Franciscan order. This account of his death is recorded by Thomas of Celano in *The Remembrance of the Desire of a Soul* (commonly referred to as *The Second Life of St Francis*), Chapter CLXII, 214 (1245–7), to be found in *FA II*, p. 386.
2. Smith, Cyprian, OSB (1987), *The Way of Paradox: Spiritual Life as Taught by Meister Eckhart*. London, Darton, Longman and Todd. Fr Cyprian is a monk of Ampleforth.
3. Cardinal Basil Hume OSB (1923–1999) was Abbot of Ampleforth, 1963–76, and Archbishop of Westminster, 1976–99.
4. Meister Eckhart (*c*.1260–*c*.1328) was a member of the Dominican order. Cyprian Smith is quoting (p. 6) from a Christmas sermon by Eckhart, who is utilizing St Augustine of Hippo (354–430) in order to reinforce the argument relating to the birth of Christ within the human soul. For the complete text of the sermon based on Wis. 18.14 see

M. O'C. Walshe (1979), *Meister Eckhart: German Sermons and Treatises*, Vol. I. London and Dulverton, Watkins, pp. 1–13. This reference is from p. 1. For a contemporary assessment see Roy, Louis (2017), 'Meister Eckhart's Construal of Mysticism', *The Way*, 56/1, pp. 77–88.

5 Smith, *The Way of Paradox*, Chapter 3, 'The Silent Desert', pp. 29–42.
6 *Ibid.*, p. 56.
7 St Thérèse of Lisieux (1873–97) was a Carmelite nun. Her most famous work is *The Story of a Soul*. In 2009 I delivered two homilies and a lecture at Westminster following the countrywide progress of the relics of St Thérèse. The sight of the huge number of people who came to pray and to honour her life and example stimulated me to revisit the implications of the concept of the lure of God and to discern how God is working graciously in our lives. The homilies were preached on 13 October (the feast of St Edward the Confessor) and on 15 October in the presence of the relics of St Thérèse. The lecture was delivered on 22 October as one of the series 'Silence in the City'.
8 See *S of S*, MS B, 3v, 19–29, p. 302.
9 See Smith, *The Way of Paradox*, pp. 113f., where reference is made to two of Eckhart's Maundy Thursday sermons to be found in O'C. Walshe, *Meister Eckhart*, Vol. I, in particular, pp. 235f. and 241f.

## 2

## *The Mystery of Christ*

*For God so loved the world that he gave his only Son.*
JN 3.16

When I was a child, my mother taught me to begin the day by making the sign of the Cross: 'In the name of the Father and of the Son and of the Holy Spirit. Amen.' This act of devotion ensured that the day was offered in the service of the Triune God. Just as all life flows from the Father, through the Eternal Word, in the creative power of the Holy Spirit, so too my day was to be shaped by the will of the Father, in company with the Son, Jesus, in the strength of the Holy Spirit.

At the heart of this devotion is the fullness of the revelation of Jesus, Son of the Father, to the world. This revelation comes in historical events at a point in time, the late first century BC and the early years of the first century AD in Palestine, which was part of the Roman Empire. Luke refers to the census which was undertaken during the reign of the Emperor, Caesar Augustus (Lk 2.1), while Matthew describes the tyranny of the Emperor's client ruler, Herod (Mt 2.1). Many of the

Jewish people were restless and engaged frequently in rebellion against this regime (Acts 5.35–7).

Following the ministry of John the Baptist, the engagement of Jesus in public preaching (c. AD 27, Lk 3.1–3) took the form of declaring that God's appointed time had arrived, that his reign was dawning and that as a result, the people should 'repent, and believe' in this message of good news and salvation (Mk 1.15). The ministry of Jesus followed the pattern of the blessedness of God's way (e.g., Mt 5.3–12) and of demonstrating that God's power was at work through the mighty acts of Jesus (e.g., Mk 1. 21–8). Such a ministry was bound to incur the wrath both of the Jewish religious leadership and the Roman authorities, a situation which led ultimately to the crucifixion of Jesus (e.g., Mk 15.1–15; 27ff). Yet at the heart of the Christian faith is the belief that God raised Jesus from the dead (e.g., 1 Cor 15.3–11). This conviction means that Jesus was not merely fully man but also totally God (*CCC*, 464). As a result, we declare that Jesus is the Christ or Messiah of God (*CCC*, 436–40), his only (unique) Son, and that Jesus, the Son, shares with the Father divine lordship over all creation (*CCC*, 436–51).

Although unknown to me at the time, my mother's daily act of love, devotion and understanding opened a treasure house of spiritual grace which will remain with me throughout my life. One way in which this precious gift is shared and strengthened is through the celebration of the Mass and the preaching of the Word. How clearly this is seen at the major seasons of the Church's year, when we celebrate the saving events of the life of Christ: his birth at Christmas, his death on Good Friday and his resurrection at Easter.

As Archbishop of Birmingham and latterly as Archbishop of Westminster, I have been privileged to celebrate these splendid liturgies in the Cathedral Church. This ministry has allowed me to explore and present these great truths to large congregations and, on occasion, to wider audiences through the media of radio and television. I always try to offer to all an invitation to take up again the way to salvation and eternal life that is found in Jesus Christ. The path for discipleship also offers a foundation for the good ordering and harmony of society. Thank God these celebrations always strengthen my faith and bring a blessing into my life, often in an unexpected way.

For many people, Christmas and Easter are associated mainly with a chance for a rest from work and a few days' holiday. These moments in themselves can be stressful, adding to the fundamental anxiety many sense in the face of the multiple difficulties of life today.

Such weariness is not confined to personal family life. It is not hard to sense a deeper tiredness with our public life and institutions: promises quickly made, impossible to keep; expectations inflated for short-term gain but leading only to long-term disappointment.

Where does the weary soul go for refreshment? Of course, my answer is to come to faith as the wellspring of life. But for some that can be a step too far: I believe that an approach to the great traditions of art may assist us on our journey. The best art does not merely present us with a witty idea or a passing pleasure. It teaches us to see and to understand. Art reorganizes things, even familiar things, so that we come to appreciate them in a wholly new and unexpected way. The best art is generous: it gives us something without our asking; it often takes us by surprise. There are so many examples from which to choose, but the one that has caught my attention is a picture in the National Gallery, *The Nativity with Saints* (c.1485–95) by the Sienese artist Pietro Orioli (c.1458–96).[1]

This picture not only explores the wonder of the birth of Jesus but also points to the events with which his earthly life will end and the new, eternal, resurrection life, which will begin. Let us see what this picture reveals in terms of Jesus' nativity, death and resurrection, and let us begin this exploration in the name of the Father, the Son and the Holy Spirit.

## *The Nativity with Saints* Altarpiece, by Pietro Orioli

### The Nativity of Christ

*And they [the shepherds] went with haste, and found Mary and Joseph, and the babe lying in a manger. And when they saw it they made known the saying which had been told them concerning this child; and all who heard it wondered at what the shepherds told them. But Mary kept all these things, pondering them in her heart.*

LK 2.16–19

In my article 'Christmas: When the Sacred Becomes Real'[2] I have demonstrated how Orioli's altarpiece *The Nativity with Saints* combines a wonderful delicacy with a deep, mystical artistic imagination. It makes us pause by inviting us to step out of the rush of life, leaving our anxieties and bringing us to an attentive stillness. At the centre of the scene of the nativity is the child Jesus newly born, with Mary and Joseph (Lk 2.7). The mother, of course, is rapt in adoration of her new son. Mary is aware that this birth is unique because, according to St Luke, she has responded to God's call, given by the angel Gabriel at Nazareth in the power of the Holy Spirit, to be the mother of Jesus (Lk 1.26–38). This prophecy of Jesus' birth and ministry (Lk 1.31–3) provides Mary with the assurance that she is able to perceive the deep significance that this birth is revealing the mystery of the incarnation, and she is captivated by the coming in our flesh of the Eternal Word of God (Jn 1.12–14). Jesus, as God's Messiah, has come to make his home with us, in this poor, exhausted world. It is surprising that Joseph seems distracted and overawed as he has also, according to St Matthew, been given the news in a dream by an angel that he is to take Mary as his wife and the promise that Jesus, the son to be born, is to save his people and be God's divine presence in the world as Emmanuel (Mt 1.18–25; Emmanuel, Mt 1.23, a quotation from Is 7.14). Although Joseph obeyed God's command (Mt 1.24), his eyes are, nonetheless, directing us to the figure of St Nicholas, the original Santa Claus. Orioli is here portraying Joseph as in need of the encouragement and support of the saints; we also require their inspiration in our lives. Why has Orioli portrayed Nicholas (*c*. AD 270–343), Bishop of Myra, as a witness to the birth of Christ? We see Nicholas offering the gift of a golden ball (one of three) because he is the great giver of gifts, especially to the poor and distressed. This action affirms the theology of the incarnation offered by St Paul when he declares that 'for you [the Corinthian Christians] know the grace of our Lord Jesus Christ, that though he was rich, yet for your sake he became poor, so that by his poverty you might become rich' (2 Cor 8.9). With the figure of St Nicholas the artist is telling us that in the birth of Jesus Christ we are being given a revelation of God who is love and whose nature is that of total self-giving.

In becoming human, Jesus, the Son of God, is experiencing poverty both actual and spiritual. He is showing us something which is essential, not only concerning the nature of God the Father, but also about how our human nature is to be understood. We are, in our essential make-up, beings who are destined to give from our bounty (2 Cor 8.7) and, in doing so, to find our fulfilment. By this act of charity we are seen to be made in the image and likeness of God (Gen 1.26).

Our capacity to give is not merely seasonal, something for Christmas only. Rather, giving is part of who we are as beings both human and spiritual. In the birth of this child, Jesus, this capacity is restored in us, in a deeper and more radical way. Orioli shows us that the birth of Christ is, in a unique way, timeless. By placing Nicholas in this painting, the artist is demonstrating that we can know Christ at any time and in any place. This universal understanding of the nativity shows how we can become part of his family and receive his gift of salvation, eternal life and the riches of God's glory. In this way we are able to become givers and find our fulfilment in this generosity.

True generosity, however, comes only with freedom. Only when I place my own needs into another perspective, only when they cease to dominate my thinking, am I able to respond selflessly to the needs of others. In this way, paradoxically, this offering leads to true freedom. This new perspective is found supremely in the Christ child. If God acts in this way in the finest use of his divine, almighty power, then, in this incarnational spirit, I am able to use my limited, human power in the same way. Indeed, God never coerces us but waits for our consent to this act of revelation. The Christ child does not force humanity into any submission. He offers in creative generosity that which we need and then waits, helplessly, for our loving response. Such a response is not only individual; it is also corporate. Imagine a society in which we could discover again these realities of our humanity: gift and freedom. In this context the gift is not tied to any contract. Here freedom is mature enough to take responsibility for wider needs: those of each other and of our planet.

By surrounding the nativity scene with saints Orioli is revealing the great fruit of this new freedom. Whereas we are tempted to put our trust in the autonomy of the individual, Christ offers us a freedom that creates and sustains community rather than treating it as a type of utilitarian constraint. Here, the profoundly relational character of our human nature is again asserted. In reality we belong to each other: born into a family; growing through relationships; finding challenges and meaning in shared enterprise; and depending on others in childhood and old age. In this understanding individualism is nonsensical and is harmful to human development.

Like the Gospel itself, Orioli's painting, with all its mystical calm, illustrates abundant realism which recognizes the cost of human loving. In order to illuminate this theme Orioli includes the deacon and first martyr, St Stephen (Acts 6.3–6, 7.54–8.1), the prophetic figure, forerunner to the Messiah and martyr St John the Baptist (Mk 1.4–8; 6.14–29) and the ascetic figure of St Jerome (*c.* AD 345–420). They were all aware, each in his own context, like the Christ child they follow, that neither love nor freedom achieves its goal except through sacrifice and a willing self-restraint for the sake of others. This painting respects our reality and offers us the opportunity to enter into the depth of its spiritual meaning, while being dissatisfied with any superficial understanding of Orioli's representation.

There is something delightful and timely at its centre: an ox, determined to see the Christ child. The animal has such gentle eyes and a smile that is almost seraphic. Today we must be challenged to protect the needs of our environment and to consider the threat that our selfish actions pose to all living things. In this nativity scene a harmony is suggested between the different dimensions of our world, a harmony that we struggle to establish. The truth is here proclaimed that the incarnation is a redemptive act for the whole universe (Rom 8.18–25; *CCC*, 668).

When we continue to indulge in lifestyles that threaten this harmony, and when, consequently, political leadership struggles to take the decisions necessary to sustain our world, this vision of the stable scene of Bethlehem can invigorate our efforts of restoration and conservation. The Christ child and our faith in him can give us a new moral energy and a renewed sense of justice to create a restored relationship with creation. This perception will help us to find the vision for a life lived happily with simplicity because it is free from the tyranny of greed.

When we are weary, we find refreshment in such works of art as this nativity scene. When viewed with the eyes of faith, it shows us how the truth is able to renew us. For tired eyes and for an exhausted heart and mind, Orioli reminds us of the beauty at the centre of the Christian faith. The incarnation ensures that this understanding is not a distant beauty that takes us out of the universe but a beauty that lives within this world. This beauty is named 'Emmanuel', God with us (Mt 1.23). This is the beauty that saves us and our world.

The Christmas story is not a myth but provides us with the basis for historical and theological exploration. This foundation gives us a vision of the community which we are meant to be, and sometimes, even when faced with crises and disasters, we are able to achieve this goal of harmony. The Christmas message does not deal in tired political clichés or disguise reality with spin. Rather, the Gospel offers us a truth about God, about ourselves and our world which is fresh. In his love God has made this world his home. In doing so he has made a home for us. With generosity and genuine freedom that is not afraid of commitment and effort we can work to make this world truly a home for all because it is always his home.

In the words of the poet Robert Frost,

> [...] Earth's the right place for love:
>     I don't know where it's likely to go better.[3]

The Christ child teaches us this truth and, in so doing, directs us on the pathway of faith and life, and is revealing by his birth the loving purposes of God for all ages.

FAITH FINDING A VOICE

# The Passion of Christ

*He [Jesus] said, 'Abba, Father, for you all things are possible; remove this cup from me; yet, not what I want, but what you want.'*

MK 14.36 (NRSV)

*'Could you not keep awake one hour?'*

MK 14.37 (NRSV)

*'So when he [Judas Iscariot] came, he went up to him [Jesus] at once and said, 'Rabbi!' and kissed him.*

MK 14.45 (NRSV)

*When Jesus saw his mother, and the disciple whom he loved standing near, he said to his mother, 'Woman, behold, your son!' Then he said to the disciple, 'Behold, your mother!' And from that hour the disciple took her to his own home.*

JN 19.26–7

*So he [Joseph of Arimathea] came and took away his [Jesus'] body [...] Now in the place where he was crucified there was a garden, and in the garden a new tomb where no one had ever been laid [...] they laid Jesus there.*

JN 19.38, 41, 42

[...] Earth's the right place for love:
  I don't know where it's likely to go better.

These lines of Robert Frost are only part of the truth: the fullest expression of the truth of love is to be found in the life of Jesus, who is the entire love of God in our flesh and blood walking on our earth, and evoking from our broken humanity all the ambiguities and dissonance that we often experience. Through faith in God we can affirm that the record of Jesus' life on earth is the account of what happens when the love of God comes into our world. The presence of evil, however, reveals that this love is being rejected. This rejection brings chaos to the natural ordering of the world. God's will for all creation will be restored when the harmony which he brings is recognized, taken to heart and lived ethically. This tension between rejection and acceptance, and between chaos and harmony, is portrayed evocatively on the predella of Orioli's masterpiece. The first four scenes deal explicitly with rejection and chaos. They represent the agony of Jesus in the Garden of Gethsemane outside Jerusalem, his betrayal by Judas, his ignominious death on the gibbet of the Cross and the heart-breaking embrace of his dead body by his mother, Mary. This iconography invites us to enter into the tragedy and futility that threaten to overwhelm the life of every person and also to face the certainty of death and the emptiness which is released. In the final scene, however, through the reality and vision of the resurrection of Christ, the gravity of the rejection and chaos of the passion are embraced within the totality of eternal harmony which humanity is offered by God when he raised Jesus from the dead (1 Cor 15.4, 20–24).

The scenes on the predella have been preserved, and we are able to read them as a continuous narrative. As a result, a close scrutiny of their details will bring us great rewards.

In the first scene (see Mk 14.32–42; Mt 26.36–46; Lk 22.39–46) Orioli is revealing the encounter of Jesus with his heavenly Father (the ancient Aramaic word, *abba*, is retained by Mk 14.36a, which indicates the spirit of intimacy) in relation to his forthcoming suffering and death, which is necessary for the salvation of humanity. In this moment when the vocation of Jesus as the Son of God is being tested (Mk 14.35–6), his three principal disciples, Peter, James and John, sleep (Mk 14.37). Orioli is showing us by his division of the picture space the comparison between the faith of Jesus and the faithlessness of the disciples. Jesus is here facing his true fate. He sees with utter clarity the cost of his loving embrace of the will of the Father; sweating blood (Lk 22.44), he cries out 'Father, if you are willing, remove this cup from me' (Lk 22.42 [NRSV]). By the presence of an angel from heaven (see Lk 22.43), Orioli is here linking the agony of Jesus with the nativity scene through the ministry of God's angelic messengers (compare with Lk 2.9, an angel appearing to shepherds), and thereby the link is being made between the birth of Jesus and his approaching death, thus symbolizing his total embrace of the cycle of life. In portraying the angel as offering the cup of suffering to Jesus, Orioli is, ironically, revealing how Jesus is being strengthened in his moment of anguish by the ministry of the angel (Lk 22.43–4). The tension between Jesus and the disciples is further heightened when they are perceived as representing Christian believers. Like them, each of us has a full repertoire of avoidance techniques. We know how to protect ourselves with skill and determination. We develop a hard skin of indifference, from behind which we are able to express words of solidarity with those who are facing their agony. We keep a safe distance, at least emotionally, faced, for example, with the tragedy of human trafficking Pope Francis believes that 'We [should] incarnate the duty of hearing the cry of the poor when we are deeply moved by the suffering of others' (*EG*, 193). Such a response is the only way in which wounds in the body of humanity, in the body of Christ, will be healed.

By contrast, it is in the very nature of love that it wants to know the truth and to face the truth. This is why true love always wounds us, because the truth in our broken world is often painful. Love desires to know and embrace the truth, and in this way to share its pain. Jesus is the fullness of love, and he faces resolutely the totality of experience with humility and trust, even the truth of his own rejection and death. In this situation he demonstrates both his divinity and his perfect humanity for, in his vocation, there is no avoiding the ultimate sacrifice, and he shows no equivocation in his desire to conform to the will of the Father. Jesus accepts and embraces his fate, 'yet, not what I want, but what you want' (Mk 14.36b [NRSV]).

In the second scene (see Mk 14.43–52; Mt 26.47–56; Lk 22.47–53; Jn 18.2–11) Orioli shows how the ideal of the garden of paradise is broken when it becomes the abode for violence and betrayal, and ceases to be a place of apparent security.[4] This juxtaposition finds its origin in the creation narratives. God placed Adam in the garden of paradise – Eden (Gen 2.8). He failed, however, together with Eve, who was beguiled by the serpent (Gen 3.13), to be obedient to God's will and, as a result, was expelled from the garden of paradise (Gen 3.24). Adam's sinfulness and alienation from the divine will are represented here by the behaviour of Judas and the soldiers, whose aggression turns the garden into a place of chaos, equating it with human depravity. Orioli brings this perception to our notice by portraying this crowded scene at the front of the picture space, thereby highlighting the horror which is occurring in the attempt to arrest Jesus (Mt 26.47).

Within this context the theme of betrayal by one of the twelve disciples, Judas Iscariot (Mk 3.19), is brought to our attention through the psychological encounter between Jesus and his betrayer (Mt 26.49). Orioli heightens the emotional tension through the particular gestures and juxtaposition of Judas and Jesus. Their embrace is revealing that the motivation of Judas is both cunning and deceitful, as shown, ironically, by his outstretched arms in an apparent act of welcome. The band of soldiers accompanying Judas (Jn 18.3) show by their great number (Mt 26.47) and venomous behaviour that the action of such a crowd is far in excess of what is required to arrest Jesus, whom they have seen teaching daily in the Temple (Mk 14.48–9). During this emotional interaction Jesus is moving forward to accept the embrace of Judas, which demonstrates symbolically that Jesus is continuing to fulfil the will of the Father and the ministry of salvation. The intensity of this moment is highlighted by the kiss of Judas (Mk 14.45). Orioli combines Judas' kiss of affection with that of betrayal. In terms of faith and experience the viewer is able to contemplate this gesture, which exposes the tension between justice and injustice, sincerity and falsehood, faith and faithlessness, love (see Jn 13.34) and avarice (see Mt 26.14–16, 'thirty pieces of silver') and good and evil, revealing the dialectic between the righteousness of Jesus and the villainy of Judas.

Within the conflict of this drama Jesus alone remains the perfect example of virtue. Orioli's iconography shows the disarray of the disciples. Simon Peter enters impetuously into the violence of the moment by cutting off the right ear of the high priest's slave (Jn 18.10), which Jesus heals (Lk 22.51). The other disciples flee in terror (Mk 14.50). The horror of the situation is highlighted by the physiognomy of one of the disciples, who is transfixed by fear but who, at the same time, is turning to escape from the garden (alluding to Mk 14.51–2). Orioli is demonstrating here how human expression is linked to the loss of human motivation (compare with Mk 1.20 and 3.13–19) revealing the faithlessness of the disciples in the time of trial.

These activities mark a turning point in the Gospel narrative, in that Jesus ceases to be the subject of his actions and becomes the object of what others are doing in relation to him (compare also Lk 22.52–3, 'Jesus said', with Lk 22.54, 'they seized him'),[5] actions that will lead ultimately to his crucifixion.

In the third scene Orioli moves our consciousness to the cross (Mk 15.21–39; Mt 27. 32–54; Lk 23.26; 32–49; Jn 19.17–30). By removing the soldiers (see Jn 19.23, 19.25; 19.34) from the picture, he allows a serenity to pervade the action and captures a moment of intimacy between Jesus, his mother Mary, and John, the beloved disciple, as recorded in the Gospel according to St John. Mary, standing at the foot of the cross, is gazing in anguish at the suffering of her Son, and the gesture of her hands shows how she is pleading to God for succour in her torment. Her Son is helpless, nailed to the brutal wood of the cross; he is innocent of any wrongdoing (in fulfilment of Is 53.9b). In this moment of total surrender there is, however, a glimpse of light. It is to be found in the words of Jesus to his mother, 'Behold, your son!' and to the beloved disciple, 'Behold, your mother!' (Jn 19.26–7) and in the comment 'from that hour the disciple took her to his own home' (Jn 19.27). Orioli reveals here the immensity of the ministry now given to the beloved disciple. The gesture of his right hand indicates the existential moment of realization for him of how his role as a leader and supreme witness to the testimony of Jesus (Jn 19.35; 21.24) is being placed on his shoulders. This moment also marks the beginning of the Church, the new community of faith and light. Now, as the fruit of Jesus' death, a new pattern of relationship is born. In the person of the beloved disciple, the Church, which is the community of the disciples, receives a new mother, a mother not in the order of nature but in the order of grace. Mary, therefore, is our unique mother, always leading us to her Son (see Jn 2.5), always present and always holding us in love. We are no longer alone. Mary is always best understood in the company of the Church. She is the first and best of all the disciples, the Mother of the Church (*CCC*, 495). In this community of faith and light we each pursue the pathway of discipleship: encouraging, inspiring and at times correcting each other on the way. In this journey of love we all come to the cross of Jesus on the hill of Calvary. Our own encounter with pain, dismay, isolation and death is offered there in order that in this community our hope is kept alive and the promise of victory over death (1 Cor 15.26) never destroyed.

The sacrificial death of Jesus also offers forgiveness and healing (in fulfilment of Is 53.4–6; see also, in particular, *CCC*, 604, 608–9). Orioli shows us the figure of Mary Magdalene (Jn 19.25), who is kneeling at the foot of the cross and embracing the feet of Jesus. Through this action she is contemplating the meaning of his passion, and she is depicted in red, symbolizing how redemption is achieved through the blood of Christ, which represents the totality of love which we should follow. Orioli draws us into this scene and brings to our attention the narrative as recorded earlier by St Luke (Lk 7.36–50). This narrative relates to the action in the house of Simon the Pharisee regarding a woman (believed traditionally to be Mary Magdalene) 'who was a sinner' (Lk 7.37) and who wet the feet of Jesus with her tears and 'wiped them with the hair of her head' (Lk 7.38). As a result, Jesus declares that her 'sins are forgiven', that she is saved by her faith and can 'go in peace' (Lk 7.48; 7.50). In the same way, at the foot of the cross, Mary Magdalene is manifesting how the repentant sinner can be granted forgiveness and healing. On Good Friday we approach the cross and kiss the feet of Jesus as he hangs in death. By our sins being placed upon him, our broken love is refashioned and the offence which we have caused to God is forgiven through the shedding of the blood of Jesus, 'the Lamb of God, who takes away the sin of the world' (Jn 1.29). From the cross, Jesus also offers forgiveness and healing to all humanity, as shown by his words, 'Father, forgive them; for they know not what they do' (Lk 23.34). Thus, human suffering is to be seen in terms of faith born in union with Jesus, which becomes part of the mysterious love across the face of the earth, touching the hearts of many souls.

Out of the suffering and death of Jesus a victory is being born, as expressed through his final words from the cross, 'It is accomplished' (Jn 19.30, my rendering). Jesus is here the herald of a new era. From his wounded side life-giving water and redemptive blood will pour forth (Jn 19.34). Jesus will strike the rock of suffering with the rod of his cross (alluding to Ex 17.5–6). Then we shall know that death is split open and destroyed, giving way to new, everlasting life. This redemptive sacrifice is being performed in the name of God the Father, whose will is never without purpose. His sovereign will is being fulfilled by Jesus in that his death inaugurates the possibility of the radical transformation of humanity and the whole created world. In the death of Jesus, the Father is making 'all things new' (Rev 21.5).

In the fourth scene (Mk 15.42–7; Mt 27.57–61; Lk 23.50–56; Jn 19.38–42) Orioli portrays the dead Christ, who has been taken down from the cross and is being prepared for his burial. Mary, his devoted mother, is manifesting her pity for her dead Son. Orioli is continuing to reveal the emotional tension here by concentrating upon Mary's lamentation and sorrow as she draws our attention to the sacred heart of Jesus, in order to indicate the heart of love in its fullness through sacrifice (Col 1.19–20), by which we are bathed in the beauty of redeeming light. No wonder this scene evokes her title as Mother of Sorrows. In this moment Mary discloses the unfathomable depth of maternal love. I can still recall feeling as a child the terrors of the night, during which I would cry out. My mother always came to me, banishing my childish fear and restoring normality, the life-giving normality of love with which my life was blessed. This picture evokes in me a prayer of praise and thanksgiving for every faithful mother who gives of their utmost for the sake of their children, often in the harshest of circumstances. Mary is the mother of us all, God-given and utterly faithful. We can call upon her at any moment, and she is with us. From the moment of the Annunciation (Lk 1.38) Mary realized that she would play a pivotal role in the unfolding of the Father's plan for our salvation. For this vocation and ministry she was preserved from sin from the time of her conception (*CCC*, 490–94), in order that she might be a fitting dwelling in which the Eternal Son of God could be endowed with his human nature. As in the scene of the crucifixion we behold Mary as a mother with a broken heart who is a source of strength and compassion for us all in her desolation; but Jesus, however, has ensured that she does not stand alone.

The beloved disciple, John, is beginning his watchful care of Mary and the community of believers. Here, despite his bewilderment at the events which are unfolding before him, his hands are together praying earnestly over the dead body of his Lord. Mary Magdalene in faithful devotion is kissing the wounded feet of Jesus, symbolizing the joining of her anguished soul with his tortured body. Orioli portrays Joseph of Arimathea sharing in the community of faith (Jn 19.38) as 'a good and righteous man' (Lk 23.50), while also being a rich (Mt 27.57) member of the Jewish Sanhedrin (Mk 15.43; Lk 23.51). Joseph, through his seeking 'for the kingdom of God' (Mk 15.43; Lk 23.51), has perceived during the trial and death of Jesus that he is the king of the new age of God's reign of righteousness and love (Jn 18.36).

As a result of this new understanding Joseph requests that Pontius Pilate give him the body of Jesus (Mk 15.43) so that he may not be buried in an unknown common grave but be given a royal burial (Lk 23.53) by being laid in Joseph's own, new rock tomb (Mt 27.60). He is portrayed wrapping Jesus in a shroud to indicate further his royal status. The realism of this scene is brought to our attention by Joseph's attributes: the pincers, hammer and nails, being laid at the front of the picture space. These physical means of death ironically become the means of salvation in that the sinfulness of humanity has been 'nailed' upon Jesus, through whom redemption is offered.

Orioli provides a connection with the fifth and final scene by placing the city of Jerusalem in the background of both events. He is implying that this city, its leaders, inhabitants and pilgrims for the Passover, who condemned Jesus to death and have apparently banished him from their lives, will have the possibility of living in the new age of the Spirit of Pentecost, when the action in the final scene is known.

## The Resurrection of Christ

*This Jesus God raised up [...]*

ACTS 2.32

*'You [guards] must say, "His disciples came by night and stole him away while we were asleep."'*

MT 28.13 (NRSV)

In the final scene the Risen Christ is depicted standing alone. Orioli is emphasizing here that the resurrection was a totally divine event and was not witnessed by any human being. At this moment our eyes are drawn back to the apex of the altarpiece. At this high point below the frame is the figure representing God the Father, reigning from heaven with his messengers, the angels, on either side. He is portrayed as presiding over the entire drama of salvation, one hand held in a gesture of protective peace (Heb 13.20), the other hand held in blessing (Num 6.24–6). God sees all that is taking place in the universe. He endows us with the supreme gift of freedom (*CCC*, 51–2). He is not a tyrant who imposes an iron will, reducing us to the status of automata. Rather, God is a loving Father who watches over his children as we struggle, fall, recover, fall again and reach to achieve the deep desires written into our souls by God (Ps 8.4–5).

Between the apex of the centre piece and the resurrection scene on the predella there is established an intrinsic relationship between God's victory in heaven and Christ's victory on earth, given that the resurrection of Jesus, the only begotten Son of God, demonstrates God's transcendent intervention of himself in creation and history (*CCC*, 648). As a result of the obedience of Jesus to his heavenly Father's will for the restoration of creation and humanity, Jesus has been raised body and soul, having conquered death; which is the ultimate frontier, 'the last enemy' (1 Cor 15.26), and Jesus of Nazareth, the Christ, is the only person in the entire sweep of human history to have broken the power of death. Jesus, through his resurrection is inaugurating a new form of life, no longer subject to the fact of dying but opening a new dimension, the possibility of a new heavenly future for humanity.

In comparison with the previous scene Orioli is producing a contrasting emotional effect by changing the position of Jesus as seen in the *pietà*, lying dead, to that of being dynamic, seen bursting out of the tomb, the weighty lid having been thrust aside. Jesus is standing erect, holding in his hand his staff and flag of victory; the mood of poignancy has been changed from despair to the confirmation of triumph. Orioli is revealing here that by this unique, miraculous and redemptive action of God, through the resurrection of Jesus, a new order has been created. This new order represents a form of existence which is no longer subject to the fact of death, one that opens a new dimension and offers a new heavenly future for humanity.

By portraying the Risen Christ in this manner Orioli is, by implication, unlocking the door to the occurrences which follow the resurrection. The immediate events relate to the presence of the disciples at the empty tomb (Mk 16.1–8; Mt 28.1–8; Lk 24.1–12; Jn 20.1–10) and the appearances of the Risen Christ to his chosen witnesses (e.g., Jn 20.11–18). With this understanding the viewer is able to connect the resurrection with the ministry of St Peter and St Paul, and the angel Gabriel and Our Lady, who are shown paired on the pilasters of the centre piece. Orioli demonstrates the link between the appearance of Jesus at the resurrection to Simon Peter (Lk 24.34; Jn 21.7–8), who is holding the book of the Gospels and the scroll of the Scriptures. This iconography portrays the confirmation of the resurrection faith as declared by Peter in his homily in Jerusalem on the day of Pentecost (*c*. AD 30). This event was foretold in the Old Testament (Ps 16 [Vg 15].8–11), and Peter is able to testify that 'this Jesus God raised up, and of that we are all witnesses' (Acts 2.32). The apostle Paul received the revelation of the Risen Christ at a later date (*c.* AD 34), while journeying to Damascus to persecute Christians (Acts 9.1–3). Paul heard the divine voice of the risen and glorified Christ, who declared 'I am Jesus, whom you are persecuting' (Acts 9.5). Paul was commissioned by Christ to proclaim the Good News of salvation to both Jews and Gentiles (Acts 9.15). Orioli depicts Paul holding his letters written to the early churches, which contain the saving truths of the Gospel, and the sword which symbolizes his martyrdom (*c.* AD 64–7) during the reign of Nero (54–68). As a Roman citizen and according to custom, Paul was beheaded (*HC*, 2.25). His martyrdom represents identification with the death of Jesus. The manner of Paul's death shows the continuity with his preaching of the saving power of crucifixion of Jesus (1 Cor 2.2) and his glorious resurrection (1 Cor 15.20), which reveals the pathway to God's redemption offered to humanity through Christ. St Luke records that at the time of the Ascension the disciples were commanded by the Risen Christ to return to Jerusalem, where they would be 'baptised with the Holy Spirit' (Acts 1.4–5). Mary, the mother of Jesus, accompanies the disciples to the upper room, where in prayerful unity they are awaiting the Pentecostal Spirit (Acts 1.14). Orioli is linking this action of the Holy Spirit with that which occurred at the Annunciation, when the angel Gabriel declared to Mary that she is to be the mother of the Son of God, through the descent of the Holy Spirit upon her (Lk 1.30–35).

Through the links between resurrection, chosen witnesses and the coming of the Holy Spirit, Orioli is affirming that the resurrection of Christ is a universal event (1 Cor 15.20–28) which opens the possibility of an eternal future for all humanity in all ages, in every part of the cosmos. God's promise of the renewal of creation is demonstrated by Orioli in his representation of the Garden in the resurrection scene (Jn 19.41). This Garden manifests the restoration of the Garden of Eden (Gen 2.8; Ezek 36.35) and the return to paradise (Rev 22.1–2). Orioli believed that every aspect which he has portrayed is dependent upon the resurrection from the dead of Jesus Christ and from faith in the resurrection experience.

Despite the fact that the Risen Christ did not appear to his persecutors – Pontius Pilate and the Jewish religious leaders – nevertheless, Orioli is revealing in two ways the juxtaposition between the Risen Christ and the soldiers, the representatives of the Roman Empire. First, the iconography of the sleeping guards, who are scattered like ninepins, is demonstrating symbolically that the greatest power on earth at the time had been defeated. These proud representatives of the Roman political and social order, the *pax romana*, have been reduced to fear, confusion and helplessness and resemble men who have 'died', while the Risen Christ is portrayed as victorious and alive eternally. Such divine power had not been encountered before; nor had humanity had to reckon with God's Gospel of salvation.

Second, Orioli is showing, by implication, how both the Jewish leadership and the Roman authorities wished to prevent the spread of the Gospel of the Risen Christ. St Matthew records (Mt 28.11–15) that, following the realization of the empty tomb (Mt 28.11), the guards returned to the city of Jerusalem (portrayed in the background). By accepting a bribe from the Jewish elders in return for protection from Pilate, the soldiers agreed to lie about the fact of the resurrection by spreading a false rumour that while they were sleeping the disciples had stolen the body of Jesus (Mt 28.13). This morally corrupt behaviour was worthless and counterproductive because the disciples were given authority by the Risen Christ to proclaim the Gospel to 'all nations' and to receive followers into the new community of the kingdom through baptism 'in the name of the Father and of the Son and of the Holy Spirit' (Mt 28.19). Thus, nobody is excluded from the kingdom; its borders are open to all who wish to enter and to embrace the Risen Christ who is its king.

At his trial Jesus had announced the coming of this kingdom and its spiritual power in answer to the Imperial representative, Pilate, by saying 'Mine is not a kingdom of this world' (Jn 18.36 [NJB]). Now we begin to see the nature of God's kingdom and the reign of Jesus within this new age. The kingdom which Jesus brings is one of life and not death, of dignity not servitude, of mercy and compassion not retribution, of forgiveness and not domination, which will be realized fully at the end of the age, in heaven.

This discussion relating to the worldly kingdom of Pilate and the spiritual kingdom of Jesus presents us with the dichotomy between the darkest depth of human depravity and the sinless humanity of Christ. Human depravity which emerges from the caverns within the human heart is manifested in many different guises. Sometimes it comes in a stream of hatred aimed in fury at an innocent victim; at other times it can emerge in a diabolical cunning which systematically divides people and nations, setting them at odds with each other and exploiting the subsequent chaos for their own advantage. In this situation, slowly but surely, families and communities will lie in ruins. Alternatively, it is the Eternal Word of God alone who is present in our flesh (Jn 1.14) who can face and embrace every last expression of the depravity of our fallen humanity (1 Cor 15.45–50, the Risen Christ as the New Man, Adam). Becoming 'truly man' at the Incarnation 'while remaining truly God' (*CCC*, 464), only Jesus Christ in his divinity is able to embrace humanity without destroying human nature. It is through this wonderful mystery of two natures, human and divine, in one person that Christ is able to be truly the Saviour of humanity (*CCC*, 469). Without his divinity he could not claim victory over sin and death. Without his humanity we could not have any part in his victory; it would always be beyond our reach. In this one, unique person, however, in whom total divinity and humanity are found, we behold our only true Saviour (2 Tim 1.10; in terms of the kingdom, see 2 Pet 1.11), who seals our salvation by his resurrection (1 Cor 15.20). As we walk on our pilgrim journey we know that the fruits of these saving acts of Jesus enable the spirit of love to continue to flow into our human drama as it is unfolding through time and experience.

Orioli, a man of deep faith which was innate within him, has tried to capture this spiritual wisdom. He has used his craftsmanship and enormous talents to bring us this radiant painting, which is his prayerful gift 'in the reverence of God, and of The Virgin Mary'.[6] Orioli believed that his offering was inspired by the work of the Holy Spirit. This Spirit is expressed through the will of the Father, who found in Mary and all the saints the faithful instruments through whom the Father's message of redemption for humanity is to be found.

This redemptive power is achieved in the Son, born in a stable, betrayed into the hands of his enemies, pierced through unto death, embraced by his faithful and grieving Mother, and raised victorious to the new life of his kingdom. This drama of salvation is celebrated in the liturgies of the Church, which are a source of refreshment and hope for a wearied world.

My mother too was inspired, Yes! She set me on the right path when she encouraged me to begin each day 'In the name of the Father, and of the Son and of the Holy Spirit, Amen'. For it is on this path that we journey to find the fullness of life.

*The Altarpiece: A Lay Perspective – Elaine Parsons*
The exploration of the ministry of Jesus Christ – Christology – is further enhanced by the consideration of the context of this altarpiece (*c.*1485–95) in terms of location and genre.[7]

It is thought to have originated from the small chapel of St Stephen and St Nicholas, Cerreto Ciampoli in the Val-d'Arbia district of the province of Siena. This tempera-on-wood composition measures 187.5×155 cm and, being located upon the altar, would have dominated the chapel.[8] The symbolism in the altarpiece offers the worshipper an interrelated dual perspective: first, as an aid to personal devotion through meditation upon the scenes; and second, to contemplate the divine action by attending the public offering of the Mass. Here the spiritual significance of the altarpiece is reflected through the ministry of the priest, who stands '*in persona Christi*' (*CCC*, 1548; see, in particular, n. 25, the comment of St Thomas Aquinas) and mediates his grace. In the offering of the Mass, for both the living and the departed, the priest '*re-presents*' (*CCC*, 1366) the sacrifice of Christ on the cross, and through this sacrifice the faithful know that they are united with their departed loved ones in heaven. The focus of the centre piece is the infant Jesus, and we are here reminded that, at the dominical words in the Eucharistic prayer and by the invocation of the Holy Spirit, the bread and wine are transformed into the real presence of the body and blood of Christ (*CCC*, 1377). Thereby, we are able to recollect that the Eucharistic bread which we shall receive is the same body of Jesus. Through this understanding we are able to relate our experience to the historical events of the birth, death and resurrection of Christ. We are also able to perceive that the body of Christ received in Holy Communion is being related directly to his incarnate, wounded, risen body, as seen through the progression of the narrative represented both on the centre piece and the predella. Through this insight the experience of God's history of salvation through Jesus is being revealed.

Orioli's altarpiece also assists the worshipper to develop Christian virtue by following faithfully the way of Christ, who is manifested through the action of God the Father, who gives to us the Holy Spirit, the Father's life-giving wisdom. Through God's love expressed in terms of the Trinity the supernatural blesses the natural, heaven reaches to earth and the faithful are guided in their response to the heavenly vision. Orioli is here revealing this truth through the action of John the Baptist, who by pointing to Jesus as *Ecce Agnus Dei* (Jn 1.29[Vg]) is illustrating how the divine revelation is being mediated through the Christ child, God and man. By entering into this heavenly vision we understand that in life and prayer, both in joy and sorrow, we need the intercession and encouragement of the saints. The primary focus for this support is to be found in Our Lady, Mary, Mother of Jesus, Mother of God, who is declared by the Church to be *theotokos* because through the action of the Holy Spirit she gave birth to God's incarnate Son, who is truly God and truly man (*CCC*, 495).[9] Orioli is portraying the infant Jesus gesturing towards his blessed Mother. This action of Jesus symbolizes the recognition of Mary's indispensable role in God's plan of salvation. At the same time Jesus is conveying this truth to the worshipping community by looking outwards from the scene and drawing us into the mystery of divine love. Mary is also portrayed here as the Madonna of humility, praying in adoration to her Son and thanking God for his birth. In the crucifixion and deposition scenes on the predella, Mary is seen as our Lady of Sorrows standing at the foot of the cross and assisting in the burial of her Son. In all these experiences between the Son and his Mother, Mary shows us the way in which she is the Mother of the Church by including us in this relationship (see Jn 19.26–7; *CCC*, 964), through the demonstration of her maternal love for us as our guide and comforter (*CCC*, 969). Orioli is drawing us into all these scenes and demonstrating how humanity is able to share in the salvation which

Christ is bringing, through his birth, death and, ultimately, his resurrection.

The resurrection scene, in particular, is confronting us as to how the divine status might be restored and renewed within a sinful world by anticipating the final judgement. Through the gesture of his right hand the risen Christ is symbolically drawing all people into his final victory over death (1 Cor 15.57), which is 'the last enemy' of humanity (1 Cor 15.26; 15.54–5). Thus, in the pilgrimage of faith the believer is bidden to walk in the way of Jesus Christ as guided by the teaching and life of the Church. By the inclusion in the centre piece of the face of, possibly, a shepherd, Orioli is illustrating the nature of the Christian pilgrimage. The shepherds were the first pilgrims, who, after experiencing the vision of the angels, visited Bethlehem in order to offer worship to 'Christ the Lord' (Lk 2.11). In a similar way we, the Christian faithful, are invited to walk on our pilgrim journey through life whilst entering symbolically into the totality of the life of Jesus, keeping our minds and hearts 'fixed on him' (Lk 4.20) in order that in heaven we may experience God face to face.

This understanding reveals again the engagement between the supernatural and the natural worlds. Orioli portrays this engagement through the harmony expressed in the nativity scene of Christ's incarnation by placing the characters in unity with each other, under the ubiquitous eye of God the Father: in particular, the members of the Holy Family – Jesus, Mary and Joseph – who are portrayed within a circle of sacred love. This harmony shows symbolically the unity of the faithful within the arc of the Church and its teaching office represented here by Bishop St Nicholas, who, being portrayed traditionally as in middle age, is seen as a figure of both experience and wisdom. Orioli pictures Nicholas looking towards the Christ child from whom episcopal authority to be a shepherd and teacher (wearing the vestments of a Bishop and holding a crozier) is received (*CCC*, 888). Nicholas' devotion assures the faithful that these dual actions will ensure that our faith is able to grow in wisdom and love and be preserved always from error and evil. The Bishop exercises this ministry under the authority of the Pope, who is 'the sign and servant of the unity of the universal Church' (*CCC*, 1369). This universality is based fundamentally on the incarnation, which is the source from which salvation is offered by God to humanity. Kneeling before this altarpiece at the Mass in the small chapel of Cerreto Ciampoli, the faithful would have known, as we know today, that we are a microcosm of the universality expressed in the Eucharistic sacrifice which is being offered throughout the world. The validity of this unifying experience is seen through the ministry of the Pope, successor of Peter (Mt 16.16–19), who is named in every celebration and thereby brings the whole Church together under the harmony which Christ brings through his incarnation, death and resurrection, and which through the inspiration of Orioli is being revealed with such grace and beauty.

The deacon and martyr St Stephen (wearing a dalmatic) is portrayed as a young man owing to his zeal for mission (Acts 6.8). He is holding the Book of the Gospels, which contain the totality of the records of Jesus' birth, ministry, death, resurrection and ascension into glory. Stephen is pictured looking outwards from the scene. This action symbolizes that the ministry of the deacon, commissioned by the apostles, is evangelistic: to announce, preach and live the life of the Gospel and to proclaim its message to the world (Acts 6.2, 6.6–7). Here the faithful are called to imitate the example of Stephen in both his life and also in his death. The stone on his head symbolizes the nature of his execution (Acts 7.58), during which he, completely, offered his life to the 'Lord Jesus' (Acts 7.59), and, following his example (Lk 23.34), Stephen forgave his persecutors (Acts 7.60). Through his prayers and by hearing and reading the Gospels we are able to find the encouragement to follow the way of Christ in both his mission and through his suffering.[10] In conjunction with meditation upon the messages contained in the altarpiece we are also able to fulfil our obligation to engage in the mission of the Church and to present Christ by bringing the joy of the Gospel to everyone whom we meet in our daily lives.

St Jerome, kneeling in homage to the Christ child, is holding a stone used to beat the breast in mortification for sin and symbolizing penitence. Here the faithful are being shown the way of humility through negation and asceticism. This perspective reveals how Jerome is attempting to imitate the pattern of the self-emptying of Jesus Christ (Phil 2.6–8). By following this example we are able to understand how we should live by possessing the mind of Christ (1 Cor 2.16; Phil 2.1–5)[11] and how we may overcome evil, renounce worldliness, grow in virtue (Gal 5.22–4) and practise humility (Phil 2.5–6; Thomas à Kempis, *The Imitation of Christ*, Chapter 2, 'On Personal Humility', *c*.1418).

Meditating upon these scenes, the worshipper may appreciate both the material and the spiritual aspects of light. When viewed, for example, by candlelight, a rich and brilliant meaning would be produced, which is highlighted by the golden effect, giving atmospheric depth, drawing us into the emotive experience which is being offered. In a spiritual way the affirmation that God gives light through Jesus would also be revealed. Orioli's craftsmanship here is giving us a vision for life and faith which has been radiated through this glorious painting for many centuries. He believed and understood that the truths about God are mediated constantly to the world through the mission of the Church. By contemplation upon the scenes in this altarpiece we are able to see that Orioli knew that it was the purpose of his life that he should always give love and praise to God (Ps 150. 1,6). In our lives we likewise are bidden to follow this example as we walk on our pilgrimage of faith (Mt 22.37–40; 25.40).

*The Altarpiece: A Priest's Perspective – Fr Richard Parsons*
Orioli is inviting the priest to consider his pastoral service through reflection upon the redemptive ministry of Jesus Christ and the benefits that this redemptive mission offers to humanity.[12] The ministry of the priest is centred upon the celebration of the Eucharist, which proclaims the reality of the historical Gospel and the continuing pilgrimage of the Church towards heaven. Through the contemplation of this reality the priest is able to unite his continuing theological vision, manifested in the study of God's divine revelation in Christ to the world, with the priest's offering of spiritual worship and the ministry of *caritas*.[13] These perceptions relating to the ministry of a priest are proclaimed by Orioli, on the centre piece, where he is presenting us with the

great and cosmic mystery of God's salvation concentrated in the incarnation of Christ (Gal 4.4–6). His birth is truly a hinge upon which the entirety of human history is opened to us with the invitation to enter into the new and transforming phase of God's redemptive activity. The deeper meaning of the mystery of the birth of Christ for salvation is revealed by the link with the crucifixion scene on the predella. When the priest offers the Eucharist he is re-enacting and re-presenting the unique sacrifice of Jesus mediated through God's act of self-giving love (e.g., Rom 8.32) revealed in the birth of the divine Word, who has taken on flesh and blood in the person of the human Jesus (Jn 1.14), the Father's only begotten Son (Jn 1.18). Orioli is here encouraging us to contemplate these scenes, which are presided over by the figure of God the Father with his love, compassion and glory. The entire universe and the whole of humanity, its creation and redemption, flow from him and are directed by him. The golden rays of light surrounding him and radiating from him to the Christ child symbolize the immovable bond which is shared by the Father and the Son (Jn 14.11). The gestures of God's hands show us that here all is taking place according to his will and under his creative blessing (Num 6.24–6). In response to this blessing all life is directed to him through the ministry of Jesus, portrayed here by Orioli in terms of the birth of our Saviour and Lord (Phil 2.11), which is intrinsically linked to his passion, death and resurrection, as represented on the predella.

Orioli is offering us the splendour of the divine plan of creation, revelation and salvation. As a result, the priest in his sacramental and pastoral ministry is able to perceive by implication how his calling might be deepened and challenged and to understand more fully his ministerial vocation against the background of the entirety of God's activity towards humanity. This understanding is linked to the teaching outlined by St Thomas Aquinas. According to his interpretation, all life proceeds (*exitus*) from God as its source and is given the opportunity of returning (*reditus*) to him as its goal. Thus, creation is the great *exitus* from God, as is his revelation in the incarnation. All creation has been broken and impaired by sin, but, through the work of salvation wrought in Jesus, creation is able to be drawn back to its origin and source, God the Father. All life is to be returned (*reditus*), offered to the Father in, with and by the Son in the power of the Holy Spirit. Thus, the origin and goal of existence are the same: union with God.[14] The pattern of God's plan is, therefore, circular. Its motion is perfect through God's revelation in Christ because, as a result of his saving power, origin and goal are truly united through his sacrifice. As the priest meditates on the profundity of this saving vision, he is challenged to respond positively through faith by our deepened love and service to Christ, through whom all divine worship is channelled. In this vision the revelatory basis for creation, salvation and blessedness is clear, yet our human response in love and generosity is, as a result, presupposed.

It is within the symbolic nature of Orioli's special gift to us that we are able to understand this teaching in terms of our ministry. When we look at the person of Jesus in his incarnation, life, sacrificial death on the cross and resurrection, we know that there is an intrinsic link between the priest and our divine Lord. Orioli is portraying these Christological scenes in order to reveal the totality of God's redemptive plan for the world. This interpretation becomes a reality when a priest offers the holy sacrifice of the Mass, which is the foundation stone for all his evangelistic and pastoral work.[15] By reflecting upon the depth and richness which accompany every celebration, 'priests as ministers of the sacred mysteries, especially in the sacrifice of the Mass, act in a special way in the person of Christ who gave himself as a victim to sanctify men' (*PO*, 13) and thereby the mystery of salvation is revealed. It is the greatest privilege and joy in the life of a priest to celebrate these sacred mysteries. It never ceases to amaze me, and to challenge me, that God chooses to use my voice, my hands, to do this work. These thoughts, however, must be seen always within the corporate body of the ministerial priesthood, which ought to be understood as a company of brothers who represent Christ in order that they 'can represent the Church' (*CCC*, 1553). It is Jesus who speaks his words at the moment of consecration; it is his hands that take the chalice and offer it again to us for our salvation. The priest is only a poor instrument; we are 'earthen vessels, to show that the transcendent power belongs to God and not to us' (2 Cor 4.7).

How, then, does reflection upon Orioli's altarpiece encourage and strengthen our ministry as priests? First, the symbolism of the golden rays of light from the Father which are surrounding Jesus reminds us that all the events of our lives – birth, death and eternity – are encased within the entirety of his birth, death and resurrection, and if we open our hearts to this reality he takes us up into a depth of life which is beyond human achievement. Thus we are bound together by him living within us, given by the Father in the unfolding mystery which took its decisive step in the stable in Bethlehem. Through this revelation we are called to love him more and to serve him and all his sons and daughters with more fervour. Second, the rich symbolism given to us here helps us to appreciate more fully the living tradition of the priesthood in which we stand and which finds its origin in Jesus, the High Priest (Heb 7.25, 9.11). This understanding embraces all priests within the unfolding love of Jesus from the apostolic age until now and in the future.

Central to the office of the priest is his ministry of prayer[16] and mediation.[17] The teaching proclaimed on these scenes by Orioli becomes a vehicle whereby the priest can communicate through word, sacrament and pastoral care the truths revealed by God to the world and his love for humanity. The mediatory role of the priest, however, should be seen always in relation to the unique office of Jesus Christ as mediator,[18] who acts as the 'one mediator between God and humankind, [...] himself human, who gave himself a ransom for all' (1 Tim 2.5–6 [NRSV]). In this understanding the priest acts as a slave and apostle of Jesus Christ in the service of the Gospel (Rom 1.1). Thus every action of the priest must be performed 'in Christ Jesus' (Rom 6.11) in order that through the priestly ministry the freedom which God offers might become a living reality through the work of the Holy Spirit. In this narrative framework Orioli is giving us a vision of the events of Christ's life with which the priest must identify: incarnation, death, resurrection and glorification. This revelation is portrayed through the drama of the Mass, where liturgically all that we offer to God is taken from what he has already given to us; the things that come forth from God: the bread, the wine, our joys, our sorrows, our very selves, are offered back to him. This pattern can only happen when we allow ourselves and material objects to be transformed by the action of the Holy Spirit and taken up as part of Jesus' own offering of himself, the acceptable sacrifice which takes away the sins of the world.

Orioli assists us in our understanding of how the priest, by participation in the divine mystery of salvation, leads us into the timelessness of God's love and of the heavenly life which sheds its rays of light upon earth. In the Mass we are reminded that we are in communion with the angels, saints, apostles and martyrs whom we venerate, and pray for a share in their fellowship. Through this communion and by the invocation of their prayers our earthly pilgrimage is united with the assurance of heavenly timelessness. We ask God to accept our prayers as mingling with the praise of heaven. In every celebration of the Mass we bring to him those who have gone before us and for whom we ask for his mercy. Orioli encases the divine revelation within the framework of the saints found on the pilasters. Each of the saints has a particular message of encouragement and support for the priest: the angel Gabriel and Our Lady of the Annunciation assist us to remain faithful to our vocation (Lk 1.26, 1.38); St Peter strengthens our communion with the Holy Father and the body of the Church (*CCC*, 863), and St Paul inspires us to pursue further our ministry of evangelization (e.g., Rom 15.15–17), while St Lucy and St Francis (in their different contexts) show us the way of sacrifice and suffering and set us an example of how we should care for the poor. These saints, together with St John the Baptist, the forerunner (e.g., Jn 1.29), St Stephen the beloved deacon (Acts 6.3–6), Bishop St Nicholas, who offers episcopal authority for the apostolic priesthood, and St Jerome, who helps us to love the divine Word revealed in sacred Scripture,[19] indicate the key role of the ministry of the Church in bringing everything back to the Father in and through Jesus Christ. Orioli, by drawing us all in and around the figure of the infant Jesus together with his blessed Mother, Mary, and her spouse and guardian of the child, Joseph, is directing us to the truth of the perception of Julian of Norwich when she declared that 'I saw the whole Godhead concentrated as it were in a single point, and thereby I learnt that he is in all things.'[20] For the priest the whole purpose of God's will is focused in the historical moment of the incarnation of his beloved Son, and through the whole of the Father's plan for the salvation of all humanity. Orioli in his artistry is teaching the priest that his ministry should be understood in the 'single point' of the sacred moment of the incarnation of Christ, and also through the 'single point' by the continual intercession of the priest in Christ's name for humanity; in order that the whole created order may be embraced and renewed in the beauty and holiness of the blessedness of God. By entering fully into the divine vision which Orioli is giving us here the priest himself is being renewed, and is becoming a transformed man for good in the service of the Gospel.

## ITE, MISSA EST

> 'their voice [the apostles] has gone out to all the earth, and their words to the ends of the world.
> Rom 10.18, quoting Ps 19 [Vg 18].4

In the celebration of the Mass the great triumph of God, the declaration of his acts of salvation (see The Liturgy of the Word at the Easter Vigil) are fulfilled and personalized in Jesus Christ.[21] Yet on leaving the altar we are conscious of our mission to proclaim this victory of God as we re-enter the world. The recognition of this hope, however, is glimpsed only occasionally and fleetingly by many in society. The harmony which we see between the human and the spiritual, between the natural and the supernatural, so beautifully portrayed by Orioli, is not often confirmed in daily experience. Despite this experience, however, there exists in every heart a movement towards God, the lure of God. Thus Christian people through our Baptismal vocation are given the mandate for the divine task of evangelization as 'missionary disciples' (*EG*, 120) within the Church. As we continue to deepen our faith in the service of the Gospel (Phil 1.27) the nature of our mission becomes clearer: we are to proclaim the victory of Christ and the effects of the outpouring of the Holy Spirit (Acts 2.17–21, quoting Joel 2.28–32).

The work of mission, however, presents us with a twofold challenge: on the one hand, we must not be so lost within the efforts and dramas of daily life that the proclamation of the Gospel in words and deeds loses its distinctive Christian character. On the other, our presentation of the Gospel must be related to the experience of the daily life of those to whom we address the Gospel and minister the saving grace of our Lord Jesus Christ.

This challenge is resolved only when we grasp fully the truth that nothing truly human ever fails to find an echo in the heart of the disciple, and no human sorrow or joy fails to resonate with the community of Jesus, the Church (*GS*, 1), 'the one People of God' (*LG*, 13). The heart of the missionary disciples (*EG*, 120), filled with the sacred mysteries of the Eucharist, is open to all humanity. We know that the world is God's field in which the great treasure of the kingdom lies hidden and that this treasure is found in the light of Christ, through his gift of grace, by the guidance of the spirit working especially within the Church (Acts 13.52). The disciple is also aware of the treasure, the pearl of great price, for which every sacrifice is to be made with a joyful heart (Mt 13.44–6), as the means whereby the Church is able to grow (Acts 9.31) and all humanity is blessed by God. 'So what are we waiting for?', as Pope Francis asks us in *The Joy of the Gospel* (*EG*, 120), a challenge which also faces us very clearly in the iconography of the altarpiece *The Nativity with Saints*, which has been given to us to contemplate through the exceptional artistry and devotion of Pietro Orioli.

## Notes

1 For information relating to Orioli's contribution to Sienese painting see Christiansen, Keith, Kanter, Laurence B. and Strehlke, Carl Brandon (1988), *Painting in Renaissance Siena, 1420–1500*. New York: The Metropolitan Museum of Art, pp. 335ff. 'Documents reveal Orioli to have been a highly devout man [...] admired by his contemporaries both for the sanctity of his life and for his artistic talents' (p. 335). On the original context of *The Nativity with Saints* altarpiece, see Fattorini, Gabriele, and Paardekooper, Ludwin (2002), 'Committenza a Siena nel secondo Quattrocento.

La famiglia Cerretani, Alberto Aringhieri e due opera di Pietro Orioli', *Prospettiva*, 106–7, pp. 2–33. I should like to thank Sean Ryan for bringing this article to my attention.

2 Printed in the *Daily Telegraph*, 24 December 2009, as 'When the Sacred Becomes Real'.

3 For 'Birches', see, *Mountain Interval*, Frost's third collection of poetry. New York, Henry Holt & Co., first published in 1916.

4 I am grateful to Elaine Parsons for assisting me with the analysis and interpretation of this scene, and also for discussing with me the iconography of *The Nativity with Saints* altarpiece. For further understanding relating to physiognomy and character, see Norman, Diana (ed.) (1995), *Siena, Florence and Padua: Art, Society and Religion 1280–1400*, Volume II: *Case Studies*. New Haven, CT, and London, Yale University Press, in association with The Open University, p. 102.

5 See Vanstone, W. H. (2006), *The Stature of Waiting*. Harrisburg, PA, and New York, Morehouse, p. 20 (1st published 1982).

6 Cennini, Cennino d'Andrea (1960), *The Craftsman's Handbook*: *'Il Libro dell' Arte'*, trans., Daniel V. Thompson, Jr. New York, Dover, p. 1.

7 I should like to thank Elaine Parsons for this lay perspective.

8 For further information see www.nationalgallery.org.uk/artists/pietro-orioli. At the time of writing *The Nativity with Saints* altarpiece was not on public display. Fr Richard and Elaine Parsons would like to thank Rosalind McKever and the staff of the National Gallery, London, for allowing a private viewing of the altarpiece and for their generous assistance. For the religious importance of sacred art see *CCC*, 2502. See also *Letter of His Holiness Pope John Paul II to Artists*, from the Vatican, Easter Sunday, 4 April 1999.

9 For further information on the Marian title *Theotokos*, see Pelikan, Jaroslav (1996), *Mary Through the Centuries: Her Place in the History of Culture*, New Haven, CT, and

London, Yale University Press, chapter 4, 'The Theotokos, the Mother of God', pp. 55–65, where the title is translated as 'the one who gave birth to the one who is God' (p. 55). Note also that the concept of *Theotokos*, established in the fourth and fifth centuries AD is a natural progression from Elizabeth's question to Mary, 'And why is this granted me, that the mother of my Lord should come to me?' (Lk 1.43). As *Theotokos* comes from the Church's understanding that Jesus is God incarnate, *theotokos* combines the language of Christian worship with that of Christian theology to give a rich interpretation of the incarnation and of Mary's role within this unique revelation of God's salvation (see Pelikan, p. 58).

10  An example of how we are able to find encouragement through the mission and suffering of Christ is seen in the work of the Sue Ryder Foundation. In 1972 on a visit with Fr Richard – whom I married in 1973 – to Hickleton Hall (see https:/en.wikipedia.org/wiki/Hickleton_Hall, now sadly closed as a Sue Ryder home), I was given a copy of this prayer which I have offered to God throughout my life:

> O Lord, remember not only the men and women of goodwill, but also those of ill-will. But do not only remember all the suffering they have inflicted upon us, remember the fruits we bought thanks to this suffering, our comradeship, our loyalty, our humility, the courage, the generosity, the greatness of heart, which has grown out of all this, and when they come to judgement, let all the fruits that we have borne be their forgiveness.

This prayer was found on a small piece of paper near the body of a child who had died, together with many thousands of women and children, in Ravensbrück concentration camp. See Ryder, Sue (1975), *And The Morrow Is Theirs*, Bristol, The Burleigh Press, p. 110. By the example of this martyrdom Sue Ryder through her inspiration and compassion sought to further the love of God and proclaim the Gospel of Our Lord Jesus Christ by devoting her life to the relief of suffering on the widest scale. See Ryder, Sue (1997), *Child of My Love: An Autobiography*. London, The Harvill Press, p. xii (first published 1986). Also http://www.sueryder.org

11 For St Paul, in 1 Cor 2.16, to enter into 'the mind of Christ' is to be open to the wisdom of God which is given through Christ (1 Cor 1.30) and necessary for the apostolic mission. In Phil 2.5 Paul instructs the Philippian believers that they should have 'this mind [...] which is yours in Christ Jesus'. Here they are given an injunction that they should both imitate Christ and behave with humility (Phil 2.3), sympathy, love and unity, and in the fellowship of the Holy Spirit (Phil 2.1) within the Church community.

See also Dalrymple, John (1991 [1st edn 1975]), *Costing Not Less Than Everything: Notes on Holiness Today*, London, Darton, Longman and Todd, Chapter 13, 'The Mind of Christ', pp. 74–8.

12 I should like to thank Fr Richard Parsons for this priest's perspective.

13 See also Ramsey, Michael (1985 [1st edn 1972]), *The Christian Priest Today*, London, SPCK, pp. 10 and 102.

14 The *exitus–reditus* pattern could be seen to form the basic framework of *Summa Theologiae*. See Davis, Brian (2014), *Thomas Aquinas's Summa Theologiae: A Guide and Commentary*, Oxford, Oxford University Press, p. 14. Given that not all the topics discussed by Aquinas fit easily into this pattern, modification is needed (p. 15).

15 *ST*, III, q 65 a 3c.

16 Wojtyła, Karol, Pope John Paul II (1979 [first published in Italian in 1977]), *Sign of Contradiction*. London, Hodder and Stoughton, pp. 134f.

17 *ST*, III, q 22 a 1c.

18 Ratzinger, Cardinal Joseph, Pope Benedict XVI (1987 [first published in German in 1982]), *Principles of Catholic Theology: Building Stones for a Fundamental Theology*, trans.

Sister Mary Francis McCarthy SND. San Francisco, CA, Ignatius Press, pp. 280f.
19  *Commentary of Isaiah*, prologue, cited in *DV*, 25; text, *DO*, III, pp. 301*f.
20  Julian of Norwich (1966), *Revelations of Divine Love*, trans., (into modern English) Clifton Wolters. Harmondsworth, Penguin Books, Chapter 11 (p. 80); see also Chapter 81 (pp. 206f.). A new translation has been given by Elizabeth Spearing with an introduction and notes by A. C. Spearing (Penguin Books, 1998), for information on *poynte* (single point or instant), p. 181, n. 6.
21  *1 Apol.*, 65.3–67.8.

# 3
# The Holy Spirit: Community and Creation

> *Come, Holy Spirit,*
> *fill the hearts of your faithful*
> *and enkindle in them the fire of your love*
>
> CCC, 2671

The concept of the Holy Spirit is difficult to explain, given that its roots are to be found in the idea of the breath or wind of God, which produces creative and renewing energy in relation to the beauty of the world and humanity (Ps 104 [Vg 103].30). We say, 'Look at that wind' when what we really mean is that we both feel and see its effects, as with trees falling to the ground in the midst of a storm. In order to explain the concept of the Holy Spirit perhaps we should begin by examining how we interpret the symbols relating to the Holy Spirit. St Luke in the Acts of the Apostles describes how the Holy Spirit came upon the apostles on the day of Pentecost (Acts 2.1–4), giving them divine power in fulfilment of an ancient prophecy (Joel 2.28–32; Acts 2.16–21) to preach the Messiahship and Lordship of Jesus (Acts 2.36). Accompanying this proclamation is the understanding of the offering of forgiveness of sins through repentance and baptism 'in the name of Jesus Christ' (Acts 2.38). The new believers will receive the gift of the same Holy Spirit (Acts 2.38), who will empower them to live according to the teaching of the apostles (Acts 2.42), both in unity (1 Cor 12.12–13) and with the sharing of possessions (Acts 2.44–5).

To understand the profundity of this activity of the Holy Spirit who, within Christianity, is believed to be the third person of the Blessed Trinity, 'consubstantial with the Father and the Son: "with the Father and the Son he is worshipped and glorified" (from the Nicene Creed)' (*CCC*, 685), is to portray the totality of the divine action of the Trinity in relation to the world. The unparalleled nature of this relationship demonstrates the work of the Holy Spirit, who, through the ministry of Jesus (Lk 4.18–19, the fulfilment of Is 61.1–2), reveals the love and saving power of God in a unique way. In order to perceive the depth of this confession of faith, symbols are needed to highlight its particular character. In addition to 'mighty wind' (Latin: *spiritus vehementis*) St Luke uses the image of 'tongues as of fire' (Acts 2.2–3) in order that through the creative action of the Spirit the first apostles (Acts 1.12–14, 1.26) might be able to proclaim the Lordship of Jesus, the Christ (*CCC*, 684). This proclamation was preached first to the Jewish pilgrims assembled in Jerusalem for the feast of Pentecost (Acts 2.1, 2.14), fifty days after Easter-Passover.

In *The Nativity with Saints* altarpiece Pietro Orioli is portraying the Holy Spirit as rays of golden light which are emanating from the heart of God the Father. The purpose here is to return the viewers' imagination to the scene in Nazareth of the Annunciation of the Lord to the Blessed Virgin Mary which prophesied the nativity of Jesus (Lk 1.26–38), proclaimed to be 'the Son of the Most High' (Lk 1.32). This divine child would be conceived as a result of the work of the Holy Spirit. In this way God was offering Mary everything (Lk 1.28). Her 'Yes' to God was the fruit of her cooperating and responding to the Spirit who came upon and overshadowed her (Lk 1.35). It was as if she was being enveloped by the Holy Spirit and her will was being united to that of the Father. She could say with utter conviction 'You see before you the Lord's servant, let it happen to me as you have said' (Lk 1.38 [NJB]). In the same way we can know the Holy Spirit coming upon us and overshadowing us (Ps 91 [Vg 90].4) in order that the Lord's work may be continued through our ministry. For this task God wants to reveal to us the deep mysteries of the faith. Through the Holy Spirit he asks everything of us (Acts 2.37–9), and even though, unlike Mary, we do not always respond as we should, nevertheless, in return God gives us everything – every grace and every blessing. In this regard the work of the Holy Spirit helps us to revere the living memory of the Church as she celebrates these key moments of salvation. These celebrations are occasions for us of rebirth as, following the Annunciation and the nativity, we are able to focus on the ministry of the Holy Spirit in his role of bringing to birth God made Man in Jesus. In giving God praise and thanks, we receive an inner conviction of peace and the spirit of joy which imparts grace, strength and power (Phil 4.4–7) which surrounds us and carries us forward on our journey to him.

## Community

> *Go therefore and make disciples of all nations, baptizing them in the name of the Father and of the Son and of the Holy Spirit.*
>
> MT 28.19

This verse, from the final section of the Gospel of St Matthew (Mt 28.16–20), where the Risen Christ speaks to his eleven remaining disciples on a mountain in Galilee, reminds me of the idea of rebirth and renewal (in relation to baptism, see also Tit 3.4–7) through the ministry of the Holy Spirit. When preparing to address the Proclaim 15 conference in Birmingham on 11 July 2015, the question arose in my mind as to how the Church of today is measuring up to this command of Christ. I realized that the whole Church should regard herself as being placed on a missionary footing, as declared by Pope St John XXIII before the opening of the Second Vatican Council in December 1962 and more recently by Pope Francis (e.g., *EG*, 19). This ministry of evangelization is conferred upon 'all the members of the People of God' who become 'missionary disciples' by 'virtue of their baptism' (*EG*, 120), and through the work of the Holy Spirit who enriches every culture 'with the transforming power of the Gospel' (*EG*, 116).

First, we receive the command of the Risen Christ to 'Go therefore and make disciples of all nations' (Mt 28.19a). This command is central to the ministry of Jesus because it summarizes the primary purpose of his incarnation, life, death, resurrection and return to the Father. His will is to return humanity to the place that we held when we were created: total obedience to God, together with salvation and eternity within the arc of faith. This ministry is now offered to his disciples through the prayer which Jesus addressed to the Father: 'As you have sent me into the world, so I have sent them into the world' (Jn 17.18 [NRSV]). This is our mandate, our mission, and we have to understand how central it is to our identity.

Second, another aspect of the mission of the disciples is to baptize with running water in the threefold name of the Trinity: the Father, the Son and the Holy Spirit (Mt 28.19b). Baptism is the sacramental means by which we encounter the inner life of God, the heart of the divine mystery manifested through the Holy Trinity. As a result of its baptismal faith the Church is empowered to continue the divine mission. The Father has entrusted this mission to Jesus, his Son. Through Jesus, the heart of the Father, the overflowing of his creative love and his eternal mercy is communicated to us. Through this communication the ministry of the Holy Spirit can be discerned as the energy, the love and the fire which descend upon us. In the new Pentecostal age it is the Spirit who guides and teaches us (Jn 14.26) and offers us divine forgiveness.

Third, this relationship between the Trinity, baptism and the mission of the Church helps us to explore the mystery of the faith in terms of *communio*. Primarily the divine *communio* is the sharing within the mystery of the Trinity the perfect life, love, truth, goodness and beauty which are to be found at the heart of the one God. It is, therefore, from the inner heart of God that the mission of the Church arises. It is from this heart that our mission finds its purpose, shape and energy, which the Holy Spirit is providing. In the words of Mother Teresa, we are to do something beautiful for God, which is of God, and for God. It is from this divine foundation that the Church can be described as a *communio*. This foundation ensures that Christians are not merely a group of like-minded people who agree upon a particular programme of action but, rather, participants in fellowship with the mystery of God (2 Cor 13.14).[1] To believe in the Trinitarian Godhead is to affirm the *communio* of faith within the whole Church. In this way the individual profession of faith becomes part of the corporate declaration of faith as expressed, for example, through the proclamation of the Baptismal promises. It is in this regard that parish communities should focus on the celebration of Baptism as 'the gateway to life in the Spirit' (*CCC*, 1213) and thereby on the celebration of the Mass as its central act of worship, as the real presence of Jesus Christ is received through word and sacrament (*CCC*, 1349 and 1355). Thus, in this way the *communio* of the parish flows from the *communio* of God, the sending forth of the Son by the Father in the power of the Holy Spirit (Gal 4.4–6).

I should like to offer two particular examples to illustrate the precise role of the Holy Spirit within the totality of *communio*. First, the Holy Spirit sends us into areas of life which are unexpected and precedes us on this pilgrimage of his mission by preparing us to speak the words of the Father in the power of the Spirit (e.g.,

Mt 10.20). This grace is offered so that those who hear us might respond in love to our Spirit-filled proclamation. Before we embark on our journey, however, we should seek the wisdom of the Spirit (Is 11.2) in order to perceive whether or not what we intend to do is truly the will of God and not the result of our desire for gratification and pleasure (Gal 5.16–17). If we are truly engaged in the work of God, our endeavours will be blessed and bear fruit, the fruits of the Spirit (Gal 5.22–3), usually in ways which we do not expect. Second, the Holy Spirit will give us the gifts (1 Cor 12.4ff.) that we need for our mission. The Holy Spirit will give us the discernment of what to do, of what to say and of how to bring faith to life at any particular moment.[2] Jesus told his twelve disciples (Mt 10.1), especially in times of persecution, that they need not worry about their defence because it is not they who will be speaking but 'the Spirit of your Father speaking through you' (Mt 10.20). For us evangelization is not about superior planning, greater efficiency and high-class management but about being open to the freedom which is to be found in Christ (Gal 5.1) and the love and trust which the Holy Spirit offers.

Through baptism we are incorporated into Christ (Rom 6.5) and become part of his body (1 Cor 12.12–13) and are called to enact the pattern of his life within our own lives. This formation is possible only through the ministry of the Holy Spirit. Being one with the Trinitarian God through the baptized life, and engaged in the evangelizing mission of the Church, we are called to be sharers in the work of recreation through the power of the Holy Spirit given afresh in the life of grace.

## Creation

*When you send forth your spirit, they are created;
and you renew the face of the ground.*

PS 104 (VG 103).30 (NRSV)

*[…] and the Spirit of God was moving over the face of the waters.*

GEN 1.2

*This responsibility for God's earth means that human beings, endowed with intelligence, must respect the laws of nature and the delicate equilibria existing between the creatures of this world.*

Pope Francis, Encyclical Letter, Laudato Si', 68

My perception of the activity of the Holy Spirit within the created order has been heightened as a result of my presentation of *Laudato Si'* on Thursday, 18 June 2015, at Our Lady and St Joseph's Catholic Primary School in Poplar, east London.[3] The fundamental purpose of the document is to ask 'What is the purpose of our life in this world? Why are we here? What is the goal of our work and all our efforts? What need does the earth have of us?' (*LS*, 160). These questions are placed within the wider framework of the mystery of God, who is praised through *The Canticle of the Creatures*, composed by St Francis of Assisi, when he declares: 'Praise be to you, my Lord, through our Sister, Mother Earth, who sustains and governs us' (*LS*, 1).[4] In the world of today, however, 'Mother Earth' is being plundered continually, and the dignity of human beings and their place within the created order are being threatened. This situation has arisen because 'we have come to see ourselves as her [Mother Earth's] lords and masters, entitled to plunder her at will' (*LS*, 2). Such human sinfulness means that 'the whole creation has been groaning in travail together until now; and not only the creation, but we ourselves' (Rom 8.22–3, partly quoted in *LS*, 2). St Paul is using the image of the pain associated with childbirth to illustrate how this painful experience is in the process of being removed both for creation and humanity through continual adherence to the Christian Gospel, which has been established once and for all by the death and resurrection of Christ (Rom 5.1–5; also *LS*, 99–100) and which gives new birth through our 'adoption' (Rom 8.23) as children of God. The reference to 'groans in travail' (*LS*, 2) should be interpreted in terms of the sum of Paul's thought found in Romans 8.18–25. There is a tension here between the past sinful age and God's future glorious age. The background to the past age is to be found in Genesis 3.14–19, where God reveals how the glory of creation is corrupted by disobedience to his will, as seen in our age, for example, through the pollution of the planet, waste of the earth's resources and climate change caused by human greed (*LS*, 20–26). The future age can be grasped partly in the present, and it is possible to reverse the situation of decline by turning to God and accepting the 'adoption' and 'redemption' offered through Christ (Rom 8.23). This gift is a cause for hope (Rom 8.24–5; *LS*, 61) not only for society but also for all creation, as human beings are now able to understand how they should care for all people as

God's beloved sons and daughters and the world as his 'loving gift' (*LS*, 220).

The tension between the ways things will be and the way they are now is bridged by the ministry of the Holy Spirit. Through this perception we are taken to the action of God in creation where his Spirit, word and wisdom are manifested to the world (Gen 1.2). We can appreciate the ways in which God is continually renewing his created order when we recite the ancient psalm (Ps 104 [Vg 103]) in worship, and we are able to understand how the earth is always being blessed by the divine Creator through the ministry of his Spirit. It is the responsibility of humanity, especially those in positions of power, to cooperate with God in ensuring that the planet is preserved for future generations (for positive examples see *LS*, 58). St Paul believes that the Spirit 'intercedes' for the world and identifies with its 'weakness' and 'searches' the mind and heart (Rom 8.26–7). Here we see Paul articulating an understanding of the created order which combines the saving ministry of Jesus with the activity of the Holy Spirit in a way that ensures that the whole created order may be redeemed by God. Paul also perceives that, given the action of the Spirit, we are able to recognize his work, allowing this new creation to enjoy freedom (Rom 8.11). This action of the Spirit is summarized through the concept of 'groaning' (Rom 8.22). Paul refers to this concept three times: the groaning of all creation (Rom 8.22); the groaning of humanity (Rom 8.23); the groaning for humanity of the Spirit himself (Rom 8.26).[5] Thus, by using this idea of groaning, those who respond to the ministry of the Spirit are able to perceive how, by their 'fellowship in [of] the

Holy Spirit' (2 Cor 13.14), they are a part of God's plan, by which the totality of the universe becomes renewed through the action of the Creator Spirit.

This ministry of the Holy Spirit, therefore, informs the conscience of humanity and enables us to serve and practise the will of God with regard to the care of creation. Given that the Holy Spirit represents the outpouring of the Father's love for his world, creation is able to respond to the invitation to participate in this divine love in action. Such action is seen through respect for the ecological life of the planet and for the upholding of the dignity of all human life. Since the Second Vatican Council the Church has affirmed that the 'Spirit of God [...] directs the course of time and renews the face of the earth'. The Spirit, therefore, is at work within the political and social life of the world in order to ensure that the 'social order and its development must constantly yield to the good of the person'. Inspired by the Spirit, it is the mission of the Church to ensure that social conditions are improved in terms of justice and goodness. Our aim must be to undertake this ministry armed with the 'ferment of the Gospel', which 'continues to arouse in [our] hearts' the 'unquenchable thirst for human dignity' (*GS*, 26). It is in this context that *Laudato Si'* should be placed, as Pope Francis maintains that 'The Spirit of God has filled the universe with possibilities and therefore, from the very heart of things, something new can always emerge' (*LS*, 80). It is the spiritual detection and realization of these 'new things' that are at the heart of Pope Francis's vision for the created world.

My reflection on *Laudato Si'* has enabled me, in three particular ways, to perceive further the ministry of the Holy Spirit within creation. First, the Spirit challenges us to construct an ethical framework within which creation and humanity might flourish.[6] In this task recourse to consider 'the fruit of the Spirit' from St Paul's list is essential: 'love, joy, peace, patience, kindness, goodness, faithfulness, gentleness and self-control' (Gal 5.22–3); the acquisition and the living of these God-inspired virtues will ensure that life on the planet not only demonstrates his glory but also enables both animals and humans to manifest their interdependence with each other for the common good (Is 11.6–9 and *LS*, 80). Sadly, the converse is also true: that there are many ways in which we can close ourselves to the work of the Spirit by the pursuit of selfishness for personal gain, by rigid legalism and by living the Christian life not as service to God and to each other but by following our personal inclinations and interests. In this way we have constructed a destructive ethical framework which assumes that perennial progress is for ever possible, seen, for example, in the desire to possess the latest piece of technological equipment. This mentality means that we make endless demands on creation, we exceed its capacity, and, in the end, nature will be destroyed. We must return to consider 'the fruit of the Spirit'. By the daily examination of conscience we need to look at how we have behaved towards the environment and each other and, in the power of the Spirit, to examine the lifestyle in which we are engaged or to which we aspire.

Second, we should allow the Holy Spirit to mould our lives in order to engage in 'ecological conversion' (*LS*, 216–21). One of the attributes of the Spirit is to transform the character of human beings in relation to

God's purpose. Through the ministry of the Spirit we have the potential to become wise (Prov 1.2–3), to be truly prophetic by proclaiming and living the word of God by receiving 'another heart' (1 Sam 10.9–10), to proclaim, by being anointed by the Spirit, freedom to the broken-hearted and to prisoners, which in itself is the manifestation of God's good news (Is 61.1) and to share in the Spirit-filled ministry of the Messianic king (Is 11.2) by responding to 'the gaze of Jesus' (*LS*, 96–8). As a result of being open to the Spirit we have again enthroned God at the centre of our lives, perceiving 'that the world is God's loving gift' (*LS*, 220). Through this perception we can contemplate the mercy of God both in the patterns of creation and in the simple actions of kindness and acceptance shown to us, and which we are able to demonstrate to others.[7] In a multiplicity of ways we are touched by the hidden presence of the Holy Spirit, who is at work everywhere in order that we might seek and find friendship with God. Through the ministry of the Spirit and by his grace our fellowship with God is renewed, allowing us to follow the path of true conversion.

Third, the Holy Spirit assists us to enter into true dialogue on environmental issues in the ways envisaged by Pope Francis – with the international community (*LS*, 164–75), with political leaders concerning national and local policies (*LS*, 176–81) and in a spirit of openness and transparency (*LS*, 182–8). The purpose of this dialogue is not to achieve agreement 'at any price' but, rather, to engage in discussion following the fundamental principles which are outlined in *Laudatio Si'*: creation as the work of God (e.g., *LS*, 77), respect for the dignity of every person on the planet where no one is 'superfluous' (*LS*, 84), especially not the poor (*LS*, 48–50), and corporate action to ensure that the quest for 'human fulfilment' (*LS*, 189–201) is paramount. For these reasons I regard *Laudato Si'* as a challenging, timely and powerful document, but this is not the end of the story. Not only must we all think and act in the ways which Pope Francis has presented, but we should expose ourselves more thoroughly to the ministry of the Holy Spirit. For me this ministry and its challenges are summarized in these lines from 'A Christian Prayer in Union with Creation', which concludes the Encyclical Letter:

> Holy Spirit, by your light
> you guide this world towards the Father's love
> and accompany creation as it groans in travail.
> You also dwell in our hearts
> and you inspire us to do what is good.
> Praise be to you!
>
> (*LS*, 246)

## Notes

1. See Ratzinger, Cardinal Joseph (1987 [first published in German in 1982]), *Principles of Catholic Theology: Building Stones for a Fundamental Theology*, trans., Sister Mary Frances McCarthy SND, San Francisco, CA, pp. 22–3.
2. See International Theological Commission (2014), *Sensus Fidei in the Life of the Church*, London, CTS, Chapter 2: 'The *Sensus fidei fidelis* in the personal life of the believer.' The *sensus fidei fidelis* is 'a sort of spiritual instinct that enables the believer to judge spontaneously whether a particular teaching or practice is or is not in

conformity with the Gospel and with apostolic faith. It is intrinsically linked to the virtue of faith itself' (p. 49). See also the Introduction: 'By the gift of the Holy Spirit [...] all of the baptised participate in the prophetic office of Jesus Christ [...] The Holy Spirit anoints them [the baptised] and equips them for that high calling' (p. 5).

3 This venue was chosen for three reasons. First, there were the eco-friendly initiatives used in the construction of the new building: for example, everything from the old building was crushed and used as hardcore, and an eco-environment for plants and insects is provided by the incorporation of a number of green roofs. Second, these initiatives symbolize the kind of world we need to build for our children in the future. Third, the proximity to Canary Wharf reminds us of the responsibility of finance, trade and business to pursue the initiatives advocated by Pope Francis.

4 See Francis of Assisi, 'The Canticle of the Creatures' (1225), *FA I*, pp. 113–14.

5 See Turner, Marie (2013), 'The Liberation of Creation: Romans 8:11–29', in Mary L. Coloe (ed.), *Creation is Groaning: Biblical and Theological Perspectives*, Collegeville, MN, Liturgical Press, pp. 57–70, esp. p. 57.

6 Note the full title of *Laudato Si'*: *On Care for Our Common Home*. Pope Francis gave the Encyclical Letter in Rome on the Solemnity of Pentecost, 24 May 2015 (*LS*, 246).

7 See my (2015) *A Pilgrimage Companion For the Year of Mercy 2015–16*, Stoke on Trent, Alive Publishing, pp. 37–41.

# PART TWO

## *Education for Life*

If I had not been ordained a priest, I would have been a teacher. Education, teaching and learning were constant features of discussion within our family in Liverpool. My parents were both teachers. In 1935 my father travelled to what is now St Mary's University, Twickenham, to train as a teacher. He taught in both secondary and primary schools. He was a fine and gifted man, and many years later, after my ordination (in December 1969), being versatile, he typed, using an old typewriter, my MA thesis for Manchester University, *St John Fisher: Bishop and Theologian in Reformation and Controversy* (Alive Publishing, 2011). My mother was a wonderful woman. For one week in my early life she was my class teacher. When she called my name for registration I replied 'Yes, miss'. Then came the rejoinder from across the classroom – 'But she's your mum'! My aunt, Sister Magdalene, a Sister of Charity of St Paul, was a head teacher. Even during the summer holidays there was continual talk about schools and the processes relating to teaching and learning. My brothers and I had to submit to the discipline of the teacher; homework had to be completed before we were allowed to play!

Years later, as a priest, I became involved in the educational work of the Church. During my time as the Secretary to the Bishops' Conference of England and Wales the Conservative administration of Margaret Thatcher passed the Education Reform Act of 1988. This Act defined new powers for local financial managements of schools and their independence from local authorities. The Act also required an enhanced role for Religious Education, which included regulations for collective worship, which should be of a 'broadly Christian character', and the establishment of a Standing Advisory Council on Religious Education (SACRE) within every Local Authority.[1] I found myself sharing in the responsibility for the organization of Catholic education in England and Wales and in negotiation with various governments and local authorities in order to ensure sufficient recognition and support for the delivery of Catholic education. This process proved time-consuming and complex and today seems never-ending. It is my conviction, however, that Catholic-based education at all levels (I was installed as Chancellor of St Mary's University on 27 May 2015) remains of vital importance, not merely for Catholics but also for the common good of society in its search for compassion and harmony.

# Note

1 Parsons, Gerald (1994), 'There and back again? Religion and the 1944 and 1988 Education Acts', *The Growth of Religious Diversity: Britain from 1945*, Volume II, *Issues*, ed. Gerald Parsons. London, Routledge, in association with the Open University, pp. 161–98.

# 4

## Faith in Education

*If you are willing, my child, you will be taught, and if you apply yourself you will become clever. If you love to listen you will gain knowledge, and if you incline your ear you will become wise.*

SIR 6.32–3 (ADAPTED)

As the majority of us know, the aim and objectives of education for schools are clear, and it is my desire that, when they leave school, young people should be 'confident and independent-minded'. My wish is that they realize their potential as 'unique individuals' and also that they understand their place as members of communities and society. Without this balance between individual progress and community awareness the danger of 'aggressive self-assertion'[1] looms, and the education which they receive in both rationality and the moral life of caring for others in the community will be found to have led to nothing but selfishness and vainglory. Education at its best should implant the desire to work to create an environment where justice, mutual tolerance, dialogue and harmony prevail. As a result, I believe that education holds a central place in our civic discourse, because education rightly perceived and sensitively delivered is fundamental to a sound and healthy life both of the person and of society.

Four main challenges face educators: to ensure the maximum personal and professional competence of their students; to help them explore what it means to be human, and what every human being has in common, thereby seeking a world view of the human person; to form in every pupil a personal commitment to building a better society; and to express and explore that openness to the spiritual and the transcendent which is a formative characteristic of every human being.

Thus, with regard to Catholic schools, I should like to advance further this general educational philosophy. First, I believe that individuals and communities are placed under the creative and redeeming power of God, who is the source of the life force of love and compassion. Thus, we are able to see that the inherent value of all human life is being cherished. Second, as a Catholic Bishop, I wish to affirm the importance of the continuing development of partnerships. At a fundamental level within Catholic education there is the partnership between the home, the school and the Church. Within this partnership our young people are encouraged to understand, live and practise our faith in all its aspects. In order that our educational aim and objectives might be delivered effectively, we need to uphold and reinforce the partnership that exists between school governors, staff and parents in order that every child is able to maximize their particular academic and personal strengths (including sport) and vocational aptitudes. We affirm that every child matters and that we are educating them for their journey through life because they are the beloved children of God. In this regard and within the local community I should like to see more partnerships developing between differing types of schools and between schools, colleges, universities and the world of work.

In my vision of Catholic school education there is nothing narrow or insular; on the contrary, by offering the Catholic spiritual treasures of the Mass, Confession and other acts of devotion, I believe that the 'door of faith' (Acts 14.27) is being opened to our young people. This loving and prayerful action will enable them to be enriched in their life of faith and thereby all whom they meet may be touched by the life and love of Christ. Through this encounter it is possible to discern 'the profound connection between evangelization and human advancement' (*EG*, 178), and as a result, the enrichment of the common good will bring unity to society (*EG*, 228). By conformity to Christ we shall become more truly human and able to achieve our true goal: the hope of glory in heaven.

I should like to explore faith in education in two ways. First, I am asking if it is possible to have faith in education and, if so, on what basis should education be understood? Second, I am enquiring if there is a role for matters relating to religious faith in education today.[2] As a preliminary, however, I should like to offer some remarks about the context in which these considerations arise.

At present the context for any serious debate on public matters is that of our collective search for deeper social responsibility in a time of economic stringency. These difficult circumstances are bringing to the fore crucial questions that, to some extent, we have not been required to face so sharply during the years of plenty. But those years have gone. In these new circumstances of austerity we have to be clearer than ever about our underlying sense of purpose in so many projects, not least among them education.

Is it too simple to say that many issues today revolve around an understanding of what it means to be fully human? What are we striving to achieve? What is most important for our fulfilment? What part does and should society play in this development of human potential? Does religious belief have a key role, or any role at all? And what is the part to be played by education?

Some commentators in recent years have used the phrase 'economic man' (*homo economicus*) to express one set of values and meaning underlying our existence. This expression entails the idea that we are all self-centred consumers of all possible goods, seeking the satisfaction of our preferences, however defined. As a model of what describes the richness of our lives and interactions, this understanding may seem a significantly deficient description. Yet it might be uncomfortably close to us as an indicator of how we behave. While the facts or statistics are clear that there is a lack of correlation, above a certain point, between income and human happiness or contentment, there remains a pervasive assumption within our culture that we are little more than separate individuals who happen to share the same space, who ultimately owe nothing substantial to society and who have no inescapable bonds with others. In another blunt phrase, this phenomenon is referred to as the 'unencumbered' self, leaving the suggestion that the only thing we have in common is the 'market' – or, as it was quaintly put: *'Tesco ergo sum'*.

I cannot believe that any of us actually accept this idea as a satisfactory account of what it is to be human. Such an account leads to a notion of education centred on, and judged by, the task of preparing young people to be effective and productive in the market-places of today and tomorrow. Emphasis is given to predominant links with industry and future economic well-being; now, of course, these are proper objectives for education. They are no more sufficient, however, than that account of what it is to be human, but this is not a true humanism.

I believe that a proper view of how we should understand humanity, the truth about ourselves in relation to God, the Absolute Being and each other, is unfolded for us in the Christian tradition. This tradition reveals the profundity of the truth relating to the depth of all human experience. This points to an inheritance upon which we may build with confidence.

The Christian understanding of the human person is that we are each created in the image and likeness of God (Gen 1.26). Thus the root of our dignity, of our purpose, lies deep within us, within that abiding presence of God of which St Augustine spoke so clearly when he said: 'And see, you were within and I was in the external world [...] You were with me, and I was not with you.'[3]

Each of us, then, is endowed with this capacity to go beyond the immediate, beyond the world of sense perception: we have a capacity for self-transcendence. In other words, we are each in the process of becoming, existentially, the person who we are essentially already by nature. Thus we are able to be open to the 'beyond'. Instinctively, we reach out for more. We seek love. We seek truth. We hold them as qualities to be attained. In many ways this orientation to truth and love is key: each person has a God-given capacity to search for the truth and to live by it in love. Similarly the gift of freedom allows us to exercise our conscience in both discerning and living the truth. Human life, in fact, makes no sense without this desire to seek what is true and to live in freedom.

But what is truth? In Part Two of his book *Jesus of Nazareth,* Joseph Ratzinger, Pope Benedict XVI, offers a valuable discussion of the concept of truth through his interpretation of Pilate's question to Jesus during his trial ('What is truth?', Jn 18.38). Pope Benedict believes that an important perception as to how this question may be interpreted today is to be found in the scholastic definition of this idea as utilized by St Thomas Aquinas, who argues for the conformity between intellect and reality. In this context Pope Benedict states: 'If a man's intellect reflects a thing as it is in itself, then he has found truth: but only a small fragment of reality – not truth in its grandeur and integrity.' The totality of the truth, however, according to Aquinas is to be found only with God, who is 'truth itself, the sovereign and first truth'.[4] When we share and understand this perception, then the truth becomes our possession, but only derivatively. We are, however, paradoxically, led closer to what Jesus, the teacher, means when he says that he came into the world 'to bear witness to the truth' (Jn 18.37).

The posing of the question 'What is truth?' within the context of the Passion of Jesus (Jn 18.1–19.42) brings into focus Pope Benedict's belief that: 'The world is "true" to the extent that it reflects God: the creative logic, the eternal reason that brought it to birth. And it becomes more and more true the closer it draws to God. Man becomes true, he becomes himself, when he grows in God's likeness. Then he attains to his proper nature. God is the reality that gives being and intelligibility [...] Bearing witness to the truth [...] means making creation intelligible and its truth accessible from God's perspective.'[5]

In this way we come to see that in mathematics and in the human genetic code, for example, we are recognizing the language of God. In contrast, an education concerned with merely 'functional truth' denies itself the whole language.

Thus, functional truth becomes by itself insufficient, as Pope Benedict comments further:

> The functional truth about man has been discovered. But the truth about man himself – who he is, where he comes from, what he should do, what is right, what is wrong – this unfortunately cannot be read in the same way. Hand in hand with growing knowledge of functional truth there seems to be an increasing blindness towards 'truth' itself – towards the question of our real identity and purpose.[6]

On this basis, therefore, true education must help us to see that our identity and dignity as free beings are found in our relationship to this first sovereign truth, to God. Moreover, recognizing this relationship enables us to affirm that we are all members of a single human family, each with a unique identity and a unique calling.

We are, therefore, inherently social beings whose identity is in part constituted by the relationships we have with others. In fact, none of us can find our true fulfilment entirely apart from other people.

It is not merely that we are born into relationships of dependency, or even that without our relationships we could not grow or develop. Rather, it is that only through our relationships – of love, friendship, the enlargement of our social ties – that we can be fulfilled. To be fully human is to be more than an individual: it is to be a person in relationship, self-transcendent, creative and emergent. These are the very bonds that enable us to understand and fulfil our freedom to be ourselves.

Now this understanding gives us a very different purpose as a basis for education. Now we are talking about the development of the whole person, understood in this 'self-transcending' manner, reaching out from within a complex of relationships, building more relationships of every sort and seeking fulfilment precisely in the depth of relationship and community, and being conscious of God.

The deepest purpose of our efforts, then, is not self-promotion but service of this complex web of interdependent persons. Our efforts are at the service of others, at the service of their and our fulfilment. It is for this purpose that education exists, especially in those very formative years up to the early twenties.

This claim is simple but rather radical. Education has a subsidiary function – it should be at the service of the common good of all: first, those around us with whom we share our lives, and then those in the wider perspective, which includes ultimately the whole human family.

This belief is the foundation of Catholic social teaching: the flourishing of all, respecting their dignity. This affirmation represents the overall purpose of Catholic social thought.[7] Each person matters, and no one is to be excluded. There is a job to be done, and we each have a part to play in doing it. Catholic teaching utilizes these ideas to express the conviction that education is here to serve the common good. Yet this language of the 'common good' is used so widely, with such different meanings, that its distinctive meaning is not easy to capture. There is here a useful image from mathematics. In a utilitarian calculus, maximizing the common good would be like an addition sum. In Catholic social teaching it is more like multiplication. You will understand that, in a multiplication, if there is a zero, then the total is also and always zero. So too if, in society's efforts at progress, the good of anyone is completely excluded – a zero – then the total is also zero and the true common good cannot be realized. The emphasis on the human dignity of all, immediately takes us towards a particular concern for the weakest and to ask how well their needs are being met.

If this overall view is accepted, then the question arises as to how it shapes our understanding of the essential core of education. How are we to treat each person who takes part in the process?

In recent years there has been a growth in interest in education in terms of the formation of character.[8] Much research has been undertaken into the values and virtues upheld by young people, from the youngest age of three years up to more complex research into the views of those aged sixteen to nineteen. Resources exist, cast in non-religious terms, to enhance this aspect of education, and the publications continue to emerge, both in terms of research and classroom resources.

From a Christian point of view the effort to avoid religious language and put aside the valuable contributions of such a rich and fruitful tradition is not necessary. Fortunately, we are free of such inhibitions. While this emphasis on character education is a very contemporary approach, it is not new. Recently, I had my attention drawn to an address delivered to the National Association of Headmistresses in 1932. It was given by Mother Mary Angela Boord, then headmistress of the Ursuline Convent School in Forest Gate, east London.[9] She spoke about the central task of education as being the 'training of character' and how it was threatened by the growing number of pupils in schools and an increasingly uniform approach to learning. She highlighted how, in response, another philosophy of education had emerged, centred on a 'doctrine of self-expression'. This sounds rather familiar, so it is worth following Mother Mary Angela's comments a little further. She expressed doubt about this new philosophy because, as she said:

> [I] cannot believe that the method of self-expression, carried to its logical conclusion, provides any real safeguard to an individuality valuable to the individual himself or to society. For, at least in its more advanced forms, self-expression ignores the fundamental difference between repression of impulses and control of impulses. Secondly, by placing the good or convenience of others as the only limit of its action, it ignores objective standards of right and wrong and so must lead, if not to unrestricted egoism, at best to a weak humanitarianism. Moreover it ignores the

practical fact that the young child soon exhausts, not merely that which it has worth expressing, but also that which it is able to express at all.

This quotation provides considerable material for further research. The good headmistress continues: 'The deepest fact, which is often ignored when character training is approached from the angle of self-expression, is the distinction between individuality and personality.'

In making and elaborating on this distinction in 1932 Mother Mary Angela touched on many contemporary themes: the use of the term 'individual' often amounts to the psycho-physical aspects of each person: body temperament, instinct and consequent reactions to experience and to the world around us. On the other hand, however, to understand the term 'person' correctly is to perceive a being striving for freedom from domination by 'the entire mechanism of human nature', capable of pure thought and free will, created and sustained by God with a definite vocation and purpose. Thus Mother Mary Angela concludes these remarks by saying: 'Our task, then, in the training of character is to find means of developing, not so much individuality, which may lead to an eventual dominance of idiosyncrasy or egoism, but personality by the integration of character round the spiritual core of the person.' She sums up her view with the saying: 'Be yourself, but make that self just what God wants it to be.'

Mother Mary Angela comes across as such an attractive figure, a true educationalist, in whom one can have great faith. She recognizes the teenage years as a period of 'plasticity': 'The girl awakening to a clearer self-consciousness and a keener self-criticism grows in

[a] sense of personal responsibility, in discernment of higher values and in depth of spiritual aspiration.' The teenager, therefore, needs 'understanding and judicious' sympathy. She insists, however, that 'a lax standard is fatal to growth and freedom of her personality as [is] an over-rigid code of rules backed by sanctions of reward and punishment.' And then the words I like best. She sums up the ethos of a school in one sentence: 'Courage is born in an atmosphere of trust; sincerity in that of truth, purity in beauty and gentleness in love.'[10]

At this point I should like to introduce another theme of increasing interest to educationalists and indeed, even somewhat surprisingly, in wider circles in society. Flowing directly from the address of Mother Mary Angela in relation to the values which should be found in education, there is a growing appreciation today of the importance of the role and cultivation of virtue.

We all recognize how important it is that trust is re-established or strengthened at many levels in society, whether in government, in banking and the financial sector or simply between the generations. As Pope Benedict says in his Encyclical Letter *Caritas in Veritate*: *'Development is impossible without upright men and women, without financiers and politicians whose consciences are finely attuned to the requirements of the common good.'*[11] To act in this way requires more than not breaking rules. It demands the cultivation of moral character, the development of habits of behaviour that reflect a real respect for others and a desire to do good works. This activity is what we would hope for from the efforts of all of us in education. What we are seeking, then, is the practice of virtue. This practice helps to shape us as persons because virtue strengthens who we are by nature. It empowers the process of our becoming more fully human. By virtue we act well, not because of external constraint but because it has become natural for us to do so. The cardinal virtues are 'prudence, justice, fortitude and temperance' (*CCC*, 1805), to give them their traditional names, which act as the hinges on which the good life turns. They form us as moral agents, so that we do what is right and honourable for no other reason than because it is right and honourable, irrespective of rewards and regardless of what we are legally bound to do. Virtuous actions spring from a sense of personal dignity, and the dignity of others and from self-respect as a citizen. It is doing good even when nobody is looking.[12]

Much of what I have said is drawn from the tradition of Christian teaching and life with which many of us are familiar. Similar conclusions can be arrived at by the pathways opened up in other major religions.[13] Having an appreciation of these treasure stores of wisdom and revelation is an invaluable help in the project of building the common good and of self-fulfilment. Without this appreciation we are condemned to be endlessly starting again and, no doubt, repeating mistakes and pursuing blind alleys. The gift of faith, that trusting, loving response to the revelation of God, is of the greatest importance because it puts us into the realm of a clear and conscious relationship with God, the source of all life and happiness, and into the context of a community of faith which, for all its shortcomings, will support, encourage, stimulate and guide us.

Religious Studies should be seen to be at the heart of the study of the humanities. Indeed in Catholic schools, Religious Studies is at the heart of the curriculum. It can claim to be *the* humanity, *par excellence*. In a world of increasing confusion, Religious Studies gives young people perhaps their only opportunity to engage seriously not only with the most profound philosophical questions concerning human existence and the nature of reality but also with the most fundamental ethical dilemmas of our day. Religious Studies is a demanding subject, requiring knowledge and skills in history, the critical use of texts, anthropology, ethics, philosophy and theology.

The breadth and depth of Religious Studies and its potential to enrich the lives of students are amply demonstrated by the new GCSE in Religious Studies (first taught in September 2016).[14] The new GCSE specification requires students to demonstrate knowledge and understanding of at least *two* religions. In the majority of Catholic schools, students will engage in thoughtful dialogue with Judaism alongside their own faith tradition of Catholic Christianity, attentive to the affinities as well as the differences between these two faiths. The revised Catholic Christianity component of the new GCSE specification laid out by the government was informed, to a significant degree, by detailed proposals developed by the CREDO group in partnership with the Catholic Bishops' Conference of England and Wales. The CREDO group was comprised of Catholic theologians, representing the major Catholic Universities in the UK, including Heythrop College University of London, St Mary's University, Liverpool Hope University, Newman University, Leeds Trinity University and the Centre for Catholic Studies at Durham University. The specification that emerged from this process sought to focus on a number of key theological 'beliefs' from a more integrated perspective, engaging with scripture, tradition and magisterial teaching (papal and conciliar documents, notably Vatican II) as sources of wisdom.

The result is a Catholic Christianity syllabus that engages in some depth with core Catholic beliefs and teaching on the topics of creation, incarnation, trinity and mission, redemption, church and kingdom, and eschatology. Students are encouraged to examine the layered depths of theological reflection on these central beliefs from within their own rich Catholic tradition.[15] So, for example, they reflect on the roots of Trinitarian thought in the scriptures, both the Old Testament emphasis on worship of the one God (e.g., Deut 6.4), as well as intimations of the triune God, Father, Son and Spirit in the New Testament (for example, in the theology of St Paul in Galatians 4.1–7, which describes believers as indwelt by the Spirit of God's Son, enabling believers to call God '*abba*', Father). Further depth of reflection is provided by an engagement with key thinkers from the Christian tradition, notably St Augustine's teaching on the inner life of the Trinity as an interplay of mutual love, which then flows into a discussion of more contemporary magisterial teaching, notably Benedict XVI's Encyclical *Deus Caritas Est* (2005). Here students are reminded that the entire mission of the Church – to proclaim love of God and love of neighbour – is a manifestation of the love of the Trinity, the truth that God is Love (*DCE*, 19).[16]

Flowing from this central belief that we are encouraging our students to reflect upon the religious dimension of their humanity in their Religious Studies education, I should like to conclude on a note of faith, hope and love, which forms the foundation for our prayer life and an essential part of education for us all. Our churches and chapels are constructed not only to contain the life of worship but also to be themselves an expression of that worship. Here we recognize that it is Christ Jesus who opens for us, by the will of the Father and the work of the Holy Spirit, the truth about ourselves and the unfathomable truth of God. This unfathomable truth is of God who is a dynamic communion of persons, Father, Son and Holy Spirit, each of whose unique identity is wholly constituted by their being in relation one to the other. Furthermore, the incarnation of the second person of the Trinity reveals what it is for us to be human. From Christ Jesus, who is wholly from the Father and wholly for the Father and, therefore, wholly for us too, we learn that our human personhood is a way of being entirely from and for the other. Faith in Christ Jesus, crucified and risen, assures us that God has definitively and irrevocably chosen to be for us, and that we have been set free to be wholly for God and for one another. This faith, in response to the revelation of love itself, gives rise to our sure and certain hope that our becoming more like God will reach its end, its fulfilment. Our humanity is perfected precisely by sharing in the divinity of Christ, by sharing in his being anointed with the Father's love. It is such faith and hope that inspire within us a self-sacrificing love – a love bringing healing to our fractured world, even here and now.

Building on the natural virtues, there is a place for faith in education, along with love and hope. When this fact is understood, then education serves the process whereby every person can move on the pathway of self-transcendence. This pathway, while perfecting our human nature, surpasses it with wonder. For these supernatural virtues – faith, hope and love – are nothing less than God making himself fully known, educating us, forming us, drawing us out beyond self and into the very heart of divine life, where, to use the words of Mother Mary Angela, we become the self that God wants each one of us to be.

# Notes

1. Little, Tony (2015), *An Intelligent Person's Guide to Education*. London, Bloomsbury, p. 31.
2. The substance of this chapter was given in Guildford Cathedral on 11 March 2011. I am grateful to Sean Ryan for assisting me in providing new information in relation to the revised GCSE syllabus, September 2016.
3. *Conf.* Book X, xxvii (38).
4. Ratzinger, Cardinal Joseph, Pope Benedict XVI (2011), *Jesus of Nazareth*, Part Two, *Holy Week: From the Entrance into Jerusalem to the Resurrection*, Eng. trans., London, CTS, p. 192.
5. *Ibid.*, pp. 192f.
6. *Ibid.*, p. 193.
7. Hornsby-Smith, Michael P. (2006), *An Introduction to Catholic Social Thought*. Cambridge, Cambridge University Press, in particular, Chapter 5, pp. 85–114.
8. Of the numerous studies available see, for example, Layard, Richard, Dunn, Judy and the panel of The Good Childhood Inquiry (2009), *A Good Childhood: Searching for Values in a Competitive Age*, London, Penguin Books, in particular, Chapter 5, 'Values', pp. 73–87.
9. Mother Mary Angela Boord OSU (1878–1976) was Headmistress of the Ursuline Convent School, Forest Gate, from 1925 to 1938. A memoir has been written by

Sister Mary Winefride Sturman OSU. I am grateful to the archivist, Sister Katharine Glencross OSU, for drawing this memoir to my attention.
10 I am grateful to Fr Joseph Quigley for drawing my attention to Mother Mary Angela's address, 11 June 1932, as found in the Archbishop of Westminster's archive, ref. AAW Hi 2/10 1930–42.
11 *CV*, 71.
12 *CCG*, in particular, pp. 11–13.
13 The position of the Catholic Church regarding non-Christian religions is expounded in the Second Vatican Council document Declaration on the Relation of the Church to Non-Christian Religions: *Nostra aetate*, 28 October 1965, in particular the statement that 'The Catholic Church rejects nothing of what is true and holy in these religions' (2).
14 See the Department for Education document *Religious Studies: GCSE Subject Content* (February 2015), https://www.gov.uk/government/uploads/system/uploads/attachment_data/file/403357/GCSE_RS_final_120215.pdf
15 See the excellent student textbook (AQA syllabus) edited by Anthony Towey (Director of the Aquinas Centre, St Mary's University) and Philip Robinson (Religious Education Adviser to the Catholic Education Service), *The New GCSE Religious Studies Course for Catholic Schools*, Vol. 1, *Catholicism & Judaism*, Chawton, Redemptorist Publications, 2016.
16 *Ibid.*, pp. 58–65.

5

*Faith Finding a Voice: Looking to Bede*

Proclamation has stood at the heart of the Gospel since Jesus called the twelve apostles and sent them out two by two with the authority to share in his ministry of preaching and living the kingdom of God (Mk 6.7). St Paul was commissioned by the risen and glorified Jesus (Gal 1.15–16) to exercise a similar apostolic ministry of evangelization by being called to be his ambassador (2 Cor 5.20). Christian mission, therefore, is fundamental for the life of the Church. The Second Vatican Council decree *Ad gentes divinitus*, on the missionary activity of the Church, maintains that she is 'called upon to save and renew every creature, so that all things might be restored in Christ' (*AG*, 1).

An aspect of the vocation of Christian leaders is to encourage the ministry of mission and evangelization, to be undertaken universally and within the context of British society. By his life and ministry Bishop Kevin Dunn illuminated the vision of this missionary ideal. His prophetic voice spoke to the community in the vicinity of Durham, and he inspired the formation of practical partnerships between the Churches, religious orders, a private trust and the University of Durham, in order to establish the first chair of Catholic Theology within a secular British university. Dedicated to the Venerable Bede, this chair, in conjunction with the Durham Centre for Catholic Studies, offers the opportunity for researching the challenges facing contemporary Catholicism and also provides the momentum to stimulate the practice of mission in an academic and social environment in order that faith may find a rousing voice to enable 'the kingdom of God [to be] proclaimed and renewed' (*AG*, 1).

★★★

*The spiritual man judges all things, but is himself to be judged by no one. 'For who has known the mind of the Lord so as to instruct him?' But we have the mind of Christ.*
1 COR 2.15–16, from the first reading for the feast of St Bede the Venerable, priest and doctor of the Church, 25 May

*Therefore, most beloved bishop in Christ, I exhort you carefully to strengthen with good works and sound teaching that sacred dignity which God, who has given both authority and spiritual grace, has generously entrusted to you [...] to preach God's word with great strength, helped by the king of virtues, our Lord Jesus Christ.*
Bede's *Letter to Egbert*[1]

*The voice of the turtledove is heard in our land* (Song 2.12).

# FAITH FINDING A VOICE: LOOKING TO BEDE

*The voice of the preacher is heard in the land that already began to be ours as soon as it received the word of faith.*
  Bede's commentary On the Song of Songs[2]

★★★

It was an honour to have given the Bishop Kevin Dunn Memorial Lecture. Along with so many others, I have the fondest memories of Bishop Kevin. Indeed, I still miss his presence, his vitality and his down-to-earth approach to our faith and Church. Kevin would have approved of the title of this address: *Faith Finding a Voice*. He wanted to get on with the job of preaching 'God's word with great strength' while at the same time thinking carefully about what it entailed and demanded. He wanted action rather than talking, and this maxim must be a criterion for us. I hope we can find some strength here which will enable us to proclaim and live the faith.

It is right to recall one particular and remarkable action taken by Bishop Kevin: that of the establishment of the Bede Chair of Catholic Theology in the University of Durham.[3] This truly is a lasting achievement and one which indeed typifies the importance of our theme. Bishop Kevin was determined that our Catholic faith would indeed find a particular voice in the University and in the local Church. To its credit, the University responded positively to this initiative and continues to do so. Do not be surprised, therefore, if I return to your beloved Bede later in this address.

As we begin to ponder the various aspects of the challenge of faith finding a voice in our world today, it is important to recall the wonderful, well-known reflection of St Augustine, given in reference to the role of St John the Baptist. Augustine insists that we understand the difference between what is said and who is saying it: 'John was a "voice", but in the beginning the Lord was the Word. John was a voice for a time: but Christ, who in the beginning was the Word, is the Word in eternity.'[4]

There are a number of important issues for us here. First, the realization that in finding a voice, faith – my faith, your faith – must seek to express only the Word of God, the person of Jesus. It is to him that we wish to give voice, not to ourselves. This understanding is not as easy as it sounds. Our whole frame of mind, shaped by the very air we breathe, is that we want to give voice to ourselves, to our own ideas and thoughts, to the insights we believe are rather special to us. We want to have our signature on what we say. Thus, this idea has to be borne in mind throughout our exploration: Jesus is the Word; we, in all our different circumstances, are only the voice.

Then there is a second point alluded to by St Augustine with reference to John the Baptist: we are a voice – or voices – for a time; Christ is the Word for all eternity. Our voice is crucial, for it is the voice for this day and age. We have to work hard at understanding the day and the age so that our voice has coherence, in order that what we say 'makes sense'. In doing so, however, we have to remember that the Word to which we are giving voice has an unchanging truth, an abiding grasp on reality that we, of ourselves, cannot achieve. There is a tension here. On the one hand is our creativity: we are properly explorers, adventurers even, wanting to bring to the surface, to bring into the

## FAITH FINDING A VOICE: LOOKING TO BEDE

public eye, what has been seemingly lost or hidden. Yet, on the other hand, we are not the creators of the reality we seek. Rather, we are creatures of that reality who is Himself our Creator. Thus, our own creativity is at the service of a given truth, a given goodness, a given beauty, revealed in the unfolding mystery of God, most visibly in the person of Jesus.

You will recall, perhaps, the wonderful image used to portray the work of the great sculptor Michelangelo. His creative work has been described as that of releasing, from within the block of marble, the beauty of the statue that was already hidden there, which he, by his genius, could already discern. The furious pace at which he could work was fired by his desire to set free the wonderful form already present in the stone. Musical geniuses demonstrate a similar creativity: Mozart writing frantically the score of his Requiem; Handel working intensely to complete in twenty-four days his sacred oratorio *Messiah*. Here is creativity in the service of a great, given good. Here is beauty finding its particular expression in time and space, as for us faith too must find its voice.

To summarize this first point is to state this truth: faith finding a voice is always a work of fidelity. Faithfulness to what is given is a key and essential quality of the way in which the great mystery of faith finds fresh expression. In addition, we have clear ways of understanding this faithfulness: it is faithfulness to Jesus, the Word of God, as expressed in the Scriptures and the tradition of the Church and safeguarded by its teaching role, or *magisterium*.[5] This proposition contains a complexity of understanding which cannot be explored here. I should like, however, to make one observation. Fidelity to the *magisterium* of the Church should not be regarded as a form of imprisonment (Gal 5.1). Rather, the *magisterium* represents fidelity to the gift of God – his promise of the way in which the Holy Spirit pours his grace and love into our hearts (Rom 5.5) – such bounty cannot impede our freedom in the search for the wisdom of God. Rather, it is a form, a shape, the result of a decision, through which freedom is tutored to explore ever more deeply that which it has accepted as lovely, true and beautiful. It is the harness of love which holds us to the task of faithfulness in the proclamation of the Gospel and guides us, often against our more wayward instincts, more deeply into the gift we have received.

From this spirituality flows a second and crucially important point, already implicit in what I have said so far: the voice has to be for today if it is to be a true service of the Word. Replaying the voice of the past will not be sufficient to fulfil this task of proclamation. Yearning for the familiar and having nostalgia for yesterday, emotions that can be frequently at play within us, hinder our ability to perform this ministry. In order to fashion a voice for today it is necessary to attend to the listening of the heartbeat of the age of which we are a part. In the language of the Church, therefore, dialogue is the essential partner of proclamation.

I heard recently a wonderful illustration of this point. It was a sermon given on the episode in the Acts of the Apostles in which Philip meets the Ethiopian eunuch and helps him to come to faith and be baptized. You may recall that, as the Ethiopian journeys home, he invites Philip into his chariot. The crucial phrase, as emphasized in the sermon, is this: 'So he urged Philip to get in and sit by his side' (Acts 8.31 [NJB]). It was from this position, being side by side, that Philip was able to engage in conversation and offer insight in response to questions, leading the Ethiopian to baptism (Acts 8.38). To sit side by side, therefore, is to be ready for dialogue.

In our attempt to find the art of dialogue, the art of attentive listening, I should like to make one point only. When involved in dialogue, great care should be taken to understand the interlocutor. Partners in dialogue should not attempt to distort or misrepresent the views of others, but rather, they should desire a true understanding of the others' opinions. Only then can there be a true exchange of ideas. This attitude avoids easy and superficial confrontation or pointless argument. In the contemporary world it is crucially important that this form of dialogue is embraced in order that, through the development of partnership, faith may be enabled to find its 'voice'. In our discussions we may not always be able to follow this ideal. There is a danger in allowing the pattern of much media communication to tutor our more personal manner of dialogue, even though much media communication is far from our normal way of talking together. After all, the media deal constantly with the exceptional and, of course, tend to sensationalize its message. News and comment features are designed to catch our attention and to draw us into an often confrontational interpretation of a trend or particular event. Personal communication, on the other hand, is usually about the very ordinariness of life. This communication is best shaped by the different qualities of dialogue: listening, understanding and shared empathy. The typical focus and methodology of the media should not dominate our ways of communicating. Indeed, we do well to step back from the media output which we are receiving constantly and evaluate and question its underlying assumptions. I shall be developing these ideas later.

The important point I wish to make here is that the way of dialogue is the pathway by which faith best finds its 'voice'. In our task, in our conversations, we have to be observant, not so much for the points of opposition as for the points of possible agreement, not so much for controversy as for convergence, not so much for highlighting what is missing as for seeking the good that is to be found in the other, without ignoring or glossing over important differences.[6] The pathway of dialogue is the pathway on which we are encouraged to walk, as was made clear by Pope Benedict during his visit to the United Kingdom in 2010. In our Catholic tradition there are three pathways down which faith finds a voice, three arenas or areas of dialogue in which we engage with our world and our society. These are the pathways of truth, of goodness and of beauty. I should like to say a word about each one in turn – but in the reverse order.

The first pathway concerns beauty. This pathway is perhaps the one that is most readily appealing to people today. In places and objects of beauty there remains an unobscured appeal, a quality that raises our minds, hearts and spirit above present circumstances, whatever they may be. Such beauty helps us to see our individuality within a wider perspective, loosening our preoccupation with ourselves and appreciating how our lives are but a part of a wider pattern, a wider response to the mystery of life itself. Often, but not always, that beauty has an explicit connection to the religious, to the account that faith gives of our endeavours and experiences. There are many places which are recognized as 'holy', and people still flock to them: Holy Island, Durham Cathedral or the tomb of St Cedd in Lastingham – to name a few near here. Works of art also have a great eloquence. Some of the most successful exhibitions in London have put forward the beauty of our faith: *Seeing Salvation*, *The Treasures of Heaven* and, most remarkably, *The Sacred Made Real*, the exhibition of Spanish works of art.[7] One of those pieces, a figure of the dead Christ,[8] presented a new problem to the museum authorities: visitors were kneeling beside it in prayer. They were asked gently to move on!

This situation, I suggest, highlights two points. First, we should be cautious about too easily identifying our age as one of 'aggressive secularism'. Of course there are some voices of that tone and content, but there is also a widespread and deep sympathy and search for the transcendent, for the things of God which we should note, respect and reflect upon, and to which we can respond.

Second, the beauty of our churches and homes, the beauty of our liturgy and behaviour, the beauty of our musical endeavour and the harmony we seek with others in our living together, are all parts of the way in which we express our confidence that this is indeed God's world. It was God who made it and it is 'very good' (Gen 1.31). Finding such a voice is hard work, as hard as producing any masterpiece, but it is a work in which all of us can be involved and to which we can give much thought.

The second pathway which I wish to discuss is that of goodness. This pathway is both theological and ethical, and it is also clear and practical, within the reach of each one of us. Pope Benedict, in his Encyclical Letter *Deus Caritas Est*, gives great emphasis to the importance of practical charity, rooted in and directed from the love of God, as that which gives credibility to Christianity. The words of Gospel truth are manifested when they are accompanied by the charitable deeds of kindness and goodness.[9] In his letter St James makes clear this point, 'So faith by itself, if it has no works [of charity], is dead' (Jas 2.17). Axioms such as 'Actions speak louder than words' embed this truth in everyday language, and the saints also have given it emphasis. In this context we recall the words commonly attributed to St Francis: 'Let us proclaim the Gospel always and when necessary use words.'[10]

On this basis, faith can find a voice on every street corner, in the kitchen and in the workplace, among friends and strangers, in every part of the broad pathway of life. The response of each individual should be spontaneous and personal; it is found in the work of parish groups coming together for a specific task; it is seen in the work of great organizations such as CAFOD, reaching across the world in charity. This humanitarianism operates on diverse levels and more intensively than is often appreciated. As a result, the Church needs to galvanize its organization in order to serve this witness of charity a little more systematically. This activity we are undertaking through the development of *Caritas*: a pattern of support and networking that has recognition in many countries. *Caritas* helps to develop the local work of charity and enables it to find a voice: a word of advocacy, which has a strong base in evidence and experience. A good step in this direction is for every parish to review and bring to light all humanitarian ministry which is performed and to ask how this ministry can be better supported and encouraged. Faith, therefore, finds a convincing voice through the work of practical goodness.

The third pathway, that of truth, is the most complex, for we live in an age in which truth has been largely relativized. This idea may be expressed in words such as these: 'You have your truth and I have mine and you must not impose your truth on me – though I may well expect you to accept mine!' The complexity of this cultural norm with which we are living is felt everywhere: in conflicts between the generations, in debate about the ethical and social norms to be upheld by society – such as the nature of marriage – and in the various fields of academic study. How are we to respond? How can the truth of faith find a voice in this context? I should like to make three practical suggestions.

The first concerns the practice of prayer, which is the raising of the mind and heart to God. Here is the first way in which the truth of faith finds its voice. Christian prayer is an explicit statement about the existence of God, about the gift of the Incarnate Word in Jesus Christ, and about how we live our lives in God's presence every day, every moment. In much of society today there is a great openness to the reality of prayer. Society, however, may have an unformed instinct about the totality of the nature of prayer and may not understand fully all that is involved in the work of faith. There is, however, an awareness of the reality which prayer touches. Think of the example of Fabrice Muamba, the young footballer who suffered heart failure on the pitch. There was a huge appeal for prayer for his recovery. Newspapers had headlines such as 'God is in charge'. The young man and his family have never ceased to speak about the importance of prayer alongside deep appreciation of the dedication and skill of the medical professionals. In a recent interview Muamba spoke of waking up to find his family around the bed saying psalms for his recovery. 'They were praying so loud', he laughed, 'no one could sleep through that!' Also, at a time when there is often controversy about the place of religious belief in the work place, his fiancée spoke so gratefully of 'a young African cleaner in the hospital who would come into the room every day to pray silently in the corner'. The hospital worker gives us all a good example, not only of the importance of prayer, but also of the importance of respecting the circumstances and the needs of each particular situation. Prayer is not to be imposed.

In my experience, no one has ever rejected me when I have offered to include them in my prayers, particularly when they have told me of something burdening or troubling them. Sometimes people ask for our prayers. This is an important sign. We should be ready to offer sensitively and even a little diffidently, to pray for others. To make such an offer is a simple, everyday way in which faith finds a voice in our lives and its truths are proclaimed. Its fruit is clear: Fabrice Muamba stated boldly, and it became a newspaper headline: 'If God is with me then who can be against me?' (allusion to Rom 8.31).[11]

A second way in which faith finds a voice in the proclamation of truth is in public debate. This observation could readily be a lecture in its own right, but I want to make one essential point. Often public debate produces more heat than light. Tempers rise – and people are provoked – and listening ends, and the debate becomes a battle of wills, not a meeting of minds. Of course it is not always so, but the temptation to concentrate on giving an opinion rather than seeking to understand and respond to another point of view is very real, as I know too well. In this context Pope Benedict has made a particular appeal for the part that silence and reflection have to play in communication. He said: 'Silence is an integral element of communication; in its absence, words rich in content cannot exist.' In this context, however, 'it is necessary to develop an appropriate environment, a kind of "eco-system" that maintains a just equilibrium between silence, words, images and sounds.' This reflection is confirmed by Pope Benedict's opening remarks, that

> When word and silence become mutually exclusive, communication breaks down, either because it gives rise to confusion or because, on the contrary, it creates an atmosphere of coldness; when they complement one another, however, communication acquires value and meaning.[12]

In practice, this reality may mean many things which you are well able to discern for yourselves. One suggestion from me: every radio and TV set has an 'on/off' switch. Perhaps we should use it more often and free ourselves from too much input, from the constant round of news and debate, so as to reflect a little more and then deepen the quality of our understanding and of the contribution we can make to society. Too much input into our consciousness leaves insufficient time or space for reflection. A little more stillness, space and silence in our lives will enable the 'still, small voice' of faith to find its power.

The third area in which faith can find a voice for truth is in the researching of the past. Such study illuminates the numerous narratives through which we are able to understand the ways in which history impacts on how we perceive the nature of our lives, and the circumstances that influence them within both the social and spiritual spheres in which we operate. It is, therefore, to one of your own favourite saints – St Bede the Venerable, whose feast day we celebrate on 25 May – that I should like to turn, in order to illustrate how the effects of Bede's understanding of society and of the Church have relevance for our continuing search for the voice of truth.

Bede's historical writings, the principal among them being the *Ecclesiastical History of the English People* (AD 731), are based on the overriding conviction that history concerns the work of God and how the divine operates within both society and its political organization. At the centre of this conviction is the belief that the Holy Spirit continues to operate within time. Bede placed the birth of Christ as the foundation from which the dating of world events should commence. This procedure differed from that predominant at the time, which used the foundation of the city of Rome (753 BC) as the starting-point for chronological calculation. For Bede, therefore, the interpretation of history should be perceived from the perspective of the Incarnation: God made man in Jesus Christ.[13]

This explanation might suggest to us a way of giving an account of our own personal histories, the stories we so often want to share. To speak of our lives as being under the providence of God and of having key moments recognized as part of that providence, or as a moving away from that perspective, would be a remarkable direction in which faith could find a voice in our everyday speech. This approach is not so much a question of adopting pious phraseology, in which speech is interspersed with references to the good Lord, but, rather, a way of seeing our own history as the unfolding of the gift of life, given by God, and the journey to a deeper understanding of that gift in all it entails as we journey towards our eternal fulfilment.

An illustration of a guiding principle at work in a narrative is seen each week in the *Antiques Roadshow*, when person after person overrides the financial value of an antique with the value it has for the family to which it belongs. Here value and meaning are given a specific focus. The story these people want to tell is the story of the richness of their family life and heritage, not the story of the commercial value of what they own. Things look quite different, and indeed carry different value, from the perspective that is taken on them. We can take a further step, then, and speak about the meaning of our life's experience from the standpoint of our faith in God, in our relationship with the Lord and in the perspective of the continual presence of the Holy Spirit prompting and guiding us, not only in the bigger decisions of life but also in many smaller moments. This observation is not as strange as it might seem. In my experience, those who attain to old age often adopt this view. A fine example was seen in the film *Catholics: Women*, broadcast on the BBC.[14] There an older woman reflected quite spontaneously on her whole life from the perspective of the faith that she had rediscovered recently. She spoke of sixty years of her life, years in which she had been professionally very successful, as 'wasted years' now that she viewed them again from the conviction of her faith. It was a remarkable and moving testimony: faith finding an eloquent and compelling voice.

Commenting on the life and work of St Bede the Venerable, Pope Benedict XVI has highlighted the 'timely message' given by Bede for 'scholars', 'pastors' and 'consecrated people' in the Church today. Pope Benedict broadens his argument by offering Bede's advice to the lay faithful who should 'be diligent in religious instruction [...] to pray ceaselessly' and to reproduce 'in life what they celebrate in the liturgy'. Bede's counsel here is to demonstrate that the lay faithful should offer 'all their actions as a spiritual sacrifice in union with Christ'. Within the lay faithful Bede gives particular admonition to parents, that within the home they should exercise their 'priestly office as pastors and guides' ensuring that their children receive 'a Christian upbringing.'[15]

A last thought. Of all the aspects of the Eternal Word which took flesh in Christ one strikes me of particular immediacy for our world today: it is the word of hope. Perhaps, as we struggle to enable the faith in our lives to find a voice, whether in beauty, goodness or truth, and always down the pathway of sensitive dialogue, it is the word of hope that we might most strive to articulate. Hope is the virtue by which we see all things in the perspective of the heavenly kingdom. Hope expresses that for which we strive, which is as yet not attained but which we know, on the promise made to us by the Lord, can indeed be attained and is indeed our true destiny. When we articulate that hope, then present reality takes on its deepest meaning, its true perspective.

Within this vision we human beings can maintain our true dignity, our true poise, no matter what we face. It is with the true hope of heaven in our hearts that suffering is borne with dignity, that failure is faced, that betrayal is endured and that success is celebrated properly. Christian hope strengthens our resolve and deepens our charity, for in its understanding we know that we are all truly brothers and sisters of one Father and share in a common destiny. To live without such hope is to live with vital pieces of the jigsaw of life missing. This is frustrating and annoying. We search for the missing pieces and know that until they are found we see the work as incomplete and are tempted to think of it as worthless. When they do emerge from under the sofa and are clicked into place, then the whole jigsaw becomes a thing of joy to behold. Our word of faithful hope can bring great joy to many.

Such faithful hope in finding a voice can be seen, for example, in the martyrdom of St Stephen as recorded by St Luke in the Acts of the Apostles (Acts 7.54–60), a text on which Bede has commented eloquently. Stephen died because he had proposed a new understanding of Jewish history (Acts 7.2–53), now centred on the coming, death and resurrection of Jesus, the promised Messiah of God (Acts 7.51–3). The climax of Stephen's martyrdom is revealed when, 'full of the Holy Spirit' (Acts 7.55), he declares that 'Behold, I see the heavens opened, and the Son of man standing at the right hand of God' (Acts 7.56), upon which text Bede comments: 'to strengthen the blessed martyr's endurance the doors of the heavenly kingdom are opened and, so that the innocent man being stoned may not stumble to the ground, the crucified God-man appears crowned in heaven.' The fruit of this hope is clear. Even as Stephen died he prayed, 'Lord Jesus, receive my spirit' (Acts 7.59) and 'Lord, do not hold this sin against them' (Acts 7.60). Bede believed that these intercessions demonstrate 'the virtue of the blessed martyr who was so inflamed with zeal that he openly reproached his captors for their fault in lacking faith, and burned so with love that even at his death he prayed for his murderers.'[16] Peace and forgiveness are the fruits of such hope.

Let us give thanks for every fleeting glimpse we are given of the glory of God and the goodness of the Lord. Let those moments form and deepen our faithful hope. In that light may we indeed enable faith to find a fresh and compelling voice. Bede conceives this compelling voice, for example, in his recording of the divine gift of composing religious poems granted to Caedmon.[17] This gift includes poetry in praise of God the Creator:

> Praise we the Fashioner now of Heaven's fabric,
> The majesty of his might and his mind's wisdom,
> Work of the world-warden, worker of all wonders,
> How he the Lord of Glory everlasting,
> Wrought first for the race of men Heaven as a rooftree,
> Then made he Middle Earth to be their mansion.[18]

In addition Caedmon is given the divine wisdom of perceiving the history of God's salvation from the creation of the world, God's victory over sin and death personified in the ministry of Jesus, the outpouring of the Pentecostal Spirit and the subsequent preaching and teaching of the Apostles and reaching forward to 'the joys of the Kingdom of Heaven.'[19] These manifestations of the divine voice ensured that Caedmon 'crowned his life with a happy end.'[20] Creation, salvation, divine victory, faithfulness and truth – the voice of God spoken to humanity, this is the message of hope for society today.[21]

# Notes

1. Bede's *Letter to Egbert* (5 November, AD 734) is to be found in *EH*, pp. 333–51. The quotation here is to be found on pp. 337 and 339.
2. The Venerable Bede (2011), *On the Song of Songs and Selected Writings*, trans., ed. and intro. by Arthur Holder, preface by Benedicta Ward. Mahwah, NJ, Paulist Press, pp. 77f.
3. The late Bishop Kevin Dunn was the Bishop of Hexham and Newcastle from 2004 to 2008. He led the campaign to raise £2 million to endow the Bede Chair of Catholic Theology within the University of Durham. The substance of this chapter was given on 15 May 2012 at Ushaw College, Durham. I have added here further examples from Bede's writings in relation to *Faith Finding a Voice*.
4. St Augustine of Hippo (354–430), Sermon 293, 1–3, to be found in the Office of Readings for the Solemnity of the Birthday of St John the Baptist, 24 June; *DO*, III, 68★.
5. *CCC*, 888–92; see especially 890.
6. *FS*: in particular, 'Dialogue in the Teaching of the Catholic Church', Chapter 3, pp. 25–56.
7. See the following exhibition catalogues: Bagnoli, Martina, et al. (eds) (2010), *Treasures of Heaven: Saints, Relics, and Devotion in Medieval Europe*, London, British Museum; Bray, Xavier (2009), *The Sacred Made Real: Spanish Painting and Sculpture, 1600–1700*, London: National Gallery; Finaldi, Gabriele (2000), *The Image of* Christ (catalogue to the exhibition *Seeing Salvation*), London, National Gallery.

8  *Dead Christ*, c.1625–30, a sculpture by Gregorio Fernández; see Bray, *The Sacred Made Real*, p. 27.
9  *DCE*, 31, where the parable of the Good Samaritan (Lk. 10.25–37) is quoted as an example.
10 It is probable that this maxim is a popularized and generalized form of the injunction of St Francis given in the Rule of 1221, Chapter XVII, regarding preachers: 'Let all the brothers, however, preach by their deeds', *FA I*, p. 75.
11 Fabrice Muamba, who was playing for Bolton Wanderers in an FA Cup tie against Tottenham Hotspur, suffered a cardiac arrest on the pitch on 17 March 2012. Later (22 April) Fabrice said that his subsequent recovery had been 'more than a miracle', www.bbc.co.uk/sport/0/football/17803653.
12 Message of His Holiness Pope Benedict XVI for the 46th World Communications Day (Sunday, 20 May 2012), *Silence and Word: Path of Evangelization*. Rome, Libreria Editrice Vaticana, p. 1.
13 Thacker, Alan (2010), 'Bede and history', in *The Cambridge Companion to Bede*, ed. Scott DeGregorio. Cambridge, Cambridge University Press, p. 179.
14 *Catholics*, episode 3: *Women*. BBC 4 Documentary, directed by Richard Alwyn, first broadcast 8 March 2012.
15 Pope Benedict XVI (2010), *Church Fathers and Teachers: From Saint Leo the Great to Peter Lombard*. San Francisco, CA, Ignatius Press, pp. 76–8.
16 Martin, Lawrence T., trans., with intro. and notes (1989), *The Venerable Bede: Commentary on the Acts of the Apostles*, Cistercian Studies Series 117. Kalamazoo, MI, Cistercian Publications, pp. 75–6.
17 *EH*, IV, 24, p. 248. Caedmon, who had the gift for poetry, was a monk at Whitby Abbey during the abbacy (657–680) of St Hilda.
18 Ibid., pp. 248f.
19 Ibid., pp. 249f.
20 Ibid., p. 250.

21  See Hume, Basil (1996), *Footprints of the Northern Saints*, London, Darton, Longman and Todd, in particular, Chapter 10, 'The return of the saints', pp. 80–92, and the photograph of St Bede's tomb, Galilee Chapel, Durham Cathedral, p. 88. The inscription on the wall behind, added in 1971, is from Bede's commentary on the Revelation of St John, 2.28: 'Christ is the Morning Star, who when the night of this world is past brings to his saints the promise of the light of life and opens the everlasting day.' This is the true voice which humanity needs to hear continually.

# 6

## *The Voice of Faith in Schools and Universities: Looking to Newman*

Within the midst of secular society my vision for university education has two interlocking principles. First, within the university curriculum theology and religious studies ought to be given prominence together with politics, law and sociology. This emphasis will provide the student with an overall framework regarding the issues which are involved in understanding world affairs and offer a moral basis on which courses of action and the welfare of communities may be undertaken. Second, within the totality of university provision to affirm that the Catholic university has an important collaborative role, my position as the Chancellor of St Mary's University, Twickenham, a foundation which is thoroughly Catholic in character, has assisted me to perceive the ways in which the finest traditions of Catholic education may be built. There is nothing narrow or insular in this Catholic vision of education. It is open to all truly human endeavour, to links across Europe and the world beyond, to universities in North and South America, Africa, Asia and Australia.

This Catholic tradition is fine and noble. On this basis my two principles interlock when it is seen how the Catholic university represents a most important point of contact, of engagement, between the world of higher education and the Catholic Church. This engagement, if it is to be fruitful, requires that wonderful combination of openness and faithfulness: openness to the other, to every academic discipline, together with the engagement with the wide range of challenges facing our world, facing every society and individual today. We are also called to faithfulness, to who we are and to the richness of truth and beauty that the eyes of faith reveal, in the soul of every person, and in the created world and its unfolding in wonder.

I believe that four main tasks are required in order that my vision of education may be realized and that these are fundamental to a sound and healthy life both of the human being and of society: first, to enable every student to develop their personal and professional competence; second, to help them to explore and understand what it means to be a human being and to have a broad world view of a shared humanity; third, to prompt in every student a commitment to the building of a better society, one entrusted to bring justice, harmony and compassion to the world; and fourth, to express and explore the openness to the transcendent, to the spiritual, which is a formative characteristic of every human being, revealed in its fullness in the person of Jesus Christ.

To develop and maintain these tasks presents a challenge: to understand that strength is best used in compassionate service and that if we place ourselves at the centre of our world we end up worshipping idols that do not bring true peace. To help face the challenge, as students, teachers and members of the university staff now and in the future, we need to regard the university as a lifelong home in terms of the friendships made, of the ongoing opportunities for research in all areas of life and in order to provide the impetus as lives and careers unfold. We have been educated in a place which remains a home, a place for loving human engagement, prayer and study. I am much influenced by the educational principles of Cardinal John Henry Newman, who thought of the university as a community, universal in scope – 'a University is the home, it is the mansion-house, of the goodly family of the Sciences, sisters all, and sisterly in their mutual dispositions'[1] – a family of subjects, undertaken by the family of the university in the loving environment of the family home, a place to which we are always welcome to return.

★★★

*University training is the great ordinary means to a great but ordinary end; it aims at raising the intellectual tone of society, at cultivating the public mind [...] to detect what is sophistical, and to discard what is irrelevant.*
John Henry Newman, *The Idea of a University*,
Discourse VII, section 10[2]

★★★

When I think about the work of the university, my thoughts go immediately to the Blessed John Henry Newman.[3] His thoughts about the university are, I believe, very pertinent to the theme of evangelization and education: thus the title of this chapter, 'The Voice of Faith in Schools and Universities'. I wish to comment within the context not only of Cardinal Newman's recent beatification, on Sunday 19 September 2010, but also of the Apostolic Visit of Pope Benedict to the United Kingdom, during which the beatification was celebrated.[4] As you will understand, and as our celebrations of its first anniversary made manifest, this Visit continues to be an event of great importance for the Catholic community in England, Wales and Scotland. It has also had a lasting significance for the wider society of the United Kingdom – a society in which many cultures meet, not least within its schools and universities.

Pope Benedict, during his Apostolic Visit, paid special attention to education. On the morning of Friday 17 September he led a 'Big Assembly'. It was a unique event, presented in the presence of 3,500 schoolchildren but linked to every Catholic school in the United Kingdom, together with over 800,000 other participants, via an internet broadcast of the event. It truly was a 'Big Assembly'!

I should like to quote from the Holy Father's address, even though many of his words were addressed to children. He invited them to think about the deeper meaning of their lives and of their education. My experience tells me that words addressed to children are nearly always attractive to adults, although the opposite is not always true! So here are some of the insights offered by Pope Benedict to the children at St Mary's University College, Twickenham:

> In your Catholic schools, there is always a bigger picture over and above the individual subjects you

study, the different skills you learn. All the work you do is placed in the context of growing in friendship with God, and all that flows from that friendship. So you learn not just to be good students, but good citizens, good people [...] Never allow yourselves to become narrow. The world needs good scientists, but a scientific outlook becomes dangerously narrow if it ignores the religious or ethical dimension of life [...] We need [also] good historians and philosophers and economists, but if the account they give of human life within their particular field is too narrowly focused, they can lead us seriously astray.

A good school provides a rounded education for the whole person. And a good Catholic school, over and above this, should help all its students to become saints.[5]

Earlier that morning the Pope had addressed teachers and religious:

As you know, the task of a teacher is not simply to impart information or to provide training in skills intended to deliver some economic benefit to society; education is not and must never be considered as purely utilitarian. It is about forming the human person, equipping him or her to live life to the full – in short it is about imparting wisdom. And true wisdom is inseparable from knowledge of the Creator, for 'both we and our words are in his hand, as are all understanding and skill in crafts' (Wis. 7:16).[6]

This vision of education is the necessary context for our consideration of the relationship between evangelization and the culture of our schools and universities. Often the work of evangelization is that of the formation of a culture, and a culture draws its characteristics from the vision or expectation which lies behind an enterprise. The culture of education, then, can only be changed if the vision of education is clear and well founded. In this context I should like to concentrate on university education, bearing in mind that university life presupposes that experienced at school and also prefigures the world of work and professional life.

The vision of education expounded by the Holy Father is, of course, in good measure drawn from the vision of the Blessed John Henry Newman. Between 1826 and 1831 Newman was a tutor at Oriel College, Oxford. There he took a rather distinctive line: that the duty of the tutor and, therefore, the task of education, was to keep in view the whole development of the student, including his moral and spiritual well-being. The tutor had to undertake the pastoral care of his students and see them not simply as 'units' of education. This insistence did not make Newman particularly popular, especially when Edward Hawkins was elected Provost of the College in 1828.[7]

Yet, for Newman these intellectual and educational ideas were to come more to the fore later in his life. Given his scholarly past and commitment to education it was not surprising that the Archbishop of Armagh, Paul Cullen, invited Newman in 1851 to develop a Catholic University in Dublin and to become its first Rector.[8] This foundation lives on today as University College Dublin. In anticipation of taking up his appointment, Newman wrote a series of lectures which explained his thoughts about university education. It is these lectures which now constitute the substance of the book entitled *The Idea of a University*. These ideals he attempted to implement at the new Catholic University of Ireland.[9] This particular context, however, should not deter us from the fact that Newman's thoughts are important for the educational discourse of the twenty-first century. In seeking to describe the work of the university in terms of 'its essence', modern interpreters are able to engage critically and sensitively with his ideas because they are flexible and they have the ability to stand the test of time, despite massive social change and the existence, thankfully, of mass educational provision.

Newman recognized rightly that it was by including within the curriculum the study of the classical civilization of Greece and Rome that the capacity was provided 'to strengthen, refine, and enrich the intellectual powers'.[10] Newman saw philosophy, which he believed 'embraces and locates truth of every kind, and every method of attaining it',[11] as the basis required to encompass the total learning activity provided by a university. In the contemporary world this total learning activity has been broadened to include historical study, which assists in the analysis and interpretation of world events.

Theology was considered by Newman to merit a place, given that it is concerned with the truth that locates human endeavour in its wider relationship with God, rather than the pursuit of subjectivity or sentiment. Newman defined theology as 'the Science of God, or the truths we know about God put into system'.[12] On all of these subjects Newman wrote long specific discourses which merit further careful study, although it is not possible to consider them in detail here. The principle of cultivating the holistic mind, open to the widest body of knowledge and connected with the integrated vision of humanity in its relationship with God, is the basis of Newman's vision of a university.

Thus, the core principle of Newman's vision can perhaps best be described as the truth that is unifying. He maintained that all the modern sciences and learned professions had a place in the university. It needed to be a place of 'universal *knowledge*.'[13] He provided for schools of arts and sciences, as well as medicine, engineering, classics, theology and philosophy. A chemical laboratory and astronomical observatory were included in the buildings. Far from being threatened by those thinkers, such as Charles Darwin, who were making advances in scientific discovery, Newman would have recognized their place within the universal search for knowledge.

At the same time, however, he was taking a contrary view to the contemporary philosophical and educational position known as utilitarianism. This tradition was developing as a result of the ideas of Jeremy Bentham (1748–1832), Henry Brougham (1778–1868), James Mill (1773–1836) and his son, John Stuart Mill (1806–73). This utilitarian philosophy was based on the earlier thinking of John Locke (1632–1704) and was disseminated through the journal *Edinburgh Review*.[14] With regard to university education, utilitarian thinking held that, within the university curriculum, dogmatic theology should not be taught and the prominence given to classical languages should be reduced. These educationalists believed that the object of learning should rather be to provide the student with the necessary skills to perform a trade or profession. The implication of these arguments was that university education should be offered regardless of race, gender, political belief or religious conviction. These ideas came to fruition between 1826 and 1836 with the foundation of University College, London, in which both Bentham and Brougham were influential.[15]

Newman's response (in 1852) to this educational standpoint was to unmask what he believed to be the faults in this contemporary philosophical tradition by analysing the educational philosophy of John Locke.[16] With regard to the unsuitability of the teaching of Latin, for example, Locke asked 'Can there be any thing more ridiculous [...] than that a father should waste his own money, and his son's time, in setting him to *learn the Roman language*, when at the same time he *designs him for a trade* [...]?'[17] On the contrary, Newman believed that he could demonstrate 'how a liberal education [including Latin] is truly and fully a useful [...] education.'[18] His method was to employ sections of the utilitarian educational philosophy and turn them around and interpret them in terms of his own idea of what a university should encompass within the Catholic framework. Within the sphere of a Catholic university the strength of Newman's position is illustrated by the fact that 'It teaches *all* knowledge by teaching all *branches* of knowledge',[19] and as a result the intellect is nourished and thereby gives purpose to all employment and the student is able 'to be more useful, and to a greater number.'[20]

In the light of these observations it is now possible to see the reasons for Newman's concern regarding the fragmentation of the curriculum as proposed by the utilitarians. Newman argues that 'if you drop any science (including theology) out of the circle of knowledge, you cannot keep its place vacant for it; that science is forgotten'.[21] The implications here of the utilitarian approach show how the self-promotion of each secular discipline makes the totality of the curriculum unbalanced. Secular science would be able to set itself up as the centre of all truth to the neglect of all other reality, including, fundamentally, religious truth. Newman's corrective to the utilitarian position was to propose that the true purpose of university education was to impart the capacity to achieve a connected grasp of the totality of knowledge. Newman used the image of the British Empire to illustrate 'the philosophy of an imperial intellect'.[22] This intellect should produce 'a philosophical habit of mind'[23] because a university, like an empire, should embrace many disciplines and a university should map 'out the territory of the intellect, and [see] that the boundaries of each province are religiously respected, and that there is neither encroachment nor surrender on any side [...] It is impartial towards them all, and promotes each in its own place and for its own object.'[24] For Newman, then, questions of meaning were as essential a part of university education as were questions of explanation or the structure and operation of every facet of the universe.

On this understanding, the present-day university is the ideal environment where different cultures may enter into dialogue on terms of mutual respect, promoting the common good, and where the evangelistic mission of the Church may be enhanced. In 1990 Pope John Paul II discussed the place of Catholic universities in his Apostolic Constitution *Ex Corde Ecclesiae,* where he argued on the specifics of university education as serving humanity. In the Apostolic Constitution he referred to Newman and drew modern equivalents in terms reminiscent of Newman: the crisis of the university as a crisis of truth and alienation, and of modern technological society, where the individual is reduced to the status of an instrument. Universities are expected to turn out useful products fit for production, rather than promote learning. In a modern, mechanized and consumerist society, says Pope John Paul, 'It is essential that we be convinced of the priority of the ethical over the technical, of the primacy of the person over things, of the superiority of the spirit over matter.'[25]

This theme was utilized and developed by Pope Benedict when he applied it to the wider cultural context of civil society in his address in Westminster Hall on the afternoon of Friday 17 September 2010. The Holy Father began by identifying an underlying problem which as a society we have to face:

> Each generation, as it seeks to advance the common good, must ask anew: what are the requirements that governments may reasonably impose upon citizens, and how far do they extend? By appeal to what authority can moral dilemmas be resolved? These questions take us directly to the ethical foundations of civil discourse. If the moral principles underpinning the democratic process are themselves determined by nothing more solid than social consensus, then the fragility of the process becomes all too evident – herein lies the real challenge for democracy.[26]

He continued:

> The central question at issue, then, is this: where is the ethical foundation for political choices to be found? The Catholic tradition maintains that the objective norms governing right action are accessible to reason, prescinding from the content of revelation.

In this context faith and reason are seen to be working together, faith helping to 'purify and shed light upon the application of reason to the discovery of objective moral principles.' Reason is able to assist in the correction of 'distorted forms of religion' which 'arise when insufficient attention is given to the purifying and structuring role of reason within religion [...] Religion, in other words, is not a problem for legislators to solve, but a vital contributor to the national conversation.'[27]

If this coming together of faith and reason is crucial for the well-being of our society, then it is fair to assume that in a similar fashion it is crucial for the well-being of the university. Indeed, the well-being of society may depend, to some extent at least, on this partnership being recognized and honoured in the university.

In the dialogue between faith and reason it is important to grasp the contemplative quality of both faith and reason. The contemplative quality of faith is not difficult to understand, but there is a contemplative aspect to reason too, which can easily be lost. Indeed, as has often been shown, the positivist understanding of reason and of truth is that they are based on empirical evidence. They are, in other words, based on the findings of science and of physical observation. This understanding is, for the most part, the meaning given to the notion of truth in many university settings. Of course, empirical evidence has a crucial part to play, but, left to this evidence alone, our own reason becomes a kind of scientism.

One example of this inappropriate use of empirical evidence can be seen when the notion of 'nature' and 'natural law' are taken to mean the observable patterns of human behaviour and development. This position may be illustrated by the interaction between Christian teaching and evolutionary theories. The true notion of natural law is more the product of contemplation than of scientific analysis. Natural law is concerned more with philosophy than biology. Only by contemplation and reflection do we come to an understanding of what is meant by our deepest human nature and the claim it has on us.

This theme is broadened and developed by Pope Benedict in his address entitled 'The Listening Heart: Reflections on the Foundations of Law', given to the German Parliament on Thursday 22 September 2011. The framework for this address is provided by reference to the Biblical story of King Solomon. God invited Solomon, 'on his accession to the throne, to make a request.' He chose not 'Success – wealth – long life – destruction of his enemies' but, rather, he asked 'for a listening heart' in order that he might demonstrate wisdom and 'discern between good and evil (cf. 1 *Kg* 3:9)' in the governance of his people.[28] On this basis Pope Benedict argues that this discernment should form the foundation for the establishment of justice and the promulgation of law. Both the objective and the subjective aspects of reason, nature and conscience (forming the language of being), rooted in the creative power of God, provide the conceptual basis for Pope Benedict's argument. On the other hand, the breakdown in this structure of law can be traced to the emergence of a positivist understandings of nature and reason, which are both subject to the rules and limitations of science. Dramatically, he goes on to describe the effects of relying on positivism, which recognizes as objective only the phenomena that are functional. Pope Benedict believes that this understanding is like living in 'a concrete bunker with no windows, in which we ourselves provide lighting and atmospheric conditions, being no longer willing to obtain either from God's wide world.' Then he continues: 'And yet we cannot hide from ourselves the fact that even in this artificial world, we are still covertly drawing upon God's raw materials, which we refashion into our own products.' Then comes his appeal: 'The windows must be flung open again, we must see the wide world, the sky and the earth once more and learn to make proper use of all this [creativity].' Then he asks the question 'How can nature reassert itself in its true depth, with all its demands, with all its directives?' He continues:

> The importance of ecology is no longer disputed. We must listen to the language of nature and we must answer accordingly [...] Man too has a nature that he must respect and that he cannot manipulate at will. Man is not merely self-creating freedom. Man does not create himself. He is intellect and will, but he is also nature, and his will is rightly ordered if he respects his nature, listens to it and accepts himself for who he is, as one who did not create himself. In this way, and in no other, is true human freedom fulfilled.[29]

In the conclusion, by reference to King Solomon, Pope Benedict is returning full circle with his plea that contemporary politicians and lawmakers should be making the same request as Solomon: the desire for 'a listening heart' in order 'to discern between good and evil, and thus to establish true law, to serve justice and peace.'[30] Thus, in our public discourse, in the work of evangelization within the setting of the university, we need much more of this quality: a listening heart, listening to the deepest longings which bring us in touch with our shared human nature rather than our individuality, in touch with the spiritual realm rather than only the positivism of logic and science, in touch with the wisdom which is God, the Creator Spirit. This understanding enables our nature to be not only an 'is' but also an 'ought', not only an experience but also a command, which, in the tumult of our emotions and efforts, we may find difficult to discern and obey.

In order to bring the necessary focus for humanity on justice, peace and law, Pope Benedict has demonstrated in these addresses how the meeting of cultures plays an essential role in the right ordering of public affairs. Within multicultural environments – for example, the United Kingdom and Germany – part of the ministry of evangelization issuing from the Catholic Church is the proclamation of these theological ideas: the awareness of God and the acquisition of divine wisdom in the service of humanity. Crucial to this understanding of evangelization today, not least within our schools and universities, is the fashioning of 'The Listening Heart'. In this search for truth three most important themes arise: dialogue, rationality and the acquiring of knowledge. Thus through openness to divine guidance and the embracing of others in compassion we are able to create a world where, hopefully, 'Steadfast love and faithfulness will meet; righteousness and peace will kiss each other' and where 'Faithfulness will spring up from the earth and righteousness will look down from heaven' (Ps 85 [Vg 84].10–11).

The exploration of these matters is, I believe, pertinent to the university if it is to be understood as an institution and community dedicated to the expansion of knowledge, pastoral care and the service of the common good. In this exploration we are brought directly back to the challenges initiated 150 years ago by John Henry Newman, which remain equally as important today. Are our universities (and schools) able to understand themselves as being at the service of truth, fired by the conviction that reason, understood as the capacity of every human being to transcend the empirical, able to lead us forward not only in search of that overarching truth but also in our response to that truth in love?

Let us pray they can. For meeting precisely this challenge, I should like to propose, is central to the theme of 'The Voice of Faith in Schools and Universities'. To respond to this voice means that our schools and universities become places in which various cultures are able to interact freely, and where evangelization in the sense of quiet witness to God can be manifest.

## Notes

1 Of the numerous editions of the *The Idea of a University*, that produced by I. T. Ker, Oxford, Clarendon Press, 1976,

is the most comprehensive. I have used this edition for the references which follow (cited as 'Ker, *University*'). The quotation here is from p. 421.
2. Ker, *University*, p. 154.
3. There are numerous biographies of John Henry Newman (1801–90) including: Dulles, Avery (2002; 2009 edition), *John Henry Newman*, London and New York, Continuum; Gilley, Sheridan (1990), *Newman and His Age*, London, Darton, Longman and Todd; and Ker, Ian (1988 [paperback edn 1990]), *John Henry Newman: A Biography*, Oxford, Oxford University Press.
4. *SV*, pp. 160–69, for the record of the Mass of Beatification, together with the Holy Father's 'Angelus address'.
5. *Ibid.*, pp. 79f.
6. *Ibid.*, p. 76.
7. For details of the controversy see Ker, *John Henry Newman*, pp. 37–41. On the role of Newman as a college tutor at Oriel see Cornwell, John (2010), *Newman's Unquiet Grave: The Reluctant Saint*, London and New York, Continuum, pp. 45f.
8. For details on the background and genesis of this appointment see Ker, *John Henry Newman*, pp. 376–8.
9. Another edition is that edited by Frank M. Turner (New Haven, CT, and London, Yale University Press, 1996). This volume contains a group of useful interpretative essays entitled 'Rethinking *The Idea of a University*', pp. 257ff.
10. Ker, *University*, p. 221.
11. *Ibid.*, p. 428. This quotation is to be found within Discourse V, 'General Knowledge Viewed as One Philosophy' (1852), which Newman removed from later editions; for details, see Dulles, *John Henry Newman*, p. 137, and Ker, *University*, pp. xxxiiff.
12. Ker, *University*, p. 65.
13. *Ibid.*, Preface, p. 5.
14. *Edinburgh Review* was founded in October 1802 and published quarterly. Its contributors favoured political, social and educational reform. Influential in its day, by 1818

circulation reached 13,500. It ceased publication in 1929. See https://en.wikipedia.org/wiki/Edinburgh_Review.
15  For further details see Chadwick, Owen (1966; third edn 1971), *The Victorian Church,* Part I, London, A. & C. Black, pp. 81, 94f.
16  Ker, *University*, pp. 141–3.
17  *Ibid.*, p. 140.
18  *Ibid.*, p. 143.
19  *Ibid.*, p. 145.
20  *Ibid.*, p. 146.
21  *Ibid.*, p. 73.
22  *Ibid.*, p. 371.
23  *Ibid.*, p. 57.
24  *Ibid.*, p. 370.
25  Apostolic Constitution of the Supreme Pontiff John Paul II on Catholic Universities, *Ex Corde Ecclesiae*, 15 August 1990, n. 18. For reference to John Henry Newman, *The Idea of a University*, see nn. 7 and 19.
26  *SV*, p. 103.
27  *Ibid.*, p. 104.
28  Address of His Holiness Benedict XVI, Reichstag Building, Berlin, 22 September 2011, 'The Listening Heart: Reflections on the Foundations of Law'.
29  *Ibid.*
30  *Ibid.*

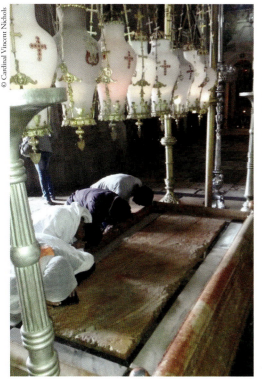

The Church of the Holy Sepulchre, Jerusalem: Stone of Unction. Pilgrims are lured by God to pray with loving devotion at the place where Jesus was anointed and clothed for burial.

In Rome with Pope Francis and Bishop Peter Doyle, here representing the collegiality of the episcopal office symbolising the unity and the faith of the Church.

The wilderness of Judaea where the devil tempted Jesus to deny his divine vocation. Through faithfulness to his heavenly Father, Jesus emerged victorious and opened the path to eternal salvation for us.

We are called by God to create a desert in the heart so that in our lives we may concentrate solely on him.

This map illustrates the strategic position of Gaza within the Middle East. I pray daily for peace and stability within this region, especially for the wellbeing of every member of the community.

*The Nativity with Saints Altarpiece*, Pietro Orioli, reveals the panorama of the history of God's salvation through his Beloved Son, Jesus Christ our Lord. The voice of the everlasting Gospel is proclaimed here by the messages which Orioli is giving through the beauty and solemnity of his artistry.

# PART THREE

*Religious Dialogue and the Hope for Humanity*

During my ministry I have developed a greater awareness of the inherent sacredness of the world and of human life. Personal encounter with numerous religious leaders and their congregations has led me to realize that such dialogue is of vital importance for religious harmony and the good ordering of society across the world. To this end I should like to suggest three principles as a basis for further discussion. First, it is necessary to understand the fundamental importance of the dignity of every human being. The acknowledgement of this dignity is the first requirement for every form of truly human dialogue. Fundamental human dignity comes from God, the Creator. It is important that the source of dignity innate to every human soul is recognized as being divinely given. Human dignity cannot be bestowed by governments, politicians and legal systems. It is the task of the powerful to recognize human dignity, and it is not for them to believe that it is they who are granting such bounty. Second, we should learn that every participant in a dialogue of inter-religious cooperation has to be able to show how their desire is to serve the good of humanity. We have to be able to give an account of how our religious belief and observance can be understood as part of a vision of the common good for all society. Third, we should recognize that the road of inter-religious cooperation is long and difficult to travel and requires much patience and good will on the journey. With regard to the Catholic Church, the promulgation of *Nostra aetate,* at a time in which I was a seminarian in Rome, was a vital step in the attempt of the Church to reach out in fellowship to adherents of other religions. I was aware that this undertaking was a moment of grace when all God's children could be brought together in an atmosphere of mutual respect in order that we might serve one another more lovingly. We need the vision of 'the holy city which is illuminated by the glory of God, and in whose splendor all peoples will walk (cf. Apoc. 21.23ff.)' (*NA*, 1).

I shall then attempt to consider how St Paul's vision of salvation and hope in Romans 8 not only acts as a fulcrum for the whole letter but also informs the issues of religious dialogue which I shall be considering. This vision of reconciliation and hope in Romans 8 informs the next section (Rom 9–11), in which Paul envisages that God will offer a new covenant of unity to both Jews and Gentiles (Rom 11.25–6) which will establish holiness (Rom 11.26–7, quoting Is 59.20–21). Paul understands *caritas* as a fulfilment of the precepts of the Jewish law (Rom 13.8–10) which has its origin and purpose in 'the love of God' (Rom 8.39). In terms of both preaching and writing he believed that by speaking in the name of God apostles are armed with the grace of the Gospel of Jesus Christ (e.g., Rom 1.8; 15.16–17) with which they are entrusted. Being successors of the apostles, bishops – and through their ministry of ordination, priests and deacons – receive the same apostolic commission: to declare the victory wrought by God in Christ Jesus (Rom 8.37–9) and, with all believers to manifest the fruits of that victory: faith, hope and love.

# 7
## *The Journey to God and Faith Today*

*I am coming [says the Lord] to gather all nations and tongues; and they shall come and see my glory, and I will set a sign among them.*

IS 66.18–19

In presenting the theme 'The Journey to God and Faith Today',[1] I should like to offer four interconnected aspects relating to this idea. First, I shall present a broad reflection on the sacredness of our world and how awareness of the sacred has fashioned much of our understanding of the environment in which we live. Second, I shall explain the basis on which the efforts of the Catholic Church are shaped and guided with regard to inter-religious dialogue.[2] In relation to parts three and four I shall attempt to apply the insights gained in order to offer observations on two particular issues: (i) how religious faith may contribute to public debate in relation to the moral order; and (ii) to emphasize the importance of the spiritual quest in matters of faith and our journey to God.

## Sacredness and Our Religious Heritage

In order to illustrate this theme I should like to begin by referring to a contemporary book by Martin Palmer, entitled *Sacred Land*.[3] Here Palmer is inviting us to look again at our world and observe its almost hidden sacred character. He also argues strongly for the conservation of the environment. He insists that this country abounds with very familiar places whose sacredness we can easily forget. He indicates 'four kinds of sacred place'.[4] First, there are those buildings made sacred by acts of dedication: mosques, synagogues, ghudwaras and churches. Second, there are those places which have become sacred because in their beauty or majesty they have the power to lift our hearts to the author of all things. Third, there are those locations which have been made sacred by an event which has given them an indelible character. He gives, as an example, Clifford's Tower in York, where in 1190 a mass suicide of Jews occurred in the face of an anti-Semitic mob. Finally, because of a defining experience or a crucial decision happening in a particular place there are those which have become sacred in a very personal way. Martin Palmer argues that we must not neglect or lose such perspectives because they form an important part of how we understand ourselves not only individually but also as a society. These places, he believes, 'are sacred because they link us to the divine and give us a sense of meaning'.[5] Ultimately, this search for identity assists us in perceiving our spiritual role within the family and society because we are able to reflect on the value of our past heritage. The awareness of the importance of the sacred place means that our horizons are broadened and we are enabled to see ourselves 'as parts of a greater narrative within which we have the opportunity to play a part'.[6]

In this fascinating book we learn how to read the layout of streets in our older towns and cities and how churches have been situated in relation to the 'geography' of the Christian faith. A church dedicated to St Michael, for example, is often found in the northern part of a town because danger and threat came from the north – at least in terms of frost and snow – and St Michael is the saint of protection against harm.[7] The author invites us to read afresh how the environment reveals the presence of the sacred and how the sacred is brought down to earth – literally.

Given that we are to see ourselves within 'a greater narrative', Martin Palmer's book presents an overarching story. He identifies five great narratives of meaning which have shaped this land: the age of ancestor worship, from 5000 to 3000 BC; the age of mysterious stone circles, from 3000 to 1160 BC; the Celtic and Roman period, from 1160 BC to AD 400; the monastic-Catholic period, from AD 500 to 1600; and the present period of Protestant individualism and the subsequent Deism of our industrialized, urbanized age.[8] To illustrate the spirit of this last period Palmer quotes the wonderful opening lines of Charles Dickens's novel *Hard Times*, in which Mr Gradgrind, the headmaster, declares:

> Now, what I want is, Facts. Teach these boys and girls nothing but Facts. Facts alone are wanted in life. Plant nothing else, and root out everything else. You can only form the minds of reasoning animals

upon Facts: nothing else will ever be of any service to them. This is the principle on which I bring up my own children, and this is the principle on which I bring up these children. Stick to Facts, sir![9]

I shall return later to discuss this view of learning, the consequences of which are not hard to see.

This division into five periods is obviously speculative and contentious, but Martin Palmer's underlying point is that each period has left its mark on our land because each has provided a grand narrative by which people have shaped their understanding of who they are and where they are located in relation to one another. He observes that four periods have faded or disappeared and the fifth is now in the process of disintegration. An absence of a coherent grand narrative is a state into which, he suggests, we are now entering.

Indeed, the landscape is changing. New buildings are, for the most part, functional and intended to have a short lifespan. The expectation is that a new £400m hospital will be replaced again in thirty years' time. In this context, which has many contributory causes, it is even more important that we understand our past and its increasingly hidden spiritual and religious inheritance in order that we are able to treasure the new expressions of religious meaning which are appearing here in our environment.

There is much to be learned from the variety contained within such experience. All across our landscape are places and buildings that speak eloquently of the richness of our spiritual quest and religious convictions. Ignorance in this area of life means that we travel with our eyes cast down, or blindfolded, depriving ourselves of so much encouragement and inspiration. At least I know that in some places children make regular visits to sacred places. They are taught to learn to 'read' them, and thus they are enabled to be inspired by all that such buildings proclaim about the divine; as a result, they are enriched by the experience. Often these are places of beauty even more than places of purpose or function, and that beauty is often the most eloquent witness to meaning and hope for life and to the quest for God. The teaching of this literacy, then, is a crucial task that lies before us. Engagement in such an educational undertaking means that the general utilitarian approach, 'Facts alone are wanted in life', with its emphasis on social economy, must be disregarded because it excludes the creative, imaginative force within human consciousness and reasoning, with the emphasis on the pursuit of virtue and the importance, educationally and culturally, of the religious environment.

## Catholicism and Inter-Religious Dialogue

In order to understand and conduct such a shared exploration of inter-religious traditions it is helpful to have some clear principles and guidance about how we understand the differences between our religious faiths and the relationships between them. This understanding is important if we are truly to appreciate the richness of each religious expression rather than simply reduce each religious belief to that which we share in common. Each faith contributes to the 'sacredness' of this land, and each adds a purpose to the 'spiritual' environment in which we live. The seriousness with which we approach our dialogue and exploration has important consequences.

You will not be surprised that I should now wish to speak from an explicitly Catholic perspective.[10] At the outset, I should like to make very clear that dialogue is not simply about study and discussion. This perception is a vital part of our journey: to understand each other more deeply. This dialogue includes all positive and constructive relationships with individuals and communities of a different religious faith directed towards mutual understanding and enrichment. In the words of the Blessed (now St) Pope John Paul II: 'Dialogue is not so much an idea to be studied as a way of living in a positive relationship with others.'[11]

Thus, inter-religious dialogue embraces simply living as good neighbours with those of other religions, or – to go a step further – trying to understand better their religious faith and to experience something of their life and culture. This dialogue also takes the form of acting together in matters of common concern and values, such as with issues of justice, peace and the good of the world as created by God, or engaging in activities which protect human life, from conception to natural death. The Catholic Church welcomes opportunities for collaborating with members of other religions in fields where they have similar values and concerns for human well-being. This broad definition of dialogue is important because we face a common task: that of speaking eloquently, in word and deed, to a society that is losing its capacity to connect with our spiritual roots and to translate that dimension of human life into concerted action.

Thus, authentic dialogue does not mean adopting a 'relativist' stance whereby all religions are reduced to 'being the same really'. Dialogue is not the diluting of belief. We must never try to smooth out or, worse, ignore irreducible differences. Indeed, true dialogue takes place between those well grounded in their own religious faith and who have moved beyond a well-intentioned, but mistaken, desire to avoid disagreement.

In this dialogue, therefore, as a Catholic Christian, I hold to my central belief that 'in the mystery of Jesus Christ, the incarnate Son of God, who is "the way, the truth, and the life" (Jn 14.6), the full revelation of divine truth is given'.[12] In my faith I know that he is the one 'in whom God reconciled all things to himself' (2 Cor 5.18–19), and in whom humanity 'find the fullness of their religious life'.[13] At the same time I know that the one and the same God is the source of every element of truth and holiness to be found within each different religion. While the Catholic Church insists that Christ is the one and only mediator (1 Tim 2.5) of the salvation which God wills for all people, the Church gladly recognizes (to use terms dating from the earliest centuries of Christianity) seeds of the Word or 'a ray of that truth' emanating from the single Creator of all that is true and holy.[14]

The positive attitude of the Church towards people of other religious communities is underpinned by our embracing of the essential unity of the human race and the need to be open to all that is true and holy in other religions which is our call to dialogue lovingly with our neighbours. Thus the theme of the unity of the human race is our shared point for embarking on dialogue. The Church teaches that:

> All men form but one community. This is so because all stem from the one stock which God created to people the entire earth (cf. Acts 17.26), and also because all share a common destiny, namely God. His providence, evident goodness, and saving designs extend to all men (cf. Wis 8.1; Acts 14.17; Rom 2.6–7; 1 Tim 2.4).[15]

This truth is the source of the dignity of all human beings and of their equality, for each is a person created in the image of God. Religious freedom flows from this equal dignity. On the basis of this dignity every person has immunity from coercion and no one should be forced to act against his or her own conscience in religious matters or, within due limits, be prevented from acting in accordance with that conscience.[16] Hence, the right to places of worship and religious associations and practice is also upheld.

This human unity and innate dignity mean the Church is open to all that is holy and true in other religions. Catholic teaching affirms that followers of other faiths can receive the saving grace of God and 'may achieve eternal salvation'.[17] Furthermore, this teaching proclaims that this grace and this salvation are essentially related to the unique saving work of Christ and his body, the Church. It is bestowed on those outside the visible Church thanks to the presence there of the Holy Spirit, who, we believe, is always the gift of the Father and the Son, Jesus Christ. We trust that the Holy Spirit will guide us into all the truth (an allusion to Jn 16.13). In this context Pope John Paul II spoke of the presence and activity of the Holy Spirit being limited neither by space nor by time. The Spirit is at the very source of our religious questioning and 'the origin of the noble ideals and undertakings which benefit humanity on its journey through history'.[18]

By insisting that this presence and activity of the Holy Spirit can be understood only in relation to Christ and cannot be separated from the particular working of the Holy Spirit in the Church, a vital point is being made: precisely because it is the same divine Spirit at work in both, the Church and other religions are positively and profoundly related to each other. Here is the true depth of our relationship; this is our common bond. Thus, within this common bond, the various religions each have their own distinctive relationship to the Church.

This understanding has a crucial consequence for our Catholic involvement in all inter-religious discussions and leads to the second theme: the need for openness to truth and holiness to be found in other religions. This position implies that our dialogue with each religion has its own particular character, which is respectful of the character of that religion. With regard to Judaism, the Church has a unique and precious affinity to the Jewish people because the origin of Christianity is embedded in the relationship that God has with the Jews. Indeed, the Church is nourished from 'the rich sap of the olive tree' on to which the branches of the 'wild olive' tree of the Gentiles have been 'grafted' (Rom 11.17 [NJB]). The Jewish people are, as Pope John Paul II has stated, the 'beloved of God', who has called them with an 'irrevocable calling', and whose covenant with them 'has never been revoked'.[19]

Christianity also shares many common traditions with Islam. During his visit to Turkey in 2006 Pope Benedict said:

> Christians and Muslims belong to the family of those who believe in the one God and who, according to their respective traditions, trace their ancestry to Abraham. This human and spiritual unity in our origins and our destiny impels us to seek a common path as we play our part in the quest for fundamental values so characteristic of the people of our time.[20]

Despite the differing interpretations, Judaism, Christianity and Islam all claim Abraham as their ancestor, honouring his close relationship with God (see Gen 12.3). All three faiths worship the one God, even if in their own traditions they understand and relate to God in different ways. This perception is vital for the objective of achieving religious and political harmony in the contemporary context.

Sikhism shares with Christianity the belief in the one Creator God and the equality of all humans as God's creatures. In the spirit of its founder, Guru Nanak, Sikhs seek peaceful relations with other religions. The strong tradition of Sikh hospitality has been enjoyed by many Catholics!

The Church also pays tribute to the ancient and richly varied Hindu traditions,[21] which give admirable witness to the human yearning for the divine and the importance of family life and to the possibility that different religions can live in peace.

The recognition by the Catholic Church of much of the value within Buddhism, not least its commitment to peace and justice, was applauded (together with Confucianism) by Pope John Paul II on his visit to Korea in 1984. In his address to spiritual leaders he declared:

> The profound reverence for life and nature, the quest for truth and harmony, self-abnegation and compassion, the ceaseless striving to transcend — these are among the noble hallmarks of your spiritual tradition that have led, and will continue to lead, the nation and the people through turbulent times to the haven of peace.

The Holy Father adding:

> Our diversity in religious and ethical beliefs calls upon all of us to foster genuine *fraternal dialogue* and to give special consideration to what human beings have in common and to what promotes fellowship among them.[22]

These ideas help towards understanding religious and political cultures, very different from our own, and assist in building harmonious relationships with the countries of the Far East.

Mention could also be made of the Church's relationships with other religious communities, such as the Jains, Baha'is and Zoroastrians,[23] with whom I have enjoyed a spiritually engaging and formative evening. I could continue with references to other such communities, but I must now consider my third theme: the call to dialogue.

What we have learned from our researching of the essential unity of humanity and religious diversity is that inter-religious dialogue requires both an honest witnessing to personal belief and also an attitude of profound willingness to listen to the belief of another. We have to engage in this dialogue with charity and with humility. We must do so because the witness of this creative dialogue is a vital factor in our search for peace and stability in our world and our society. Such dialogue is a positive contribution to the community, demonstrating that religious belief is a force for good, that religion is not inimical to our humanity but springs from the quest for truth rooted in the spirit of every human being. The witness to this truth is today very important, given that many voices denounce religious belief as divisive and demeaning.

During his visit to the United Kingdom in September 2010, Pope Benedict reaffirmed our commitment to the importance of undertaking inter-religious dialogue. Addressing representatives of other religions on Friday 17 September at St Mary's University College, Twickenham, he said:

> Let me assure you that the Catholic Church follows the path of engagement and dialogue out of a genuine sense of respect for you and your beliefs. Catholics, both in Britain and throughout the world, will continue to work to build bridges of friendship to other religions, to heal past wrongs and to foster trust between individuals and communities.[24]

This statement is the mandate of our continuing dialogue in a rapidly changing world.

## Religious Faith and Public Policy

On this basis I should now like to turn to my first practical application of the importance of inter-religious cooperation by again quoting Pope Benedict during his Visit.

Speaking in Westminster Hall on Friday 17 September to politicians, diplomats, academics and business leaders, he reflected on the proper place of religious belief within the political process. He praised our country's 'national instinct for moderation' and described this land as 'a pluralist democracy which places great value on freedom of speech, freedom of political affiliation and respect for the rule of law, with a strong sense of the individual's rights and duties and of the equality of all citizens before the law'. He continued to explain that, within this democratic tradition, each generation has to ask what are the demands that governments may reasonably impose upon its citizens, or, in Biblical language, what is owed to Caesar and what is owed to God (an allusion to Mk 12.13–17). He indicated that these questions lead directly 'to the ethical foundations of civil discourse', insisting that this philosophy is a crucial challenge for democracy, for 'if the moral principles underpinning the democratic process are themselves determined by nothing more solid than social consensus, then the fragility of the process becomes all too evident'. His illustration was weighty and telling. He said: 'The inadequacy of pragmatic, short-term solutions to complex social and ethical problems has been illustrated all too clearly by the recent global financial crisis. There is widespread agreement', he added, 'that the lack of solid ethical foundation for economic activity has contributed to the grave difficulties now being experienced by millions of people throughout the world.'

Pope Benedict then confronted the audience with the fundamental question 'Where is the ethical foundation for political choices to be found?' His answer was 'that the objective norms governing right action are accessible to reason', while they can be discerned apart from divine revelation. Thus the role of religion in this complex is to illuminate and 'purify'[25] the application of reason to objective ethics and by contributing to the national conversation relating to justice, tolerance and freedom.

These claims are bold, and there is an enormous insight within them. They represent nothing less than the search for meaning and identity, which is an essential character of the human spirit distinguishing us from other animals. In Western civilization, for example, this search has borne many fruits in a rich philosophical tradition of over 2,500 years, going back to Aristotle, Plato and the pre-Socratics.[26] Not content with the accumulation of facts alone, so vehemently advocated by Mr Gradgrind, we use our discursive faculty called 'reason' as a key tool in order to grasp the underlying truth about our world and our own humanity. The search for this truth should involve the utilization of our natural creative intelligence in order that wise and reasoned judgements and actions may result. A prerequisite for the acquisition of such intelligence is openness to receive the divine wisdom which is ultimately the source for all right thinking and action. With respect to our humanity, reason discloses to us universal, objective and unchanging truths of the moral order. These truths transcend historical and cultural conditions precisely because they are rooted in our very being. Knowledge of such truths directs our choices and actions so that we, as individuals and as a society, may flourish.

To give an example, we can reason that taking food and drink serves our own bodily health and our social well-being. No matter what we eat and drink, this fact is true in every culture. This universal norm is often transgressed by our abuse of food and drink, which when taken to excess is widely recognized as morally wrong. Recognition of the underlying pattern of our nature and the purpose of our actions gives rise to a moral code.

Even though accessible to human reason, the Catholic tradition considers our knowledge of such moral truths, and our living by them, to be an active participation in divine and natural law (*CCC*, 1954–60).[27] We forsake this tradition to our own impoverishment, a statement which I shall now explain further.

It is this high regard for the dignity and power of reason, enshrined in divine and natural law, which leads Catholicism – along with other religions, I'm sure – to affirm that religion and reason are not opposed but complement each other. Religion recognizes that reason assists a deeper understanding of its own beliefs. Indeed, it can seem that religions have more faith in reason than certain trends in our contemporary culture. That said, the search of reason for truth unaided can be difficult. Here religion may assist reason. By exploring this two-way relationship between religion and reason, the place of our religious traditions in public debate and the contribution they can make to the vitality and depth of ethical reflection in the formation of public policy may be discerned.

Referring to this relationship between reason and religion, Pope Benedict spoke, first, of the purifying role of reason in religion. He maintained that distorted forms of religion, such as sectarianism and fundamentalism, which can create serious social problems, arise when 'insufficient attention is given to the purifying and structuring role of reason within religion.' Second, he spoke of the role of religion within reason, saying: 'Without the corrective supplied by religion, though, reason too can fall prey to distortions, as when it is manipulated by ideology, or applied in a partial way that fails to take account of the full dignity of the human person.'[28]

The discussion we need here, as in many other matters, is not one of tradition, or of social consent, either old or new. It is an argument of a different kind: about our capacity to understand human nature in a philosophical sense and to derive guidance and principle from that understanding.

Religious traditions, then, can serve the common good not simply by repeating the fruit of their wisdom but also by reasoned, principled argument and attentive dialogue. The proviso, of course, is the willingness of those who disagree with the articulation of religious principles in public debate to dialogue with us. This dialogue on the tenets of religion and ethics is urgent, although it presents us with a far from easy task.

# THE JOURNEY TO GOD AND FAITH TODAY

## Our Spiritual Quest

My second practical application to our inter-religious dialogue is concerned with our shared spiritual quest. I return to Pope Benedict's address to representatives of other religions at St Mary's University College, Twickenham, where he emphasized 'the fundamental importance for human life of this spiritual quest in which we are engaged' because it 'grants an answer to the most important question of all – the question concerning the ultimate meaning of human existence.' This longing for ultimate meaning is 'the quest for the sacred', which 'is the search for the one thing necessary, which alone satisfies the longings of the human heart. In the fifth century St Augustine described that search in these terms: "Lord, you have created us for yourself and our hearts are restless until they rest in you."[29]

This quotation from St Augustine's *Confessions*[30] provides the foundation for my presentation of this theme and my comments on this spiritual quest by sharing with you the testimony of Etty Hillesum,[31] who has inspired me in my journey of faith. Etty was a young Jewish woman who made her spiritual pilgrimage during the 1940s, in the most harrowing circumstances of the Nazi occupation of the Netherlands.[32] She was deported, with thousands of other Jewish people, including members of her family, with whom she subsequently died in the concentration camp of Auschwitz on 30 November 1943.[33] Although I have met Etty only through her writings, I nevertheless have, because they are so luminous, a sense of a far more personal knowledge of her, and, as a result, I am able to identify with her spiritual quest.

Etty Hillesum was born in 1914 and grew up in Amsterdam, where she lived with her dysfunctional family in a context devoid of any explicit religious practice, experiencing great emotional instability and a fairly chaotic sex and social life. Yet in a two-and-a-half-year period from February 1941 to her death in November 1943 she came to a remarkable inner freedom and faith. She did so, initially, through a process of counselling and therapy through which she came to a deeper understanding of herself. However, the profound transformation within her resulted from her discovery of the practice of silent contemplation, silent presence before the inner mystery of her life, which she came to recognize as God.[34]

This journey of faith was remarkable, but what is more astonishing is that she made this journey in the harsh circumstances of that time, during the relentless persecution of all Jews and her work in the transit camp of Westerbork, where Jews were held for transfer to Auschwitz to be exterminated.

Etty's *Letters and Diaries* are a remarkable testimony to her inner journey of faith and to her inner strength, which was never broken.[35] Throughout her time of introspection and personal growth Etty never wavered in her attention to those who were suffering. She was a daily angel of compassion and love in increasingly desperate circumstances.[36] She rejected for herself the possibility of escape, choosing rather to stay with her people and face the certainty of death. On the contrary, she continued to exalt in the goodness of God even in the face of such utter degradation and death. Her final communication with us came when she was herded on to a train and sent to her death, together with her parents and her brother, Mischa. Then they sang with love and she managed to thrust out of the cattle wagon one last message of hope in God, a quotation from the Psalms, 'The Lord is my high tower.'[37]

In her writings Etty tells of the gradual way in which we can become aware of, and enter into, that inner space which is the place where our spiritual lives can be renewed constantly. She learned to be silent and still within herself and before the reality of God. She spoke of this spiritual renewal in these terms: 'time after time one must gather oneself together again around one's very centre. Herding together the disorderly flock of your thoughts, emotions, sensations, experiences, reactions – [...] Like the good shepherd.'[38]

In this journey of inner discovery, she learned, as we must, to first receive rather than to describe and analyse. She learned the importance of our contemplative faculty alongside our use of reason. Etty believed that 'You must live and breathe with your soul, but work and study with your mind. If you live by your mind alone, yours is but a poor existence.'[39] Her daily effort, then, was expressed in this learned conviction: 'I think I work well with You, God, that we work well together. I have assigned an ever larger dwelling space to You, and I am also beginning to become faithful to You [...] The powerful centre [which] spreads its rays to the outermost boundaries.'[40]

There is so much more we can learn from this young woman about the life of the spirit within us, but the thing that has left an indelible impression on me is this: Etty talks about a particular outward expression of this inner journey. She speaks about kneeling, an activity which becomes a metaphor for her spiritual development. She is not writing about kneeling in a church, for she never did that. It would seem that most of her kneeling was done in the bathroom.[41] But she is so eloquent in finding and describing this outward expression of inner contemplation that this expression gives her an inner joy and freedom in the understanding of her spiritual life. Here are some of her words about kneeling:

> it is as if my body had been meant and made for the act of kneeling. Sometimes, in moments of deep gratitude, kneeling down becomes an overwhelming urge [...] a gesture embedded in my body, needing to be expressed [...] When I write these things down, I still feel a little ashamed, as if I were writing about the most intimate of intimate matters. Much more bashful than if I had to write about my love life. But is there indeed anything as intimate as man's relationship to God?[42]

These experiences were the means by which Etty's spiritual growth was able to unfold into a deeper consciousness of God's creative love. Thus she was able to experience this reality: 'Some time ago I said to myself, "I am a kneeler in training." I was still embarrassed by this act, as intimate as gestures of love that cannot be put into words either, except by a poet.'[43]

In the summer of 1942 the Nazi authorities introduced further regulations against the Jews in Amsterdam which brought additional prohibitions to their freedom and thereby produced greater suffering, making the possibility of their destruction inevitable. This situation led to Etty's diary entry for 4 July, which reveals: 'I suddenly had to kneel down on the rough coconut matting in the bathroom, my head bowed so low that it nearly rested on my lap. I could remain like that for days, my body like the safe walls of a small cell sheltering me right in its middle.'[44]

Kneeling in this context is for Etty a further expression of her personal and spiritual growth. She now perceives herself to be a universal person. Although she admits that she is 'tired' and 'afraid', she knows that 'the whole world is in me all the same, it is always there and keeps growing'.[45] As she has written earlier, kneeling is for Etty the outward expression to 'allow myself to be led, not by anything on the outside, but by what wells up from deep within'.[46] The bestowal of this reservoir of divine grace becomes indispensable as Etty knows that she and her fellow Jews 'are moving toward our destruction'.[47]

Here, I think, is the beginning of a model of our common quest for holiness, a way of tutoring of the heart, and in Etty it bore much fruit. This kind of prayer sustains the daily conviction that at the root of the human heart are to be found goodness and love. It helps to develop a personal sense of vocation, even destiny.

In this context Etty's journey, and her developing sense of prayer emulating from the heart, meant that she demonstrated a readiness to bear sorrow: 'Give your sorrow all the space and shelter in yourself that is its due, for if everyone bears his grief honestly and courageously, the sorrow that now fills the world will abate.'[48] This theme of bearing sorrow meant that, for Etty, feelings should not be relieved through hatred. She believed that prayer should also be offered for her persecutors, the German soldiers, because 'There are no frontiers between suffering people, and we must pray for them all'.[49] She never withdrew from those in need of the gift of compassion. In this way, in the prison camp and even on the train to Auschwitz she was able to overcome every sense of condemning others or hating them: 'We should be willing to act as a balm for all wounds.'[50] These words form the conclusion of her diary entries, and they are a powerful reminder as to how goodness can emerge in the midst of evil.

Perhaps remarkably, in the midst of her suffering Etty's prayer gave rise within her to a keener eye for beauty, which encompassed a vast array of objects, contexts and people. She wrote of the beauty of the flowers beyond the perimeter of the prison camp – a beauty that would sustain her through the day: 'My red and yellow roses are now fully open. While I sat there working in that hell, they quietly went on blossoming.'[51] Natural beauty becomes, therefore, a metaphor for her inner dialogue which ensured that she was always harkening and listening to all reality: 'Each day I learn something new about people and realize [...] that the only strength comes [...] from within.'[52] With this perception Etty was able to write of the fleeting glimpse of compassion that she could detect in the eye of the hard and merciless prison guard, such that she also nurtured a love and a prayer for him.

Her inner life of prayer, then, bore fruit in the sense of the goodness of life, the sense of vocation, the readiness to bear sorrow, the gift of compassion and attentiveness to the hidden beauty of life.[53] As a result, the fruit of her prayer brought Etty to an eloquent and enlightening appreciation of the nature of God's presence in the world. As she struggled with the question of where was God in the midst of such destruction of human life, she declared: 'I am ready for everything, for anywhere on this earth, wherever God may send me, and I am ready to bear witness in any situation and unto death that life is beautiful and meaningful and that it is not God's fault that things are as they are at present, but our own.'[54] With this spiritual perception Etty was also able to write to a friend: 'And if we just care enough, God is in safe hands with us despite everything, Maria —.'[55]

This spirit of abandonment to the Divine will represents a subtle development from Etty's earlier reflection that humanity is able to defend the dwelling place of God within the human heart. Using the household metaphors of 'vacuum cleaners and silver forks and spoons', she perceives that, by placing them 'in safekeeping', these idols are being shielded 'instead of guarding You, dear God'.[56] Those who feel the need to protect themselves and 'put their bodies in safekeeping' and declare that 'I shan't let them [the Nazis] get me into their clutches', should understand that God is their protector.[57] Etty understands, however, that because she has surrendered herself to God's will she is able to declare that 'no one is in their clutches who is in Your [God's] arms'.[58]

At moments such as these I am struck by how much Etty might serve as an inspiration to us all, and how her thoughts prepare us to receive the main messages of Christian revelation: incarnation,[59] redemptive death[60] and resurrection.[61] Her thoughts also stand as a framework into which the Christian pilgrimage is given meaning and purpose. At the same time her Jewish heritage and its foundational importance for the understanding of Christianity, together with her appeal to humanity in general, should always be valued.[62] She illustrates in her contemporary way the importance of the contemplative aspect of human living that we stand in danger of losing. Yet this contemplative dimension, this sense of always standing before God, is what gives our lives their true depth, motivation and endurance.

The beauty of our spiritual heritage; the importance of well-structured dialogue between us; our part in public debate and our spiritual quest have been my topics in the exploration of faith today and our journey to God. I trust all I have said to the grace of God and to your gracious goodwill.

## Notes

1. In Leicester University I have had the pleasure of giving the Provost Derek Hole Lecture on 28 October 2010 ('Living the Virtues in a time of Austerity') and the Sigmund Sternberg Annual Public Lecture on 13 March 2012 ('The Journey to God and Faith Today'), a lecture that forms the basis for this chapter. Sigmund Sternberg contributed enormously to the advancement of inter-faith dialogue, especially through the work of the Three Faiths Forum (Jews, Christians and Muslims), of which he was a founder member. He sadly died on 18 October 2016, aged 95. 'The souls of the righteous are in the hand of God' (Wis 3.1a).
2. See, for example, the Address of Pope John Paul II to representatives of the Christian Churches and Ecclesial Communities and of the World Religions for the World Day of Prayer at the Basilica of St Francis in Assisi, 27 October 1986, 5 and 6.
3. Palmer, Martin (2012), *Sacred Land*, London, Piatkus.
4. *Ibid.*, p. 3. These 'four kinds of sacred place' are listed, pp. 3–6.
5. *Ibid.*, p. 6.
6. *Ibid.*

7   *Ibid.*, p. 147.
8   *Ibid.*, pp. 37f., chart, 'The Ages of History'.
9   *Ibid.*, p. 80, as quoted by Martin Palmer.
10  The Catholic perspective on inter-religious dialogue is presented in the Bishops' Conference of England and Wales teaching document *Meeting God in Friend and Stranger: Fostering Respect and Mutual Understanding between the Religions,* London, CTS, 2010, on which I shall be drawing extensively and which I invite you to read for yourselves.
11  Address of His Holiness John Paul II to the participants in the plenary Assembly of the Pontifical Council for Interreligious Dialogue, 26 April 1990, 4. See also Address of His Holiness John Paul II to the Religious Representatives at the conclusion of the Interreligious Assembly, St Peter's Square, Rome, 28 October 1999, 3.
12  Declaration *'Dominus Iesus' On the Unicity and Salvific Universality of Jesus Christ and the Church,* Congregation for the Doctrine of the Faith, London, CTS, 2000, 5.
13  *NA*, 2.
14  *Ibid.* See also the final paragraph of this section, where the core of the Church's teaching is summarized.
15  *NA*, 1.
16  *DH*, 2.
17  *LG*, 16; also *Dominus Iesus*, 22, sees inter-religious dialogue 'as part of her [the Church's] evangelizing mission'.
18  Pope John II, Encyclical, *Redemptoris missio*, on the permanent validity of the Church's missionary mandate, 28, given in Rome on 7 December 1990, being the twenty-fifth anniversary of the Vatican II Decree, On the Church's missionary activity, *AG*.
19  To be found in an address given by Pope John Paul II to the Jewish community of Rome on 13 April 1986 – the first visit of a Pope to a synagogue. On the Vatican website it is to be found in German and Italian (see paragraph 4). Reference is made to the address in *Meeting God in Friend and Stranger*, p. 28, n. 22.

20 Given in the context of the Apostolic Journey of His Holiness Pope Benedict XVI to Turkey, 28 November–1 December 2006. This address was delivered during a meeting with the President of the Religious Affairs Directorate in the Conference Room of the Diyanet, Ankara, 28 November 2006.
21 *NA*, 2.
22 Given in the context of the Apostolic Journey of Pope John Paul II to Korea, Papua New Guinea, Solomon Islands and Thailand, 2–11 May 1984. This address was delivered at a meeting of spiritual leaders of other non-Christian religions in the Chapel of the Nunciature, Seoul, South Korea, 6 May 1984, 2.
23 I am very grateful to the Zoroastrian community in Harrow for their warm welcome on 18 November 2011. It was a great privilege to share in their liturgy and hospitality.
24 *SV*, p. 89.
25 *Ibid.*, p. 102.
26 For additional evidence relating to the pre-Socratics, see Waterfield, Robin (trans.) (2000), *The First Philosophers: The Pre-Socratics and the Sophists*, Oxford, Oxford University Press, especially Anaximander of Miletus, 570 BC, and Anaximenes of Miletus, 550 BC, who introduced 'the idea of cosmic order or natural law' (p. 3). What is known of their writings is recorded at pp. 13–20, of which sections T 12, T 20 and T 28 should be noted in particular.
27 *GS*, 89.
28 *SV*, p. 104.
29 *Ibid.*, p. 87.
30 *Conf.*, Book 1.1.
31 For Esther (Etty) Hillesum, see Woodhouse, Patrick (2009), *Etty Hillesum: A Life Transformed*, London, Bloomsbury, which provides a useful introduction to Etty's life and thought. Rowan Williams has used Etty's thoughts and experiences as the lynchpin of his lecture 'Religious

Lives', published in *Faith in the Public Square*, London, Bloomsbury, 2012, pp. 313–25. Archbishop Williams uses Etty as an example for reflection upon how 'the doctrine of God' ought to be understood. My concern here is to portray Etty as a person who inspires us to think more deeply and to act more earnestly in relation to our search for spiritual growth.

32  In this context I should like to honour Edith Stein, Sister Teresa Benedicta of the Cross (1891–1942), who was taken from her Carmelite convent at Echt (with her sister Rosa) to Westerbork on 2 August 1942. Sister Benedicta and her sister were deported (with other Catholics of Jewish ancestry) to Auschwitz on 7 August and died there on 9 August. Pope John Paul II canonized Sister Teresa Benedicta on 11 October 1998 and declared that 9 August should be her feast day.

33  Woodhouse, *Etty Hillesum*, pp. 155f., has provided a chronological table of events.

34  For a helpful analysis of Etty's understanding of God see Pleshoyano, Alexandra (2005), 'Etty Hillesum: For God and with God', *The Way*, 44/1, pp. 7–20.

35  Smelik, Klaas A. D. (ed.) (2002), *Etty: The Letters and Diaries of Etty Hillesum, 1941–1943*, trans. Arnold J. Pomerans. Grand Rapids, MI, and Cambridge, Eerdmans (=*Etty*). All references are to this edition.

36  Note the evidence offered by Friedrich Weinreb in Smelik (ed.), *Etty*, pp. 767f., n. 607. Etty's own account is to be found in a letter to Han Wegerif and others, undated but after 26 June 1943: Smelik (ed.), *Etty*, pp. 606–9 (letter 42). No self-praise is to be found here.

37  *Etty*, pp. 658f., in a letter to Christine van Nooten, 7 September 1943 (letter 71). The quotation from the Psalms is probably an allusion to Ps 18 (Vg 17), 2.

38  *Etty*, p. 194, diary entry, 20 December 1941.

39  *Ibid.*, p. 139, diary entry, 27 October 1941. See also *ibid.*, p. 473, the later diary entry for 5 July 1942: 'There is

always a quiet room in some corner of our being, and we can always retire there for a while.'
40  *Ibid.*, p. 223, diary entry, 9 January 1942.
41  For the context of the bathroom, see *Etty*, p. 103, diary entry, 24 September 1941.
42  *Ibid.*, p. 320, diary entry, 3 April 1942, Good Friday.
43  *Ibid.*, p. 181, diary entry, 14 December 1941.
44  *Ibid.*, p. 469, diary entry, 4 July 1942.
45  *Ibid.*, p. 471.
46  *Ibid.*, p. 212, diary entry, 31 December 1941.
47  *Ibid.*, p. 464, diary entry, 3 July 1942.
48  *Ibid.*, pp. 308f, diary entry, Saturday morning (28 March) 1942.
49  *Ibid.*, p. 465, diary entry, 3 July 1942.
50  *Ibid.*, p. 550, forms the conclusion to her diaries, 13 October 1942.
51  *Ibid.*, p. 499, diary entry, 23 July 1942.
52  *Ibid.*, p. 500.
53  For the correlation between the external threat of terror and the protective power of prayer, note: 'The threat grows ever greater, and terror increases from day to day. I draw prayer round me like a dark protective wall' (*Etty*, p. 364, diary entry, 18 May 1942).
54  *Etty*, pp. 480f., diary entry, 7 July 1942.
55  *Ibid.*, p. 657, letter to Maria Tuinzing from Westerbork, 2 September 1943. Etty's understanding of the doctrine of God is here confused. She does not understand that God transcends all humanity; see also Pleshoyano, 'For God and with God', p. 11.
56  *Ibid*, p. 489, diary entry, 12 July 1942.
57  *Ibid.*
58  *Ibid.*, For Etty's surrender to God's will, note: 'Not *my* will, but Thy will be done' (*Etty*, p. 542, diary entry, 3 October 1942, 6.30 a.m., in the bathroom).
59  Incarnation; see *CCC*, 461–3.

60 Redemptive death; see *CCC*, 599–605, in particular: 'By giving up his own Son for our sins, God manifests that his plan for us is one of benevolent love' (*CCC*, 604).
61 Resurrection; see *CCC*, 645–6.
62 This framework has been able to be constructed on the basis of Etty's vast range of intellectual resources; for example, The Bible (in particular the Psalms and St Matthew's Gospel), St Augustine, Dostoevsky, Jung and Rilke. In the last year of her life Etty gave the writings of Meister Eckhart to her father, *Etty*, p. 613, letter 45 to Christine van Nooten, 1 July 1943. This fact encourages further the investigation of the notion of 'the Lure of God' within spirituality.

# 8
## Inter-Religious Dialogue: People and Places

> *I truly understand that God shows no partiality, but in every nation anyone who fears him and does what is right is acceptable to him.*
>
> ACTS 10.34–35 (NRSV)

St Luke is here demonstrating that, following the conversion to Christianity of the Roman centurion Cornelius and his household, St Peter is able to affirm the universality of God and his love for all humanity. To be acceptable in God's sight, however, we must be prepared to live like him and serve him and each other in a spirit of goodness, humility and truth. In the Foreword to the teaching document of the Bishops' Conference of England and Wales, *Meeting God in Friend and Stranger: Fostering Respect and Mutual Understanding between the Religions* (2010), I introduced the concepts of how, from the perspective of Catholic teaching, we ought to understand and practise inter-religious dialogue. We should acknowledge the reality that we are a part of a multi-faith environment, and that we are learning constantly how to build a society where all faiths may live together in harmony. Everyone should share in this activity because the common good of our nation is dependent on such a vision (see, for example, Is 11.6–9).

I should now like to share with you some of the experiences of the places at home and abroad which I have visited, and the people whom I have had the honour of meeting, during my inter-religious encounters. Any understanding relating to inter-religious dialogue should be based on living experiences and loving activity as well as a theoretical knowledge of the concepts involved. I am conscious that my accounts of this ministry are representative of all that is achieved by those who engage daily in inter-religious activity, often in very difficult circumstances.

### Singers Hill Synagogue, Birmingham

*If you seek after the words of the Torah as after hidden treasure, the Holy One, blessed be He, will not withhold from you your reward.*
                    Rabbi Phineas ben Jair, The Song of
                                   Songs Rabbah, I. 1.9[1]

In March 2004 I had the honour to hand over the Sacred Sepher Torah scroll to Rabbi Tann in the Singers Hill Synagogue, Birmingham. The scroll had been in the possession of the Diocesan seminary, St Mary's College, Oscott. It was only my second visit to this beautiful and historic synagogue, yet in a way that I cannot explain I felt quite at home in that fellowship. There was a real sense of homecoming about the evening, not only for the Sacred Sepher Torah but also, I suspect, for all of the

## INTER-RELIGIOUS DIALOGUE: PEOPLE AND PLACES

Catholic community as we renewed profound bonds and connections, links which had been obscured and lost for far too long. It was my privilege to participate in the liturgy and to address the faithful, and I give thanks to Almighty God who is the loving Father to us all that I was able to share in such a demonstration of unity, where love and faithfulness met and righteousness and peace embraced.

The sequence of events that brought us together that evening have such poignancy. The story has its origin in the refusal of one young man, Alfred Schilling, to accept the dictates of the Third Reich. He was forced to leave his studies for the priesthood and join the German war effort. He was a conscientious objector and, as a result, served as a member of the Red Cross. He was captured and imprisoned by the British Army, but a sensitive English general, noticing that there were a number of seminarians among the prisoners, arranged for them to be brought to England and held together in a camp at Berechurch, near Colchester.[2] It is at this point, when Alfred is behind the barbed wire of a prison, a setting that has a powerful resonance of all the hatred and cruelty that were a prominent feature of twentieth-century Europe, that a second amazing character, Fr Francis (Frank) Davis, enters our story.[3]

Francis was a young theologian of rare ability who engaged in intelligent critical scholarship; he had a doctorate in the theology of Cardinal John Henry Newman.[4] He was a man of typically English spirituality and possessed generous pastoral concern. He had been a professor at St Mary's College, Oscott, since 1930, and he responded readily to a request that he undertake the continuing theological education of over 100

German prisoner-seminarians. Every month he went from Oscott to Colchester by the only means available to him: his bicycle. He taught the young men in their native German and increased their love and understanding of the Holy Scriptures. Alfred Schilling was first among the pupils.[5] Having already an advanced knowledge of Hebrew, as well as Greek and Latin, he acted as the resident tutor. In the prison camp, like the Hebrew scholars of old in exile, Alfred taught his companions the language and interpretation of the Torah. Given the dedication and scholarship of these two men, Francis Davis and Alfred Schilling, the time spent in the prison camp was transformed. All the students returned to Germany, sixty of them became Catholic priests, two become bishops and two became distinguished professors of theology. Links with St Mary's College, however, were maintained, the group visiting Colchester and Oscott in 1990.[6]

When Alfred Schilling died, his library, a rare collection of scholarly books, was transferred to St Mary's College under the guardianship of my predecessor, Archbishop Maurice Couve de Murville.[7] In the library is this Sepher Torah, and this evening what we have received from Alfred Schilling we gladly give to you with our fraternal expression of good will.

As Catholics we share with you an understanding of the sacredness of times, places and objects. Sacredness is not separate from earthly existence. Sacredness is intertwined with our daily realities. We also know the ways in which particular objects, actions and lives are set aside and consecrated to God. This Sepher Torah is one such sacred object. It was a part of a whole library, and each book has its own particular value. I apologize to you, my Jewish brothers and sisters, that we did not recognize immediately the sacredness of the Scroll and treat it with the respect to which it is entitled as a sacred object. I ask your forgiveness for our unintended lack of reverence.

This Torah scroll now enshrined in the Ark of this Synagogue is a constant reminder to us that our faiths, Judaism and Christianity, are two brothers of the one parent, thus forming an element for us in the loving plan of God. As a result, we draw our living sap from the one tree of life. We both recognize the power and majesty of God in the wonder of creation (Gen 1–2). We are called with Noah and his descendants to perform the demands which are offered by the covenant of God (Gen 9.1–17). We are descendants from Abraham, our father in faith (Gen 12–24), and the holy Patriarchs and Matriarchs (Gen 25–50). We are both freed from slavery by the Exodus (Ex 1–15), being led on our journey by the pillar of fire and cloud (Ex 13.21–2). We are fed by manna from heaven (Ex 16.9–36) and living water from the rock (Ex 17.1–7). We receive the law (*Torah*) from God at Mount Sinai through Moses (Ex 19.3–20.17; Deut 5.1–22), and this law teaches us the immense compassion and forgiveness of God (Ex 34.6–7), to whom we must turn when we offend him by our sin and division (Ex 32.1–6; Deut 9.13–21). Both Jews and Christians share the central teaching of the law (*Torah*): love of God and love of neighbour. This understanding is summarized in the great *Shema* beloved in both our traditions: 'Hear [*Shema*], O Israel: The Lord is our God, the Lord alone. You shall love the Lord your God with all your heart, and with all your soul, and with all your might' (Deut 6.4–5 [NRSV]); and together as neighbours we believe that 'You shall not take vengeance or bear a grudge against any of your people, but you shall love your neighbour as yourself: I am the Lord' (Lev 19.18).

Christians respect and honour the Torah, clothed, crowned and placed in the Holy Ark, and we shall remember that throughout all our days we are summoned to learn more deeply how to respect God and one another. This evening provides an encouragement to this end. Jews and Catholics are resolved to promote the understanding and the peace that are God's gift to all people. It must surely be in the providence of God that he has led us to this moment of profound affinity in faith, and in mutual respect and affection, at a time when faith is under suspicion from a secular and materialistic society. At a time when religious faith is being shown as a source of division and conflict we must stand together to demonstrate to the world all that is best, all that is good and all that is noble within our communities. We affirm together that without the sacred gifts of God life has no purpose.

May I recall at this solemn and joyful moment the words of Pope (now St) John Paul II which he placed in the Western Wall of the Temple in Jerusalem on 26 March 2000:

> God of our Father,
> You chose Abraham and his descendants
> To bring your name to the nations:
> We are deeply saddened
> By the behaviour of those
> Who in the course of history
> Have caused these children of yours to suffer,
> And asking your forgiveness

## INTER-RELIGIOUS DIALOGUE: PEOPLE AND PLACES

We wish to commit ourselves
To genuine brotherhood
With the people of the Covenant.

The covenant which God made with Israel (Gen 17.7) is for all time. The new covenant initiated by Jesus (Mk 14.24) does not replace the old covenant. The whole history of God's loving action towards humanity is demonstrated by the combination of these covenants (Jer 31.31–4). This greater reality is seen in our fellowship this evening as we hand to you this sacred Torah, which represents the totality of God's love for us all – both Jews and Christians. The way in which we have lovingly cared for, studied and drawn life from this Torah takes us to the root and source of the life we have received from God and is symbolic of our response to his covenant love (Hos 6.6). The Torah, therefore, opens before us our true royal road (Is 35.8), the road of genuine brotherhood. Our hearts are raised in the song of prayer, the song of the Psalms (e.g., Ps 30 [Vg 29].4) which have enriched our ceremony this evening. We pray these psalms every day, psalms which Jesus (e.g., Mk 14.26; the *Hallel* psalms, 113–18 [Vg 112–17]) recited at great feasts, including the Passover, and the early Christians (e.g., Col 3.16) prayed, psalms which are the song of our brotherhood. As we stand together in humility before the providence of God who touches our lives with his love, let us remember that with this gift comes the task of being steadfast in our faith and compassionate in our actions. It is we, the people of faith, who must call constantly upon Almighty God and pray that he will not forget or forsake his human family in our waywardness. This evening we ask God's blessing also on all those who do not know him and all who fear that only emptiness is to be found at the heart of life. We pray for his blessing of peace on all who are suffering, and these words from Psalm 34 (Vg 33) echo again in our hearts:

> I will bless the Lord at all times,
> His praise always on my lips;
> […]
> Glorify the Lord with me.
> Together let us praise his name.
> 
> Ps 34 (Vg 33).1 and 3, Grail

We remember those who are mourning the loss of loved ones, especially those who have been victims of terrorism. Such evil acts are crimes before God, and this evening we ask for forgiveness. Ultimately we join our voices with King David, who acclaimed before the assembly of Israel:

> Yours, O Lord, are the greatness, the power,
> the glory, the victory, and the majesty;
> for all that is in the heavens and on the earth is yours;
> yours, is the kingdom, O Lord, and you are exalted as head above all.
> 
> 1 Chron 29.11 (NRSV)

## Yad Vashem Memorial, Jerusalem

*I [the Lord] will give in my house and within my walls a monument and a name (yad vashem)*

## INTER-RELIGIOUS DIALOGUE: PEOPLE AND PLACES

*better than sons and daughters;*
*I [the Lord] will give them an everlasting name*
*which shall not be cut off.*

IS 56.5

The Holocaust Memorial in Jerusalem named Yad Vashem tells a unique and dreadful story. No one can visit this place without it having a profound effect on both the soul and the mind. My visit left me with a deep sense of horror relating to the Holocaust and a long list of agonizing questions as to why such a terrible series of events occurred in twentieth-century Europe.

Yad Vashem is a monumental tribute to all who perished in this genocide and a damning indictment of all who perpetrated this hatred, directly or indirectly. Only slowly did these perceptions sink deeply into my consciousness.

The journey through the Memorial is long and demands attention. I went without a guide. The exhibits, films and explanations are arranged along a number of zigzag paths, and I soon lost touch with my companions. The visit became for me a solitary journey, and I was engrossed to such an extent that everything – time, space and wider purpose – was all forgotten. My journey led me into the history of the terrible events of Jewish persecution, in particular by the Nazis. I felt that I was entering into the closed world of the ghetto, and also into an understanding of how often many nations systematically closed their doors to the Jewish people, leaving them to their dreadful fate. Never before had I understood how they had been left so abandoned without any place where they could go or to call their own.

I was also drawn into the personal horrors of the victims of this annihilation: told and retold, city by city (e.g., Berlin, Prague, Amsterdam, Paris), family by family (e.g., Stein, Hillesum, Frank), until reduced to yet another corpse bulldozed into a pit or reduced to ash (e.g., Auschwitz, 1942–5). Never before had I felt the total degradation executed on an industrial scale and here being presented before my eyes.

My mind was flooded, both at the time and subsequently, with questions: historical, political, religious and psychological. What were the causes of these events? How have the events of the Holocaust affected those who have survived this terrible ordeal, and how have future generations come to terms with this horror? How do we live with the guilt of having been bystanders or indirect participants? One approach is to ask how we are to understand the reality of sin. Every human being is touched by sin, but this story of evil is of such a dimension as to tempt us to lose heart in human goodness. Yet even amid all the darkness there was goodness found shining forth in the indomitable endurance shown by many in the concentration camps. Goodness was also seen in the powerful bond and alliance of secrecy between the hunted and those who risked all to give them protection and shelter. Sometimes I had to read the small print to find such stories of heroism. The same heroism is also recognized today in the regular awards of the title 'Righteous Gentile' given by the Jewish people and the state of Israel as such stories of bravery continue to be brought to our attention.

I lingered long in the last room of the Memorial. In this darkened quarter, on one of the walls, are projected sayings and writings which have come from those who understood their fate and wished to reflect from the depth of their being, in words, their impending sacrifice. I was reminded of a quotation from Etty Hillesum: 'There are moments when I can see right through life and the human heart, when I understand more and more and become calmer and calmer and am filled with a faith in God.'[8]

## Gaza: The Catholic Community as a Source of Hope

Gaza is among the most forsaken places in the world.[9] My first visit there, in 2014, lasted for eight hours and was within the context of the Westminster Diocesan Pilgrimage to the Holy Land. Gaza left a deep impression upon me, which I shall always remember with sadness.

Gaza is isolated, not because it is remote from contiguous Middle Eastern states – Egypt and Israel – but because it is separated by deliberate intent; entry and exit are difficult even for those in diplomatic vehicles, and for most visitors they are virtually impossible. Entering Gaza is like visiting another world. It is a closed society, and internal tensions can be detected immediately. My impression is that it is a volatile community riven with division. Conflict is common and often violent. Opposing factions vie for authority, and internal control is exercised by those who have the means of imposing power. It appeared to me that destruction and devastation were widespread and, in some places, total. Much of the infrastructure had been destroyed, and the poverty in which people were living was an open wound.

My purpose in visiting Gaza was mainly to greet and spend time with the Catholic community, a mere 150 families among a total population of approximately 1.8 million. In the midst of such trauma and destruction the fabric of the Catholic community had not been torn apart. There was, however, deep sorrow, shadows of helplessness and profound anxiety about the future. At the same time there was also present the coherence of life, a true sense of community and solidarity and, perhaps most amazingly, a reaching out to fellow citizens who were in even greater need.

This community was energized by the presence of three groups of religious women and two priests. Their presence was sacramental, a tangible flesh-and-body sign of the abiding love of God. By their fellowship we could read, feel and touch the truth that the wellsprings of God's love and mercy are never closed, as is Gaza. They are there by choice, all committed to the ministry of this beleaguered people, who are locked away from the wider environment. The priests and religious by their presence and in the ministry help a people who are deprived of so much to find a deeper treasure from which to draw patience and endurance. One group of sisters ran a very successful high school, in which only a tiny proportion are Catholics. Another group of sisters offer love and care to the babies and children who have lost everything in the destruction of the war. The third group of sisters complemented the ministry of the priests in the pattern of parish work. It was a great privilege for me to celebrate the Sunday Mass with them, to greet them, show them signs of solidarity and see them receive practical, financial support from the Friends of

## INTER-RELIGIOUS DIALOGUE: PEOPLE AND PLACES

the Holy Land, an ecumenical charity of which I am proud to be a patron.

Frontiers may be imposed, security walls may be constructed and 'buffer zones' created which generate hardship from which many signs of normality are erased. The Spirit of God, however, is not so constrained. The Spirit flows where it wills and always seeks out willing hearts and hands through which to complete its work. We pray, 'Send forth your Spirit, O Lord, and renew the face of the earth!' (Ps 104 [Vg 103].30). Well, Gaza certainly needs radical rescue and renewal. I saw that, and I also saw those willing hearts and hands who offer all their gifts to God in the service of others. They represent a small but efficacious sign of the work of the Holy Spirit.

I returned to Gaza in November 2016 for a few hours, although the visit took most of the day. The journey to enter and leave Gaza remains difficult. In comparison with my previous visit in 2014 I felt that, despite the atmosphere being less tense, there was seemingly no more hope for the future.[10] After the Mass I met a group of young Christians, mostly Catholics. They were at that wonderful time of life, between 16 and 23 years of age: full of smiles, style, shyness and bravado. I was meeting them because they were among the beneficiaries of our charity, Friends of the Holy Land, which is providing educational and employment opportunities. Their support is enabling these young people to study and gain skills in administration and management. Jobs are being created in partnership with the Catholic parish and other centres of social concern. We hope and pray that their education bears fruit and that their employment endures.

Little is certain in Gaza, however, beyond political uncertainty. In this context two young people spoke to me and quietly expressed their deep despair at the total lack of what they believe to be their long-term prospects. They spoke in hushed tones, perhaps not to fracture the atmosphere of encouragement, gratitude and solidarity of that moment, but it was clear that their despair ran deep and could not be disguised for long. On this visit I learned that over 50 per cent of the population are under 15 years of age, and some have already lived through three wars. It takes little imagination to picture the likely future of such a huge number of young people or the attitudes and motivations that are taking root in their hearts – the future is bleak.

As we parted, we promised to pray for each other, for the strong faith that we all need to sustain hope, deepen compassion and fuel generosity. As I left Gaza City and approached the complex security and exit procedures, it was clear that I had received from the people of Gaza far more than I had given to them. Their faith in great adversity is impressive, and such faith has a gritty resilience. I am humbled again by their witness and more determined than ever before that I shall never forget my brothers and sisters in Gaza.

## Notes

1 From the *Midrash Rabbah, Song of Songs,* trans. M. Simon (third edition, 1983), London and New York, Soncino Press, pp. 10–11, being part of a nine-volume text of the *Midrash Rabbah.*

2. See Free, Ken (2009), *Camp 186: The Last Town at Berechurch*, Stroud, Amberley, in particular, Chapter VII, 'The Catholic Church', pp. 60–70 and nn. 56–75, including the role played by Archbishop William Godfrey (Apostolic Delegate), Cardinal Bernard Griffin (Westminster) and Cardinal Josef Frings (Cologne) in the establishment and recognition of the Berechurch seminary. The camp was in operation from 1944 to 1947.
3. Details from The Archdiocese of Birmingham Archives, HFD – Papers of Henry Francis Davis (1903–86); in relation to his ministry at Berechurch, see HFD/A/4. Free, *Camp 186*, has some interesting observations in relation to Dr Davis, pp. 62–3, together with an examination certificate signed by him in connection with one student, Adolf Blatha, who passed in Moral Theology, Easter 1946, p. 64.
4. Birmingham Archives, HFD/A/3.
5. See Free, *Camp 186*, pp. 63 and 70.
6. *Ibid.*, p. 70 and n. 73, for the report in the *Daily Telegraph*, 17 August 1990.
7. St Mary's College, Oscott, is a seminary for the training of priests, and a section of the library resources is dedicated to Alfred Schilling, under the title of The Schilling Library.
8. Smelik, Klaas A. D. (ed.) (2002), *Etty: The Letters and Diaries of Etty Hillesum, 1941–1943*, trans., Arnold J. Pomerans. Grand Rapids, MI, and Cambridge, Eerdmans, p. 481.
9. For details see Filiu, Jean-Pierre (2014), *Gaza: A History*, trans. John King. London, C. Hurst & Co.
10. See, for example, the report 'Executions by Hamas in Gaza', *Daily Telegraph*, 1 June 2016, but I rejoice in the good news 'A ray of hope for the suffering people of Gaza', *Independent*, 11 October 2017 and 'Egypt brokers Fatah-Hamas deal on Gaza', *Daily Telegraph*, 13 October 2017.

# 9
## Speaking in the Name of the Church and Manifesting Caritas

*Their span extends through all the earth.*
Responsorial Psalm, Ps 19.4[Vg 18.5], from the Vigil Mass for St Peter and St Paul, Apostles

*Zion shall be redeemed by justice,*
*And those in her who repent, by righteousness.*
IS 1.27

*Let love be genuine; hate what is evil, hold fast to what is good.*
ROM 12.9

*And to stand in battle in the day of the Lord is to resist the forces of evil*
*out of a love of justice.*
*If a religious leader is afraid to say what is right, what else can his silence*
*mean but that he has taken flight?*
PR, BOOK 2, 4

Should spiritual leaders speak publicly in the name of the Church about issues relating to law, politics, social conditions and economic life? It could be argued that any statements that we make should be confined to the pulpit and restricted to spiritual and pastoral matters. If we are to comment on issues of public interest, on what theological and ethical principles should we base our pronouncements? St Augustine of Hippo (354–430), for example, gives us, in the *City of God*, an important clue and guide as to how we should understand such principles when debating these questions. He believed that the foundations of society must be based on the concept of justice: 'Remove justice, and what are kingdoms but gangs of criminals on a large scale? What are criminal gangs but petty kingdoms?'[1] In developing this consideration of justice, Augustine uses the theme of how the citizens of the State are able to respond to God by the use of the metaphor of the body and soul in order to discuss the nature of reason and lust and operation of the law in respect of the 'commonwealth'.[2] The focus of his argument is found in the question 'When a man does not serve God, what amount of justice are we to suppose to exist in his being?'[3] Augustine does not advance any precise views relating to the Church and its connection with the structures of the State, as he has no particular concern as to which form of government is in power, believing that 'we must ascribe to the true God alone the power to grant kingdoms and empires.'[4] In commending to 'my dear son Marcellinus'[5] the treatise concerning the *City of God*, Augustine is reflecting here on the reason why such an undertaking is necessary to demonstrate 'the love of Christ' to the world.[6] By attempting to present the Christian message to society in relation to the State, Augustine is affirming his belief that the

Bishop has the right to speak in this context in the name of God.

In this way Church leaders should know that Christ must be at the centre of any statements or pronouncements that we make. We should present the Christian message with love and in a spirit of openness in order that all humanity might experience justice and peace. By pronouncing on matters of justice and engaging in works of charity 'in the love of Christ',[7] Church leaders, however inadequately, are able to offer a philosophy of virtue and possible plans for action which will enhance the common good (*CCC*, 1905–12).

In order to ensure the just ordering of society, it should be recognized that the State (in its numerous forms) and the Church have differing functions to perform. Jesus established this principle when he declared 'Render to Caesar the things that are Caesar's, and to God the things that are God's' (Mk 12.17; also Mt 22.21 and Lk 20.25). The fathers of the Second Vatican Council used the expression 'the autonomy of earthly affairs' to describe this proposition (*GS*, 36) in order to illustrate what is meant by the rightful establishment of the State to promote laws which lead to justice. At the Council there was the concern that this 'autonomy' might lead to an underestimation or even a denial of the role of the Creator God in human affairs, 'once God is forgotten, the creature is lost sight of as well' (*GS*, 36). In this context the prophetic work of Church leaders is clear: we must pronounce on matters of justice in the name of God, further the work of charity and promote the well-being of all citizens. We must follow the exhortation of St Gregory and not be 'afraid to say what is right' by speaking the truth about God and his loving purposes for humanity. If we remain silent, it could be assumed that we have 'taken flight'[8] and forsaken the responsibilities entrusted to us at our ordination.

Our primary responsibility is to ensure that religious freedom is guaranteed by the State. We should safeguard and promote 'religious freedom and harmony between the followers of different religions *and none*' (*DCE*, 28, my italics). Thus, religious freedom is integral for the championing and in the defence of justice, which is, in turn, the fundamental basis for defining political, social and economic life. In the execution of justice we see that public life has a 'soul'. The purpose of the just operation of the law is not merely the means by which rules and customs are enforced. It is, rather, the way of offering freedom to human beings in order that we are then able to act morally, and to become a community in which mutual fairness, respect and harmony prevail. Government by 'gangs of criminals' means the opposite: violence, intimidation, indiscipline and lawlessness. Augustine anticipates this dichotomy by asking where our true love, our basic attitude towards life, is to be found. This question follows directly from the teaching of Jesus, 'For where your treasure is, there will your heart be also' (Mt 6.21; Lk 12.34), a statement that is fundamental for understanding and living the Christian life. For Augustine human orientation can be centred in the Earthly City, which 'was created by self-love reaching the point of contempt for God' and governed by those 'exalting themselves in their wisdom, under the domination of pride' while for those who inhabit 'the Heavenly City glory [lies] in the Lord' and 'man's only wisdom is the devotion which rightly worships the true God, and looks for its reward in the fellowship of the saints'.⁹ Augustine is aware, however, that the human heart remains divided between pride and humility, between sin and glory, yet in our faithful pilgrimage through life to eternity and with openness to the Spirit of love, humanity is able to advance towards the Heavenly City and to create a foretaste of that city on earth.¹⁰ While acknowledging that we are flawed human beings, we religious leaders speak on the basis of our obligation to declare the love, peace and glory of God. By offering humanity, created in the likeness of God and given personal and corporate dignity, a vision of hope for the future (however clouded the earthly context may be) is now seen by the way in which life can be interpreted within its true perspective of living in love.

As a Catholic Bishop, my particular understanding of the ways in which the Church engages with society is based on Catholic social teaching. Such teaching, both in theory and practice, is based on the interaction between justice and faith, reason and natural law. Justice forms the foundational structure on which all civilized society is able to function with its laws, police and courts operating without favouritism for the common good. Faith, in turn, however, implies an encounter with God, who desires the welfare of every human person. Faith is able to challenge those areas of life where justice is seen to be inadequate. The Church's mission, however, must neither replace nor exercise power over the State; rather, we should act as a 'conscience', offering to society a vision of love because the Church, when she is true to her mission, 'is alive with the love enkindled by the Spirit of Christ' (*DCE*, 28). The conjunction of reason and natural law reinforces this proposition. The concept of natural law, in which is found the idea of the use of reason, is an essential element in the understanding and application of Catholic social teaching, which the Church believes should be shared with people of other religious faiths and of none. Natural law, then, can be defined as 'the original moral sense which enables man to discern by reason the good and the evil, the truth and the lie' (*CCC*, 1954). This definition needs qualification in the sense that there must be a willingness on the part of humanity to share in the wisdom, love and goodness of the Creator God and in his mission for the well-being of all humanity. The natural moral law tradition, therefore, acts as a challenge in that humanity is being requested to turn from violence and disrespect to compassion and respect for all citizens. Governments also must abandon regimes operated by 'gangs of criminals' and appoint rulers who are righteous, who manifest true justice and who care for all the people under their jurisdiction. The natural law concept, although universal in scope, is open to a variety of applications both in time and in context. Natural law and its interpretation should not be dismissed as being over-idealistic; rather, the concept and its application should be seen as vital in offering to humanity a vision of the way things ought to be, and will be, under the loving eyes of the Creator. An insight which I find challenging from *Gaudium et Spes* is that the Church, through its proclamation of the Gospel and by 'dispensing the treasures of grace', is making a contribution to world peace and harmony, through 'imparting the knowledge of the divine and the natural law' (*GS*, 89). In this regard, although natural law may be discerned by reason, that reason, however well applied intellectually, must be purified by faith because 'Faith enables reason to do its work more effectively and to see its proper object more clearly' (*DCE*, 28).

Thus the natural law tradition 'provides revealed law and grace with a foundation prepared by God and in accordance with the work of the Spirit' (*CCC*, 1960). In this observation lies another qualification, that natural law recognizes human sinfulness and the need for redemption under God (see *GS*, 78). This work of redemption represents the activity of the Holy Spirit, who offers both the fullness of the love of Christ and a new way of living in peace according to his teaching (see *GS*, 78). This understanding means that a considerable variety of subjects are included within Catholic social teaching, which is often complex and wide-ranging. They include, for example: the discussion of war and peace; international development and the care of the planet; social inclusion, including migration and community relations; welfare and human rights, especially with regard to the operation of justice; poverty and inequality, including the care of the elderly; finance and business; and marriage and the family. It is impossible to give here the depth of treatment that is desirable in relation to these issues; instead, I have decided to discuss the principles of *caritas* in order to encourage dialogue and action, to develop insight and industry, to produce a more caring society and, above all, to offer the prospect of a better world lived under the law and grace of the Creator.

As a Catholic Bishop, my ministry is established on the understanding that all engagement with society must be based on the precepts of the Gospel as enshrined within Catholic teaching. In this regard *caritas*, love, is the key concept (e.g., Lev 19.18; Mt 22.37–40; Mk 12.29–31; Lk 10.37; Rom 13.8–10) for understanding how our love for God and the world and humanity, as created by him, ought to be shown towards our neighbours, in all aspects of their lives. *Caritas* is the principle on which the Church's social organizations operate and the way in which cooperation with the State is to be perceived, based on the just operation of the law. As Pope Benedict XVI comments, 'There is no ordering of the State so just that it can eliminate the need for the service of love. Whoever wants to eliminate love is preparing to eliminate man as such' (*DCE*, 28). Thus, any attempts by the State to dehumanize its citizens in this way is a direct threat to the Gospel teaching of Jesus, the life of the apostolic Church and the total ministry of love.

In my homily during the Mass in Westminster Cathedral (10 September 2016) for ministers of charity in the Year of Mercy (2015–16) I was able to annunciate key principles on which to build the foundation for the work in exercising the ministry of *caritas*, which should be undertaken, as Pope Benedict XVI has written, alongside the proclamation of the Word of God and the celebration of the sacraments (*DCE*, 25). In engaging with these principles, let me start at the deep end. When swimming, I have always liked to dive into the pool at the deep end and not enter slowly step by step into the water! The first principle for understanding the mission of charitable engagement with society is to begin with the Holy Trinity of the Godhead. This fundamental principle encourages us to dive into the deep end of the theological and social water! Yes, 'you do see the Trinity if you see love.'[11] Every act of charity, understood and seen in its deepest dimensions, in its full beauty, lays bare the plan from the mind of God our Father, who, moved by love, sent his Son into our world to bear our burdens. Every work of charity reveals and makes tangible the pierced side of Christ and the lifeblood and water (Jn 19.34) which flow from him, the great symbol of the love and mercy of the Father. From the Risen Christ we, his disciples, receive the Holy Spirit (Jn 20.22; see also Rom 14.17). The Holy Spirit harmonizes our hearts with that of the heart of Christ, and we are moved to love others as Christ loved us when he bent down to wash the feet of the disciples (Jn 13.5) and he gave his life on the Cross for the healing and salvation of all humanity (Jn 12.32). Here, then, we see the deepest nature of the work of *caritas* which you should strive to undertake with great generosity. We must do everything possible to preserve, protect and promote this work of love. We must always build on rock so that, when the flood waters rise and put this work under threat, it does not fall because the foundation is strong, being based on the words and deeds of Jesus which are our guide in all things (Mt 7.24–7).

The second principle on which we build the foundation of *caritas* is that we know, beyond any doubt, that even before we lift a finger in love for another human being, we have been first loved and always will be loved and cherished by our heavenly Father. He knows every fibre of our being (Ps 139 [Vg 138].1–3) and pours unceasingly his love upon us in all our work done in his name. We know from experience that we must always be open to receive divine and human love; if we attempt to live by giving service alone, then we shall suffer from fatigue and boredom. Anyone who wishes to give love must first have received love. In order to become a source of love we must drink constantly anew from the true and unchanging source of love, Jesus Christ our Lord (*DCE*, 7). We see, for example, in the life and ministry of Mother Teresa of Calcutta, a saint for our age, the pattern as to how we should exercise the work of *caritas*.[12] Her demand for justice and compassion for the poor and vulnerable have taught us that Christ's love for us and our love are inseparable. When she insisted that service is the fruit of love, she was revealing the love of God.

This inseparable bond between love of God and love of neighbour is expressed most powerfully in the sacrament of the Eucharist, and leads us to our third principle in relation to *caritas*. In the Eucharist the concept of neighbour becomes universalized and challenges us to understand that 'a Eucharist which does not pass over into the concrete practice of love is intrinsically fragmented' (*DCE*, 14). The Eucharistic root for our work is sustained in our prayer life, especially in our prayers before the blessed sacrament. Mother Teresa insisted that it was vital for us to spend time in prayer in order that the practical work of *caritas* be resourced and sustained by the most powerful source and inspiration: the living presence of the sacramental body of Jesus. Through the Eucharist the works of charity find their true energy, and without the Eucharist we shall not develop the deep roots of faith and drink the living water of love which we need to renew our ministry in its freshness and spontaneity. This understanding teaches us that we must not allow ourselves to fall into the trap of allowing our ministry to become routine and heartless. Through the deep spirituality which the Eucharist offers we should learn that, together with effective help and support, those truly in need must be given love (1 Cor 13.1–3).

In the fourth principle we bear witness to the way that we manifest the work of *caritas*. Through this ministry we are proclaiming that God loves everyone, without exception (Rom 2.11), and that we seek to serve in the name of God and of Jesus, his Son. It must be clear that on this basis we are ministering *caritas* to all those in need, and without partiality. The Catholic Church is not seeking to proselytize because 'love is free; it is not practised as a way of achieving other ends' (*DCE*, 31). When we perform the work of *caritas*, we do so in the power of God and to point to his loving work in the world. We should not be seeking self-praise or affirmation, for when the ministry of *caritas* is genuine, we know that God's love is present and experienced. We have all been touched by his hand of grace simply because we have attempted to love as he first loved us. The Catholic Church offers to work in partnership with organizations both in the State and the voluntary sectors who, while not necessarily sharing all the tenets of our faith, believe in our values in relation to the sanctity of human life and its inherent worth under God. This ministry demands intellect, sensitivity and faith, and I am confident that God will bless every loving action of *caritas*.

Within this process of demonstrating *caritas* I am aware of the great value of dialogue with religious leaders of other faith traditions with whom I meet frequently in 'the desire to bridge our differences and build a world of peace, justice and friendship.'[13] The aim of such activity is to assist in the establishment of well-being and harmony among all our citizens in the workplace and in the community. This dialogue takes place in opposition to the view held by those who see society as secular and humanist, believing that recourse to religious faith in financial and social matters is unnecessary. As we journey through life, it is difficult to predict, with any certainty, how events nationally and internationally will develop in the future. What will our reactions be, for example, to political and economic change? I am conscious of a 'deep and widening sense of uncertainty' within society and that there exists 'much anxiety about the state of our world'.[14] Thus, when we experience 'uncertainty' and 'anxiety', a tension exists between social change and the timelessness which the Gospel offers. As a result, the Church through the power of the Holy Spirit is able to inject into society the practical application of the divine virtues of faith and charity. As the Church is not bound to any form of human culture or to any political, economic or society system, she is, by her universality, able to establish a close bond with the diverse human communities throughout the world (GS, 42). What remains constant, however, is the proclamation of the Christian message which is represented by Catholic social teaching. We need to evaluate again the relationship between the fundamental principles here and the ways in which they are applied in the modern world.

While the Church is attempting to enhance civic values, at the same time through its prophetic ministry and preaching of the kingdom of God, she stands as a sign of contradiction to injustice and materialism. Using the hymn of Simeon (Lk 2.33–5), Pope St John Paul II explains how Simeon prophetically proclaimed Jesus 'as a sign of contradiction' (from Lk 2.34). In this sign we see that 'Love goes hand-in-hand with poverty, its power none other than the utter weakness of the incarnate Word in the stable at Bethlehem and on the cross.'[15] In this sign humanity is given the vision of hope and the Church is given her mandate for mission.

## Notes

1. *CD*, Book IV, Chapter 4, p. 139. See also the introduction by Dom. David Knowles to the 1972 edition. Together with the Bible, Augustine was indebted to the political thought of classical authors, in particular Cicero, and his philosophy of the state. See Plato (1998), *The Republic and the Laws*, trans. Niall Rudd, with an introduction and notes by Jonathan Powell and Niall Rudd, Oxford World's Classics, Oxford, Oxford University Press. For further details see *CD*, xliii–xlvii, and Brown, Peter (2000 [first published 1967]), *Augustine of Hippo: A Biography*, Berkeley and Los Angeles, California University Press, pp. 297–329.
2. *CD*, Book XIX, Chapter 21, p. 883.
3. *Ibid.*
4. *Ibid.*, Book V, Chapter 21, p. 215.
5. *Ibid.*, Book II, Chapter 1, p. 48.
6. *Ibid.*
7. *Ibid.*
8. *PR*, Part II, 4. I have amended the translation offered here (see also *DO*, III, 609) in order to explore Gregory's interpretation of Ezek 13.4 in the light of one aspect of the episcopal ministry: to speak in the name of God for justice.
9. *CD*, Book XIV, Chapter 28, p. 593f.
10. *Ibid.*, Book XIX, Chapter 17, p. 878.
11. *Trin.*, Book VIII, Chapter 8 (section 12).

12 For a revealing insight into the life and spiritual motivation of Mother Teresa (1910–97, canonized 4 September 2016), see Mother Teresa (2008), *Come Be My Light*, ed. Brian Kolodiejchuk, London, Rider.
13 FS 226. This call forms part of the missionary mandate for all the faithful.
14 See, for example, my homily preached at the Christmas Midnight Mass in Westminster Cathedral, 2016: www.rcdow.org.uk>cardinal>homilies
15 Pope John Paul II (Karol Wojtyła) (1979 [first published in Italian in 1977]), *Sign of Contradiction*. London, Sydney, Auckland and Toronto, Hodder and Stoughton, p. 51.

## 10

## *The Hope for Humanity*

[T]*heir hope is full of immortality.*

WIS 3.4

*Through him [our Lord Jesus Christ] we have obtained access to this grace in which we stand, and we rejoice in our hope of sharing the glory of God.*

ROM 5.2

*Now faith is the assurance of things hoped for, the conviction of things not seen.*

HEB 11.1

*Let our souls, therefore, be bound by this hope [of resurrection] to the one who is faithful in his promises and upright in his judgements.*

I CLEM. 27.1

Writing to the Christians in Rome, St Paul is certain that the hope for humanity is based on the victory of God over evil, sin and darkness, as manifested through the death and resurrection of Jesus (Rom 5.2). Such hope provides strength and assurance in the present time but also reveals the glory that is to come (Rom 8.18). Paul was communicating to a small minority of Christians within the capital of the Roman Empire, in which the power and the control by the State were all-pervading. He wrote at a time (AD 57) of considerable political, social and economic insecurity. In this regard, at least, Paul is addressing our own time of seeming instability and uncertainty. We may well ask, therefore: where is hope to be found, how should we understand the concept of hope and in which ways do we facilitate the development of hope? I maintain that if we focus on the deepest nature of hope – its authentic meaning – then we shall recover the true aspirations of justice, peace and love, and find that hope is a force that is able to grow and flourish within individuals and society.

The conditions and attitudes on which such growth depends are to be found in the ways in which we engage in actions that will, ultimately, offer confidence in the virtues of goodness where humanity is in despair and distress. Hope is not the same as optimism, which may bring false hope and a failure to be realistic about the true state of human affairs. On the contrary, hope 'is the theological virtue by which we desire' (*CCC,* 1817) the coming of the justice and peace which the reign of God gives together with the hope of eternal life.[1] This desire includes 'the aspiration to happiness [blessedness] which God has placed in the heart of every' human soul (*CCC,* 1818). On this basis St Thomas Aquinas interprets hope in two distinct but intimately related ways. First, he presents hope as a natural passion arising from a desire for something thought to be good, though not yet possessed: difficult, but not impossible, to attain.[2] Hope is a movement of the will, a striving towards a future good, an appetite which stirs up confidence and grants assurance, which is often detected (thankfully) in young people. Second, hope is a quality that moves us to become pilgrims. This reality means that hope is a constant source of encouragement to the faithful, being based on the gifts and power of the Holy Spirit which brings a renewed relationship with God (Rom 8.23). We believe that this hope, although unseen, will be fulfilled in the future and that we shall receive the fullness of God's salvation (Rom 8.24) which is the goal of our journey to him. Thus, a hope-filled person is spurred into action when faced with something desirable yet hard to achieve. Hope is not the product of opinion or argument alone; rather, it is based on a vision of love (as shown by St Paul, e.g., Rom 8.39; 1 Cor 13.13), which creates an impetus to act generously. This generosity comes from within an understanding that fires our imagination, a drive exercised consciously in the effort to achieve a possible yet still future good. Hope is a partnership between both our understanding and our will which moves us to accomplish something sacrificial that will provide humanity with a renewal of purpose.[3]

Seen in this light the world is full of hope and signs of renewal, which surround us every day. These signs are found in our daily strivings to establish, maintain, express and consolidate efforts to act lovingly and to promote holiness. In human terms these good actions are difficult, if not impossible, to achieve, yet with the divine assistance of the Holy Spirit both the mind and the will may be transformed and renewed (Rom 12.1–2). This vision helps us to perceive how the countless fragments of hope in the world are being united by the action of a loving God in whose ministry we are honoured to share. But how are these fragments of hope experienced and brought into harmony? We see them, for example, in the kindness of a neighbour, the compassion of a friend, the utter generosity of a lover or the creativeness of a gifted person through a work of charity. These signs of hope enable us to respond with a warm heart and a quiet smile of gratitude and admiration. These fragments express the strivings of hope and are themselves generative of hope in others. We can perceive how each of them is a tiny masterpiece designed to strengthen a hope that something difficult will be achieved: the creation of employment and prosperity, the ending of poverty, the relief of suffering and the faithfulness of love. More challenging is to see how these tiny fragments are in fact pieces of a mosaic, the tesserae which, when brought together, are able to make a coherent and inspiring work of art.

This challenge, however, is made more difficult by the culture of cynicism in which we live. This culture urges us to view with suspicion reports of, or even experiences of, goodness. Such scepticism tutors us to attribute to others the worst of motives, or at least to entertain seriously this attitude. It is important that we learn afresh and see what is actually before us: the innate goodness of many people. Another factor that makes the formation of a coherent view of hope problematic is the way in which our culture embraces relativism. The logic of relativism means that anything that is done by anyone in the pursuit of their hopes and ideals is not necessarily related to the needs of another, since notions of what is truly good (and truly evil) are limited to individual perceptions and consideration. On the contrary, to nurture and benefit from the potential true hope initiates for humanity which is seen in the good around us, we shall need to give more attention to those fragments of faith which, if brought together, have the force to defeat both cynicism and relativism. This understanding will bring harmony within society.

Two possible areas may be detected within the various fragments of our human experience in relation to the possibilities for the strengthening of our vision of hope. First, within the family we meet our initial experience of life and love. We understand much about the conditions needed for secure attachment and the bonding of children. The disruption of family relationships and the accompanying trauma in early childhood may have lifelong consequences for future adult health and stability. Our experience has a deep influence upon our adult lives and our desire for hope and trust in others. It follows, therefore, that a society that cares about the quality of hope for the future will care greatly, in an objective and systematic way, about factors that help or hinder family life. Second, beyond but founded on the family, is the social sphere of community relationships. Jonathan Sacks, using and reinterpreting the Biblical metaphor of covenant (e.g., Jer 32.40), describes these relationships as 'covenantal', based on the agreements that we make with others as we engage in work or projects together, outside of the political or economic spheres.[4] This covenantal activity generates trust between our communities. Effective political life and creative economic activity depend on this trust. In reality such trust is not generated easily; rather, it tends to be consumed by a greedy and selfish society. Given this fact, we are made more aware that the covenantal basis for the just ordering of social relationships is crucial. The community is the place where our identity as social beings is renewed and where our fulfilment is bound with that of others and finds its expression. More importantly here, hope is something that is expressed by the community and not merely by the individual. It follows, therefore, that in the undertaking of social projects there is no place for apathy and despondency because the result of the efforts of industry should reveal the true strength of community spirit, which is always a source of hope. With this aspiration in mind we reach for another horizon which offers an instinctively emerging sense of cohesion about all things that produce a radical sense of hope. On the contrary, without this perspective we face the danger of radical meaninglessness which occurs when humanity 'makes evil use of good things', which in turn brings despair.

St Teresa of Avila portrays hope as a virtuous quality which, despite the human struggles in life, will bring from Christ 'a happiness and rapture that can never end' (*CCC*, 1821, see n. 95). Authentic hope, therefore, brings into focus the ultimate good towards which hope compels us: the mystery of God, 'by which we desire the Kingdom of heaven and eternal life' (*CCC*, 1817). Hope, therefore, has as its ultimate object our radical happiness. This happiness, in the sense of blessedness (Mt 5.3), comes with our presence both before and within the life of God. Hope directs us towards God, the source and summit of all good: goodness itself. Realizing this summit of faith enables us to recognize that among all that God gives us is the means by which we may attain this perfect happiness.

This happiness will be achieved when we place our hope in the promises that only Christ brings and rely always on the grace of the Holy Spirit to sustain us on our pilgrimage journey of faith. For St Thomas Aquinas the full description of hope translates as: 'Wherefore, in so far as we hope for anything as being possible to us by means of Divine assistance, our hope attains God Himself, on Whose help it leans. It is therefore evident that hope is a virtue, since it causes a human act to be good and to attain its due rule.'[5]

This understanding and its endeavour for good have the result that we become true pilgrims of faith (Heb 11.1). We are able to experience repeatedly that we can achieve our true and deepest purpose for life. We understand this purpose in terms of the language of faith because we have recognized that we are sons and daughters, deeply loved by our beloved divine Creator, who acts always with our best intentions in mind (Rom 8.28). This assurance gives our present existence lasting meaning, because our natural hope is infused by the grace of God as offered through the Spirit (Rom 8.27). This grace gives us a vision of heavenly glory beyond our earthly existence (Rom 8.18b), yet this glory has been implanted within us by the Creator in order that we may be able to perceive the divine hope while on earth. We know that our true home is in heaven (Phil 3.20), that our hearts and minds reach out towards that home and that the gifts of God which are being received make this hope truly attainable.

I recognize, however, there are many areas in the world today, including Britain, where hope is in short supply: in particular, in places where there is war, violence, persecution and poverty. I have seen for myself the suffering of refugees in, for example, Erbil, the capital of Iraqi Kurdistan.[6] This sense of hopelessness was especially evident when I met with families whose fathers no longer had any sense of 'self-worth' or of their responsibilities as parents. I realized that shape and purpose had disappeared from their lives, and I felt their raw anger and growing sense of despair at the dire situation in which they found themselves. They felt that their lives had been destroyed by the brutality of ISIL. Yet amid this hopelessness I found a real mode of resilience to the pain which they were suffering (Rom 8.18a). The hope for them was a way forward which combined true charity and a clear expectation of a more fulfilling life in the future. The interim aim was to give them their dignity as parents, to provide education for their children and to construct homes, however temporary and makeshift they might be. The priority for stability was that territories under ISIL should be liberated, a new rule of law established, a shattered social network rebuilt and the social care of displaced people seen as central to any future political reconstruction.

At the same time the virtue of hope is shown through the considerable efforts of the aid agency workers, including priests and religious sisters, who demonstrate Christian humanism, which proclaims ceaselessly that our reason for hope lies in the never-ending mercy of God, who pours out his life for humanity that we might see and live again. This humanism is manifested through the faith and ministry of Christ Jesus (Rom 15.5–6), which charity workers from all religious faiths or none demonstrate by their ceaseless loving kindness, for the hope of immortality is revealed through the actions of the righteous (Wis 3.4). Their work is inclusive and offered to all who are suffering. Despite having lost all their material possessions, the refugees have not lost their faith in Christ or their willingness to work together for the common good. Both agency workers and refugees provide a remarkable witness to the work of Christ in the world today. We should follow their example and provide them with the help which they need.

These acts of charity which offer hope take their meaning from, and are to be placed against the wider background of, the cosmic vision of God's plan and will, as portrayed by St Paul in Romans 8, and form a fitting concluding summary for this section, on 'Religious Dialogue and the Hope for Humanity'. Paul explains the tension here between the present reality of the world, where there is suffering, and the hope of ultimate glory for humanity created, and now renewed, in the image of God (Rom 8.18 and 8.21). Into the centre of this vision is placed the saving ministry of Jesus Christ, from whom nothing either earthly or cosmic 'will be able to separate us' (Rom 8.39). Seen in this light, hope is a source of encouragement in the midst of suffering; hope also provides the stimulus for discontentment with the present state of the world where change, renewal, goodness, compassion and love are needed urgently. Hope also challenges us to be patient, waiting and working for God's promises to be fulfilled (Rom 8.25). This way of understanding hope brings God's salvation in Christ both in the present time (Rom 8.24) and in the glorious age which we await (Rom 8.19). The resurrection and exaltation of Christ (Rom 8.34) are the ultimate guarantee that this hope will be fulfilled both now and in future. God has implanted this hope in our souls (*1 Clem.* 24.1) for the purpose of manifesting the virtue of hope, which is sustained by the heavenly intercession of Christ (Rom 8.34) and by the power of the Spirit who prays for us even in our weakness, when the force of hope seems to grow dim and we have lost hope in our divine ministry to serve the world (Rom 8.26). Thus, our task is to keep alive these rumours of hope, however we understand them, and to knit them together so that the far horizon of an eternal hope may never be lost from our sight.

## Notes

1. Pope Benedict XVI (2014 [first published in Italian in 2013]), *Virtues: Sources of Life*. London, St Paul's Publishing, pp. 33–5.
2. *ST*, II – II q 4 a 1.
3. *SS*, 30–31.
4. Sacks, Jonathan (1997 [repr. 2000]), *The Politics of Hope*. London, Vintage, pp. xvi ff.; see also Section II, 'Social Covenant', pp. 55–146, and, for ethical considerations, pp. 260–63.
5. *ST*, II – II, 17, a1c.
6. My visit to Erbil took place on 13 April 2015. I concluded the news report with the words 'They [the local population] give a remarkable witness and they need our help.' For a full account see: catholicnews.org.uk/Home/Featured/Features-2015/Cardinal-Nichols-visits-Erbil

# PART FOUR

## *Ministry: Treasure in Earthenware Vessels*

At the Easter Vigil (2016) in Westminster Cathedral I baptized six adults, and confirmed and received other Christians into full communion with the Catholic Church. This pattern was repeated throughout the world. Baptism, Confirmation and the giving of first Holy Communion are known as the 'sacraments of initiation'. They constitute entry into the fullness of the Catholic faith (*CCC*, 1234–45). The language and truth of the Easter Vigil are those of rebirth, new birth (1 Pet 2.2–3), a birth that comes from above (Jn 3.3). Those 'baptized, by regeneration and the anointing of the Holy Spirit, are consecrated to be a spiritual house and a holy priesthood' (*LG*, 10). Thus, these sacraments begin a journey for us into the heart and mystery of God, which, if we are open to the wisdom of the Holy Spirit, will enable us to enter more deeply into the wonder and beauty that the Sacraments are offering to us. Our goal is heaven; there are no sacraments there; we shall be able to experience only the totality and perfection of God when we see him face to face.

From these sacraments four others reveal their purpose: confession, asking God through the cross of Jesus to remove post-baptismal sin (*CCC*, 1427–9); anointing of the sick, which continues the healing ministry of Jesus (*CCC*, 1503); marriage, where the couple enter together into the renewal of their baptismal covenant (*CCC*, 1617); and holy orders, where men respond to the call of God to minister the sacraments in the service of his people (*CCC*, 1547). The sacrament of holy orders was entrusted to the apostles by the Lord (e.g., Lk 9.1–6; Jn 20.21–2; Acts 1.8; Gal 1.15–16), to be exercised in the Church, and through her to the world, until the close of the age, when Christ will return in glory both to judge and restore creation. This sacrament contains three orders: the episcopate, the presbyterate and the diaconate (*CCC*, 1536), which will be explored in turn.

Although the ministerial priesthood, both in essence and degree, differs from 'the common priesthood of the faithful', nevertheless they are interrelated and interlocking (*LG*, 10). The Holy Spirit distributes special gifts for ministry which are both 'charismatic' and hierarchic' (*LG*, 4). The baptized are, therefore, able to offer service in the name of God; 'by the reception of the sacraments' all exercise the 'royal priesthood' (*LG*, 10). The priest, however, represents the person of Christ (*in persona Christi*) and so is able to offer the sacrifice of the Eucharist for the salvation of all humanity (*CCC*, 1348).

In order to reveal the ways in which our 'one baptism' (Eph 4.5) and the diversity of ministerial gifts (Eph 4.11) may be understood and interpreted for us in our life today, I have selected and expanded a number of homilies. I have chosen this medium because of its essential function within Christian worship, usually though not always during the Mass, to expound the nature of the Gospel and its teaching (*CCC*, 1349). With regard to the papacy, I am not here presenting an historical assessment of an individual Pope, but rather, I am attempting to show how the papal ministry is exercised. This Petrine ministry (Mt 16.13–20; Jn 21.15–19) was and is performed in order to demonstrate 'the fullness of Christ' working within the Church and the world.

My ordination as a Bishop (24 January 1992), and my subsequent ministry as an ordaining Bishop, has often led me to reflect on the dignity, role and vocation of the episcopal office. I should like to share a few of these reflections with you. The Bishop is the successor to the Apostles: apostle, one sent out to teach. He acts as overseer of the local Church (1 Tim 1.3, Timothy in Ephesus; Tit 1.5, Titus in Crete), the original meaning of the word *episcope* (1 Tim 3.1). He is a member of the College of Bishops, a sign and source of the universal nature and unity of the Church (*CCC*, 883–5). The Bishop's office is rooted in the Trinitarian understanding of our Christian life, called by the Father, bound to the Son, filled with the Holy Spirit. The Bishop, with his triple ministries of prophet, priest and king, is demonstrating the totality of Christ's ministry. Yet the Bishop never ceases to be a priest and a deacon. Central to these ministries is the question of identity.

I remember clearly, on the evening before I was ordained a priest, my elder brother, Peter, asked 'Why are you doing this? Why do you want to be a priest?' At that moment my answer was spontaneous, and it still holds good. I replied, 'Because it makes sense of who I am, my identity.' Encased within this concept is the idea of vocation. It is right to speak of the priesthood in this way, the ordained ministry being the call of God; when men sense this call, then it must be tested by the Church and, if affirmed, acted upon in their ordination to the priesthood, a ministry for life (identifying totally with the ministry of Christ; Heb 5.6, quoting Ps 110 [Vg 109].4). Of course, our vocation and identity are complex matters. There are many different layers that make up who I am. It is possible for me to describe myself in terms of nationhood, ethnicity, family, preferences or tastes. Some of these layers are more fundamental than others, and I believe the priesthood is for me the most fundamental experience of all, dictating my identity. Principally, I am first God's servant. I am a member of his family, of his nation, of his cultural setting. That which comes from God to the priest emerges as the most fundamental stratum of his identity, the layer of rock on which everything else is built. A vocation to the priesthood gives a clear answer to the question 'Who am I?' It is seen in a calling of immense significance and service. Yet we priests always remain 'earthen vessels' (2 Cor 4.7), pots of poor clay, which the Lord in his goodness uses for his marvellous deeds.

Yet how am I to fulfil his mission faithfully? The answer is to be found in the Greek word *diakonia*, used to name the Church's ministry of charity. While the whole Church is called to exercise this ministry of *diakonia*, it is focused, however, in the holy order of Deacons, who 'share in Christ's mission and grace in a special way'. Following this path means that the deacon is united to Christ, 'who made himself the 'deacon' or servant of all' (*CCC*, 1570). The foundation for this claim is to be found in the words of Jesus that 'the Son of man also came not to be served but to serve, and to give his life as a ransom for many' (Mk 10.45; *CCC*, 1570, n. 56). This proclamation of Jesus reveals that his teaching and activity in relation to greatness in the new age of the kingdom of God (Mk 10.35–44), is to engage in Jesus' ministry of service and to offer to the world his example of humility, sacrifice and love. Deacons also have a privileged vocation of assisting the Bishop (Phil 1.1) to be a faithful missionary of charity. When I was ordained a Bishop, I resolved to show kindness and compassion in the name of the Lord to the poor, and to strangers and to all who are in need.[1] In this resolution the assistance and focus offered by the diaconal ministry are essential in order to demonstrate that the Church's work of *diakonia* is seen as a reality in action.

Within the totality of the Church's ministry there are also our brothers and sisters who share together in religious orders known as the consecrated life. This life enfolds those who profess the evangelical counsels of poverty, chastity and obedience and those who share in other forms of sacred bond. All these vocations ultimately have their origin in the endeavours of St Antony of Egypt (251–356) who, as a hermit in the desert, was joined by others to form religious communities.[2] Thus, the religious life is a calling which is lived in community. This idea goes beyond the life of the individual into one that is experienced in a group where the participants move towards each other in love. In the religious life we see that the true meaning of existence involves a total response to God in love. By the nature of this response, prayer, both liturgical and mental, has a central role and is the divine power by which the members of religious orders are able to bind their lives to God and the Church and also in the service of humanity. Those committed to the consecrated life adopt a countercultural stance with regard to the accumulation of wealth and power.[3] The arbitrary self-interests relating to personal lifestyle and the ideas of success are abandoned for the sake of the Gospel, focused in the words of Jesus to the rich young man: 'If you would be perfect, go, sell what you possess and give to the poor, and you will have treasure in heaven; and come, follow me' (Mt 19.21).[4]

To bring us full circle in relation to our ministries as members of the baptized community (*CCC*, 798), I have chosen, in the light of the declaration of Pope Francis that by virtue of our baptism we 'become missionary disciples (cf. Mt 28:19)' (*EG*, 120), to give emphasis to the ministry of evangelization and the proclamation of the Gospel. This emphasis is shown by the ways in which works of mercy are undertaken within the total framework of God's creative and redemptive order for the salvation of the cosmos and humanity realized through the mission and ministry of Jesus, the Christ. Within this understanding the people of God share in the ministry of the whole Church which Jesus has entrusted to us (Mt 28.16–20; Acts 1.8). Here the lay faithful minister in collaboration and in harmony with those of us who are called into holy orders. After the pattern of Jesus (Mk 10.45), we are to serve them – and not the other way around – in order that the

Church might be 'built up' through 'the comfort of the Holy Spirit' (Acts 9.31), that the well-being of all people might be met and the needs of the world addressed for the common good (*CCC*, 799).

## Notes

1. An idea later enshrined in the Congregation for Bishops, Directory for the Pastoral Ministry of Bishops, *Apostolorum Successores*, 22 February 2004, 194.
2. Fry, Timothy, OSB (ed.) (1981), *RB 1980: The Rule of St Benedict in Latin and English with Notes*, Collegeville, MN, The Liturgical Press, pp. 3–16, has useful information on the life of St Antony in the context of the early history of monasticism.
3. I should like to thank Sister Anthony O'Rourke PHJC for her insights.
4. To be found in the Life of St Antony by St Athanasius (probably completed by 380), Life Ch. 2–4, from *DO*, I, pp. 83★–5★. The complete life of Antony can be found in White, Carolinne (trans.) (1988), *Early Christian Lives*, London, Penguin Classics, pp. 3–70.

# 11
# *The Papacy*

## Pope St John Paul II

On 13 May 1917 Lúcia dos Santos and her two younger cousins, Francisco and Jacinta, were tending their sheep close to the tiny village of Fatima in Portugal. Suddenly, at about noon, their attention was caught by a flash of lightning. Appearing over them they saw a 'lady', shining brilliantly. She asked the three children to pray for the conversion of sinners and an end to the First World War. This 'lady' also asked the trio to come back to this place on the 13th of each month. They followed these instructions, but in September they were prevented from returning. They experienced, however, an apparition on the 19th instead. Finally, on 13 October, the 'lady' revealed herself as 'Our Lady of the Rosary'. On that day a crowd which had gathered, estimated at 30,000, witnessed the sun apparently tumble from the sky to the earth.

On this day, 13 May, thirty years ago, in St Peter's Square in Rome, Mehmet Ali Agca tried to assassinate Pope John Paul II. John Paul attributed his survival to the intercession of the Blessed Virgin Mary. One year later he made a pilgrimage to Fatima to thank Our Lady for saving his life and to consecrate the world anew to her immaculate heart. At the Mass of Thanksgiving on 13 May 1982 he spoke of Our Lady's message at Fatima as being firmly within her Son's call: 'repent, and believe in the gospel' (Mk 1.15).

The brilliant light of the Fatima apparitions is a beacon of hope inviting even the most hardened heart to welcome new life. It is a reflection of the light who is the Son, come down from heaven to earth, forming a bridge from earth to heaven; it is that light which so dazzled Saul (Acts 9.3), transforming him from being a persecutor of Jesus to becoming a fearless preacher of him as Son of God and Son of Mary; and this light of Fatima implores us to turn to Mary so that our hearts may be opened to the love and life her Son alone can offer.

This month of May is Mary's month. It is fitting that Pope John Paul was beatified at its beginning. With Blessed (now St) Pope John Paul II may we be inspired by the words of St Louis Marie Grignion de Montfort and say to Mary: '*totus tuus ego sum*, I am totally yours.'[1] For, from Blessed John Paul we have learned that this is the simplest way to belong completely to her Son. Yes, John Paul teaches us that when we are close to Mary, who trusted the angel's message not to fear (Lk 1.30), then we will never lack the courage to open wide the door to Christ when he himself says to us: 'Do not be afraid!'

The life of Pope John Paul was a very powerful witness to this truth. We know that he enjoyed the most intimate relationship with Mary, a bond nurtured especially through praying the rosary, which inspired his teaching on her role in our salvation. In his encyclical *Redemptoris Mater* he developed our understanding of Mary's motherhood of the Church. In heaven Mary's motherly love for us continues; she is our mother in the Spirit, caring for all the brothers and sisters of her Son 'who still journey on earth surrounded by dangers and difficulties, until they are led to their happy homeland'.[2] Precisely because Mary is mother of the Redeemer and hence our mother too, she shares in our struggle against the powers of darkness, radiating into our lives the brilliant light who is her Son. She 'helps all her children, wherever they may be and whatever their condition, *to find in Christ the path to the Father's house*'.[3]

Thus, we know that Mary helped Blessed Pope John Paul to reach the Father's house; and from there he still prays that we shall let her do the same ministry for us. There is much in the past life of Pope John Paul for which we rightly thank God. Yet at this Mass of Thanksgiving for his Beatification we express our gratitude that he continues to help us now on our journey. As Pope Benedict XVI has written, 'the lives of the saints are not limited to their earthly biographies but also include their being and working in God after death.'[4] Blessed John Paul now knows the truth of what he always believed: that those who have been drawn close to God do not withdraw from us, but rather become truly close to us, helping us all to serve God and to live, more effectively, the Christian life. The wonderful multitude of the blessed, who are enjoying the sight of God as he is, do not lose sight of us! Nor do they stop hearing us. Rather, in the words of Pope Paul VI, they are 'ever listening to our prayers'.[5] Their communion of life and love, in and with the Most Holy Trinity, is a communion opened outwards by their unceasing prayer. This intercession is a great help to us in our weakness. Through their union with Christ the saints and the blessed form part of that bridge between heaven and earth, proving that the bonds of love are never obliterated by death.

Blessed John Paul II, then, continues to help us not to be afraid to have faith, to be called Christian, to belong to the Church, to respond to the call addressed to each one of us: 'You shall be holy' (Lev 19.2). He helps us to cross the threshold of hope, no matter how intense our struggle and sense of inadequacy, to desire more than anything the happiness of the kingdom of heaven. He holds up for us the mother of the Redeemer as an image and model of holiness in whom we find the strength to believe in her Son. He is our Redeemer! Trusting in Christ's grace, we can live even now, in the light of eternity.

In this Mass and in every Mass the light of eternity shines into our lives. Here we are in the presence of the bread come down from heaven; here we partake of the flesh and blood that promises eternal life. In this communion with Christ through the Eucharistic sacrifice we feel closer than ever to the Church in heaven, 'sharing as it were in the liturgy of heaven',[6] participating in the celebration that Blessed John Paul is enjoying.

Yet in the Eucharist there is also a promise of a future yet to come which Blessed John Paul does not yet fully enjoy: the resurrection of the body – the fulfilment of Jesus' promise that he will raise up on the last day those who eat his flesh and drink his blood (Jn 6.54). In the Eucharist the Lord's coming is experienced, but it is also a yearning for his glorious return (1 Cor 11.26). Then there will be the redemption of our bodies as heaven finally 'forms the canopy of a new earth'.[7]

Reflection on the glorious Assumption of Our Lady Mary assists us to understand this theology more deeply. In her we glimpse our future, her body renewed in love, assumed into heaven, a promise of the new heaven and new earth that will be achieved with the second coming of Christ. The Eucharist is the pledge of that future glory, for which the body of Pope John Paul, in which he suffered so much, now lies in waiting.

At the Mass of Beatification Pope Benedict spoke movingly of his own friendship with Blessed John Paul II. May Pope Benedict's words be ours also: 'Blessed are you, beloved Pope John Paul II, because you believed! Continue, we implore you, to sustain from heaven the faith [and the hope] of God's people ... Bless us, [still] Holy Father! Amen.'[8]

[*This is an edited version of a homily preached in Westminster Cathedral on 13 May 2011, the Feast of Our Lady of Fatima, at the Mass of Thanksgiving for the Beatification of Pope John Paul II. The Readings are: Acts 9.1–20; Ps 116 (Heb 117); Jn 6.52–9.*]

## Pope Benedict XVI

This evening during the Mass we pray especially for Pope Benedict XVI. On Thursday next (28 February) we shall no longer be praying for him in the Eucharistic Prayer of every Mass in his office as Supreme Pastor of the Universal Church. Tonight, in circumstances that are remarkable, we thank God for Pope Benedict's years of service to the Apostolic See as our Holy Father (19 April 2005–28 February 2013).

I must confess great sadness at this moment. Pope Benedict is an outstanding teacher of our faith and a great guide to the role of faith in our complex world. I shall miss greatly his presence as our Pope.

Let me reflect for a few moments on his leadership, especially as a great theologian and a marvellous preacher. He is a theologian of the Second Vatican Council (1962–5).[9] From the beginning of his pontificate to almost his last words he presented the Council to us and sought to unfold its true meaning. On 22 December 2005, in an address that gave shape to his pontificate, he reminded us that the Council was misunderstood if thought of as a moment of radical change in the Church. It was not to be perceived according to such an interpretation, which he called 'a hermeneutic of discontinuity and rupture'.[10] Then, last week, on 14 February 2013, at the end of his ministry as our Holy Father, he highlighted another mistaken interpretation of the Vatican Council, one given consistently by commentators: that it was simply a Council of 'a power struggle between different trends in the Church',[11] a hermeneutic of power. Returning to the earlier defining speech of 2005, Pope Benedict tells us how to understand the Council not with 'a hermeneutic of discontinuity' but, on the contrary, with 'the hermeneutic of reform', of 'renewal in the continuity of the one subject-Church which the Lord has given to us'.[12] This sense of ongoing renewal within the Church in continuity with its great traditions is the correct way to advance the work of the Council with 'the hermeneutic of reform'. This renewal of the Christian life Pope Benedict teaches us afresh in this Year of Faith (11 October 2012–24 November 2013), when we mark the fiftieth anniversary of the opening of the Council, on 11 October 1962.

Last week he illustrated again what this interpretation means: that we understand the Church not solely as the people of God but as the people of God formed in Christ, formed as the body of Christ. Thus, we are able to understand ourselves in a truly Trinitarian manner: called by the Father, formed into the Son and animated by the Holy Spirit. In this way Pope Benedict taught us again to think of the Church not as an institution, or even as a human community, but rather as a living organism, one 'that enters my soul' and of which each of us is a constituent part.[13]

Referring to liturgical reform, Pope Benedict reminded us that priority should always be given to the worship of God, thus enabling all who participate in the liturgy to be able to do so in a radical manner. Rejoicing again at the 'intelligibility' offered through the liturgical texts being 'spoken in our mother tongue [...] instead of being locked up in an unknown language', Pope Benedict warned that this 'intelligibility' demands 'ongoing formation' in order that we 'enter ever more deeply into the mystery'[14] of God which the liturgy proclaims: which means that the liturgical texts (including the Scriptural texts) still require reflection and study.

He spoke of collegiality: that profound understanding of the fellowship of bishops in the Church, wrongly presented as a struggle between the centre and the local community. True collegiality is shaped by the fact of faith that together bishops are the successors of the Apostles and yet the Bishop of Rome alone has a specific succession: that of being the successor of St Peter. This succession is the continuing basis for renewal in continuity.[15]

Pope Benedict urged us also to recall and refresh our mission in society: to be responsible for shaping our culture, for its future, drawing always on the true hope that comes from Christ, who offers a promise of future glory in a world of enduring uncertainty. Pope Benedict encouraged us yet again to practise the disciplines of genuine dialogue, which are based on two key principles: the acknowledgement and the respect for difference and diversity (rather than a fear of difference, which seems so pervasive today) and our faith in the uniqueness of Christ and the objective reality of the Word of God to guide us on this pilgrimage. This theologian of the Council who became Pope has always been the best of teachers and we shall miss him but shall not forget his words.

As a preacher, Pope Benedict has imparted to us great wisdom. His preaching has opened a window for us into the word of God and the mysteries of the faith. I recall well going to speak to the Holy Father in early July 2010, shortly before his visit to us. I asked him if he would preach here in the cathedral on the subject of the Precious Blood of Our Lord. 'Ah,' he said, 'that is not easy. Today the image of blood is so easily misunderstood. I must think about it.' Well, of course, he did and so gave us a most outstanding homily in which he put before us that, and I quote, 'the mystery of the Precious Blood [...] leads us to see the unity between Christ's sacrifice on the cross, the Eucharistic sacrifice which he has given to his Church, and his eternal priesthood, whereby, seated at the right hand of the Father, he makes unceasing intercession for us, the members of his mystical body'. Thus the Precious Blood shed for us on the cross, the Precious Blood poured out for us in the Mass and the power of that Precious Blood in the prayer of Christ before his Father are the lifeblood of the Faith. Taking each dimension in turn, Pope Benedict then opened for us not only the understanding of the uniqueness of Christ but also our way of participation in the mystery of his Precious Blood revealed in these marvellous words:

> Here [in Westminster Cathedral] the great crucifix which towers above us serves as a reminder that Christ, our eternal high priest, daily unites our own sacrifices, our own sufferings, our own needs, hopes and aspirations, to the infinite merits of his sacrifice. Through him, with him, and in him, we lift up our own bodies as a sacrifice, holy and acceptable to God (cf. Rom 12.1).

In this way he taught us that we can become, in the Church and in our society, 'witnesses of the beauty of holiness, witnesses of the splendour of truth, witnesses of the joy and freedom born of a living relationship with Christ!'[16] The clarity of this preaching we shall miss greatly.

Pope Benedict has always directed those who attend to him to the very core of our faith, its simplicity and grandeur, its beauty and transforming quality. For me the abiding and powerful image of Pope Benedict will always be that of him in silent prayer before the Blessed Sacrament in Hyde Park. There he taught us all what is essential about our faith and our life as followers of Christ. We find our home before the Lord; we live in his presence; we trust in his love. We offer ourselves in prayer to him. As one mother wrote to me after that unforgettable evening: 'my teenage sons learned more about prayer in those fifteen minutes than in all the years of their young lives.'

On Thursday evening next the Chair of St Peter, which Feast we celebrate today, will become vacant. We know what we should do in this situation. As in Hyde Park, we must entrust ourselves and the Church to our Blessed Lord and ask for a new Pontiff, one who will continue to direct us to the heart of the Gospel in all its simplicity and magnitude; and we promise never to forget, in our prayers, Pope Benedict, Joseph Ratzinger, in his life of prayer, rest and reflection. May the Lord bless him and preserve him, and may the Lord continue to guide his Holy Church. Amen.

[*This is an edited version of a homily preached in Westminster Cathedral on 22 February 2013, the Feast of the Chair of St Peter, Apostle, at the Mass of Thanksgiving for the Pontificate of Pope Benedict XVI. The Readings are: 1 Pet 5.1–4; Ps 22 (Heb 23); Mt 16.13–19.*]

## Pope Francis

What great joy we all felt when, not long after 6 p.m. yesterday evening, the white smoke swirled into the night air, ascending high above the huge crowd gathered in St Peter's Square. We have a new pope! We have a father! A time of waiting followed. Filled with a sense of excited expectation, we wondered: who has been elected? Of course, in one very important sense it did not really matter who had been chosen as our pope, as we believe that the Papal ministry in succession to St Peter had been offered to the one chosen by the Holy Spirit through the prayer of the apostolic company (Acts 1.15, 21–6). In his final address to the College of Cardinals, having no idea who would be elected, Pope Benedict promised 'unconditional reverence and obedience' to his successor.[17] This attitude is the one that we should all take given our reliance on the power of the Spirit. With the Pope Emeritus, for whose pontificate we again express our heartfelt gratitude to God, we readily give our 'unconditional reverence and obedience' to Pope Francis.

When at last the announcement was made, many of us – and I include myself – were taken by surprise. Once Pope Francis had appeared on the balcony, however, with that lovely smile, his simplicity and his humility, which were evident, the initial surprise soon gave way to the certainty that the choice of this Cardinal is both inspired and inspiring. Pope Francis' first act, after making reference to his brother cardinals having to go to the ends of the earth to find a new Bishop of Rome, was to ask us to pray for him before he bestowed his blessing upon us.[18] The silence at this moment was a powerful proclamation of the love of God working through lives which are submitted to his will and grace. We shall continue to pray for our new Pope in the confidence that through his Papal ministry we will be richly blessed, as Pope Francis places at God's disposal a wealth of experience and many gifts.

Pope Francis was born in Buenos Aires, one of five children. His father came from Italy, near Turin, and was a railway worker. As a young man the future pope planned to be a chemist. God, however, had a different idea! Obedient to his will, Jorge Mario Bergoglio instead entered the Society of Jesus. Being highly intelligent, he studied and has taught theology, philosophy, psychology and literature. From 1973 to 1979 he was the Provincial of the Argentinian Jesuits, a period that coincided with the country being governed by a military dictatorship. He was named as Auxiliary Bishop of Buenos Aires in 1992, became Archbishop in 1998 and was created a Cardinal by Pope John Paul II in 2001. On reaching the age of 75, Cardinal Bergoglio submitted his resignation to Pope Benedict XVI. Perhaps Cardinal Bergoglio was looking forward to a quieter life? But now we know that God has a different plan![19]

Soon after his election yesterday Pope Francis enjoyed a telephone conversation with our still beloved Pope Emeritus, Benedict. Perhaps Pope Francis asked for guidance and wisdom from his predecessor? Undoubtedly, the Pope Emeritus assured Pope Francis of his unceasing and fervent prayers for him and for the whole Church. This conversation was a historic moment: a new pope speaking to his predecessor on the telephone, and thus, marking the conclusion of Benedict's papacy has its place in our great history, so also does the election of Pope Francis. He is the first non-European to hold the office for a thousand years, the first pope from Latin America, the first Jesuit Pope and the first to take the name Francis.[20]

Francis: what a beautiful name to choose. First, our minds are led to St Francis of Assisi (1181–1226) and to his love of creation,[21] simplicity of life, humility and poverty. We know that, as Archbishop of Buenos Aires, Pope Francis lived in a small apartment and used public transport. The homilies and speeches which he gave as Archbishop revealed the way in which his simplicity gave powerful credibility to the concern he expressed for the poor and marginalized within Argentinian society. He spoke against the unjust distribution of goods which creates the situation of social sin (*CCC*, 1869), '*sins that cry to heaven*' (*CCC*, 1867) and limit the possibilities of a fuller life for many of our brothers and sisters, whose rights should be protected and for whom just conditions should be created in order that they may be allowed to build their own future. I believe that we are blessed with a Pope who will follow the way of St Francis, who prayed: 'Let me, Lord, have the right feelings and knowledge, properly to carry out the task you have given me.'[22] Pope Francis has already demonstrated his commitment to justice by returning to the hotel where he stayed during the conclave in order to pay his bill!

Second, we are led to St Francis Xavier (1506–52), one of the original members of the Society of Jesus and a renowned missionary, who proclaimed the Gospel in Goa, Sri Lanka, Japan and China. In a report to St Ignatius Loyola, Francis Xavier declared, 'I have been going from village to village and every child not yet baptized I have baptized.'[23] Here we see a glimpse of what the mission of Pope Francis will be: 'to preach good news to the poor' (Lk 4.18, quoting Is 61.1). This mission is the same as that given to every pope, the same mission that we hear Christ entrusting to St Peter: 'Feed my lambs [...] Tend my sheep [...] Feed my sheep' (Jn 21.15–17).

In the first reading this evening from the book of Exodus we can see how we are able to explore further this mission of Pope Francis. The event described here occurred during the forty-year journey of liberation, when the children of Israel were led by God from servitude in Egypt to residence in the Promised Land. During this journey they remained under God's continual care and guidance. Yet what did the chosen nation do at this time? They turned away from the living God to a god of their own fashioning, the golden calf and 'worshipped it and sacrificed to it' (Ex 32.8; see also Jn 5.43). This act of idolatry denied them the authentic freedom which the 'living and true God' (1 Thess 1.9) can offer.

The mission of Pope Francis will be to lead us into an ever greater liberty by helping us to resist the attraction of the idols that we create for ourselves, idols that enslave us. He will encourage us to be faithful to God living and true: the God of Abraham, Isaac and Jacob (Mk 12.26–7), the one God revealed fully to us as Father, Son and Holy Spirit in the person of Jesus Christ (Acts 3.13–15). We are witnesses to this divine communion of love in whom we are set free to be fully ourselves.[24] Like Pope Benedict, I am sure that Pope Francis will invite us to keep our gaze on Jesus and to believe in him (Lk 4.20; Jn 20.28). Pope Francis will ask us to entrust ourselves and the Church to Christ, who was sent by the Father to lead us to himself (Jn 17.24). Pope Francis will also ask us to be open to the guidance of the Holy Spirit, who will continue to teach the Church in faith and mission, to preserve its continuity and to lead us into the charity of divine peace (Jn 14.25–7). We ought not to be surprised, therefore, when, in the tradition of his predecessors, Pope Francis will speak on behalf of the most vulnerable in society, defending the dignity of human life from conception to its natural end and also by advocating the meaning and purpose that God has established for our human sexuality: for marriage and family life.[25]

The mission of Pope Francis, then, will be to challenge every person, each one of us, to respond generously to the call to personal holiness. I am sure that this call will be accompanied by great compassion, exercised with gentleness, which recalls another St Francis, Francis de Sales (1567–1622), who wrote: 'in order that the sweetness of his [God's] mercy might be adorned with the beauty of his justice, he determined to save man by way of a rigorous redemption.'[26] Moses also knew the great mercy of God (Ex 32.14). He had confidence that God would hear his intercessory plea that, despite the sinfulness of Israel, the Lord would show mercy (Ex 32.14). In a similar way, in an address given in March 2001, after Pope John Paul II had elevated our new Holy Father to the cardinalate, it is said that he remarked: 'Only someone who has encountered mercy, who has been caressed by the tenderness of mercy, is happy and comfortable with the Lord.' When we turn away from God, the mission of Pope Francis will be to direct us to the source of mercy, 'the caress of the mercy of Jesus Christ on [our] sin'.[27]

This morning, on the radio, I was asked if I was pleased personally with the appointment of Cardinal Bergoglio as Pope Francis: is he 'my kind of man?' That is the wrong question! Pope Francis has been given to us as a great gift. We rejoice by receiving him into our hearts. My judgement here is irrelevant as is that of the media. As the Gospel tells us, only one judgement matters: that of God himself (Jn 5.36b–37a). We joyfully thank God, therefore, for the election of Pope Francis. Let us support him with our unfailing prayer and our loving fidelity. Let us join our prayers to those of our Holy Father – a man of profound prayer, who this morning went to pray before an icon of the Blessed Virgin Mary in the Basilica of Santa Maria Maggiore, invoking the intercession of the Mother of the Church. Let us pray that Pope Francis will be strong and faithful in the ministry that God has given to him to undertake, that the exercise of the Petrine ministry (Mt 16.17–19) of Pope Francis will always be to the greater glory of God. Amen.

[*This is an edited version of a homily preached in Westminster Cathedral on Thursday 14 March 2013 at the Mass of Thanksgiving for the Election of Pope Francis. The Readings are: Ex 32.7–14; Ps 105 (Heb 106).19–23; Jn 5.31–47.*]

## Notes

1 St Louis-Marie Grignion de Montfort (1673–1716) was a French Catholic priest and known for his devotion to the Blessed Virgin Mary. He was canonized on 20 July 1947 by Pope Pius XII. His feast day is 28 April. This quotation is from Grignion de Montfort, St Louis-Marie (1937), *True Devotion to the Blessed Virgin*, London, Burns, Oates & Washbourne, p. 266. See also Pope St John Paul II (2017 [5th edn]), *Karol Wojtyla, In God's Hands: The Spiritual Diaries, 1962–2003*, trans., Joanna Rzepa, London, William Collins, p. 1, n. 1.

2 John Paul II (2003), Encyclical Letter on the Mother of the Redeemer, *Redemptoris Mater: On the Blessed Virgin Mary in the Life of the Pilgrim Church*. London, CTS, p. 40, citing *LG,* 62.
3 John Paul II, *Redemptoris Mater*, p. 47.
4 *DCE*, 42.
5 Apostolic Letter in the form of *motu proprio*, Solemni Hac Liturgia (*Credo of the People of God*) of the Supreme Pontiff Paul VI, 30 June 1968, 30.
6 Homily of His Holiness Benedict XVI preached on 1 May 2011, Divine Mercy Sunday, in St Peter's Square in the context of the Papal Mass on the occasion of the Beatification of the Servant of God John Paul II.
7 An idea taken from Ratzinger, Cardinal Joseph (1988 [first German edn 1977]), *Eschatology, Death and Eternal Life*, trans. Michael Waldstein, trans. ed. Aidan Nichols OP, Washington, DC, The Catholic University of America Press, p. 189.
8 The concluding words of Pope Benedict's homily at the Beatification of Pope John Paul II; see note 6 above.
9 Ratzinger, Cardinal Joseph (2009 [first German edn 1966]), *Theological Highlights of Vatican II*, intro. by Thomas P. Rausch SJ. New York/Mahwah, NJ, Paulist Press.
10 Address of His Holiness Benedict XVI, to the Roman Curia offering them His Christmas Greetings, Thursday 22 December 2005.
11 Meeting with the parish priests and the clergy of Rome, address of His Holiness Pope Benedict XVI, Thursday 14 February 2013.
12 Address of Thursday 22 December 2005; see note 10 above. This 'double hermeneutic' interpretation of Vatican II is well explained in Boeve, Lieven, and Mannion, Gerard (eds) (2010), *The Ratzinger Reader: Mapping a Theological Journey, Joseph Ratzinger*, London and New York, T & T Clark, pp. 275–9.
13 Address of Thursday 14 February 2013; see note 11 above. Also note *CCC*, 782–6.

14　Address of Thursday 14 February 2013; see note 11 above.
15　Ibid.
16　*SV*, pp. 120–23.
17　Farewell address of His Holiness Pope Benedict XVI to the eminent cardinals present in Rome, Thursday 28 February 2013. The full sentence reads: 'And among you, in the College of Cardinals, there is also the future pope, to whom today I promise my unconditional reverence and obedience.'
18　For details of the life of Jorge Mario Bergoglio see Ivereigh, Austin (2015), *The Great Reformer: Francis and the Making of a Radical Pope*, with an updated and expanded epilogue, New York, Picador. The quotation here is from p. 365.
19　*Ibid*., pp. 3–348.
20　*Ibid*., p. 363.
21　Many of these observations now seem prophetic; see, Pope Francis (2015), Encyclical Letter, *Laudato Si': On Care For Our Common Home*; for this prophetic perspective, see also notes 24, 25 and 27 below.
22　For the prayer of St Francis before the crucifix in San Damiano, see Bader, W. (compiler) (1988), *The Prayers of Saint Francis*, London, New City, p. 19. The full prayer reads:

> Most high and glorious God,
> lighten the darkness of my heart
> and give me sound faith,
> firm hope
> and perfect love.
> Let me, Lord, have the right feelings
> and knowledge,
> properly to carry out
> the task you have given me.

23　Letters of St Francis Xavier to St Ignatius Loyola, Book 4, Letters 4 and 5, in *DO*, I, 11*.

24  See Pope Francis (2013), Apostolic Exhortation on the Proclamation of the Gospel in Today's World, *Evangelii Gaudium, The Joy of the Gospel*.
25  See Pope Francis (2016), Apostolic Exhortation on Love in the Family, *Amoris Laetitia, The Joy of Love*.
26  St Francis de Sales (2015 [first published 1616]), *Treatise on the Love of God*, London, Catholic Way Publishing, Book III, chapter IV.
27  See Pope Francis (2015), Bull of Indiction of the Extraordinary Jubilee of Mercy, *Misericordiae Vultus* (The Face of Mercy), and (2016), Apostolic Letter on the conclusion of Extraordinary Jubilee Year of Mercy, *Misericordia et Misera;* see, in particular, 20.

# 12

# The Episcopate

The last time I was in the diocese of Nottingham it was for the burial of a king.[1] Today it is for the raising up of a Bishop. This ordination is the work of the Lord and, as such, it is beyond our capacity. God alone is able to give the gifts of episcopal character (1 Tim 3.1) and ordination. Our heavenly Father, by the outpouring of the Holy Spirit, raises up this man, Patrick, to be conformed to Jesus Christ, the High Priest (Heb 4.14–16), Son of the Father (Heb 5.5–10) and to join the company of the apostles, one of whom – St Thomas (Mk 3.18; Jn 20.24–9) – we celebrate today.

Primarily, we ask the Lord to raise up for us a bishop endowed with great wisdom. The first reading, chosen by Mgr Patrick himself, from the Wisdom of Solomon, is such a beautiful text. It speaks of our utter dependence on God, a sense founded on acceptance of our true state – 'weak and short-lived, with little understanding' (Wis 9.5). Indeed the words remind us of the gulf between worldly wisdom and the ways of God, 'for even if one is perfect among the sons of men, yet without the wisdom that comes from [you] he will be regarded as nothing' (Wis 9.6). Today we do not pray for a bishop who will be popular or 'have a good press'; rather, we pray for one who will open for us the ways of God.

This text originates as a prayer offered by King Solomon. It is a prayer appropriate for anyone who has to accept a position of authority: a parent, a head teacher and certainly a bishop. For a bishop cannot avoid the responsibilities of leadership both within the community of the Church and in our society. All responsibility demands true wisdom, especially the challenge of leadership in the ways of God, in a public culture which seeks to shape society without any reference at all to the divine. Many people in our society strive to live their lives with a sense of God's presence, but rarely does that profound awareness find expression in our public life and culture. The small flame of instinctive faith may be seen in the images of broken-hearted holidaymakers on their knees in silence on the beach in Tunisia,[2] the gathering of a family in church for a baptism, not at ease but pleased to be there, and the seemingly endless procession of people who filed through Leicester Cathedral in recognition that at long last the body of King Richard III (reg. 1483–5) lay where it should – before the throne of God. Yet we need the divine wisdom (Wis 6.17–20) in order that our words and actions do nothing to quench the 'small flame', but rather nurture it into a stronger light that can begin again to guide our actions.

The moment when the new bishop takes hold of the crozier which is presented to him is, I believe, the moment when he is accepting the total reality and obligation of the episcopal office. This office requires the ministry of shepherding the faith of the people in all its authentic forms (Acts 20.28) and of shepherding the people of faith wherever they are to be found. May this prayer to God be in our hearts today for this new Bishop, Patrick; and, not only today, but whispered for him on every occasion in the years to come when he grasps his crozier: 'Give him the wisdom that sits by your throne [...] send her forth from the holy heavens [...] that wisdom may be with him and toil, and that he may learn what is pleasing to you [...] that she may guide him wisely in his actions and guard him with her glory.'[3]

Today we also ask the Lord to raise up for us a bishop whose heart is focused solely on 'Christ Jesus', who is the 'main cornerstone' of 'God's household', built on the apostolic and prophetic foundation of faith (Eph 2.19–20 [JB]). Jesus must be the cornerstone of Patrick's life, a home 'where God lives, in the Spirit' (Eph 2.22 [JB]).[4]

In my experience the step of ordination as a bishop is even more life-changing than that of ordination as a priest. I found this to be so because, as a bishop, I have always missed the day-to-day ministry of parish life. Bishops roam, like the apostles, here and there, trying to undertake God's mercy through his mercy (2 Cor 4.1). We are always wonderfully welcomed, always supported lovingly, but we are always on the move (e.g., 1 Thess 2.1–8). This missionary movement means that a bishop needs a strong heart for the Lord, a strong bond with him and a firm foundation of faith, hope and love in his providential care that accompanies the bishop everywhere. This sanctuary is the house of God which every bishop has to build, an interior dwelling for the Lord. This openness to the Spirit, this bond of divine love, is symbolized powerfully in the gift of the episcopal ring which will be given to the new bishop today and which he will wear hereafter. These are the liturgical words which will accompany this gift: 'Take this ring, the seal of your fidelity. With faith and love protect the bride of God, his holy Church.'[5]

This holy Church is built on the foundation of the apostles called by Jesus, among whom, of course, is Thomas (Lk 6.15; Acts 1.13). Perhaps he is the most reassuring of all the apostles, the one nearest to us in his doubts (Jn 20.25) and in the struggles of his heart (Jn 14.5), yet he is the one to declare his faith in the Risen Christ as 'My Lord and my God!', the greatest confession of all that can be made of Jesus (Jn 20.28). His namesake St Thomas Aquinas encourages us to go beyond the faith of St Thomas the Apostle and to believe in the Risen Christ whom we cannot see with our own eyes (Jn 20.29; *CCC*, 1381). Thomas Aquinas reminds us to trust what we hear – '*sed auditu solo tuto creditur*':

> What God's Son has told me, take for truth I do;
> Truth Himself speaks truly or there's nothing true.[6]

The truth about God's Son, Jesus Christ as 'My Lord and my God', and the way of salvation that he offers is communicated primarily to us through our hearing of the reading of the Holy Gospels. How appropriate, then, that the Book of the Gospels is held over the head of the bishop at the solemn moment of his ordination. He is to have ears for these words above all others. Every word that comes from his mouth is to be inspired and shaped by those divine words, by the Word of God himself.

In my imagination, the mitre, the symbol of the descent of the Holy Spirit in tongues of fire at Pentecost (Acts 2.3), when placed, silently, on the bishop's head, forms a continuation of the presence above him of the Book of the Gospels, with its bookmarks still hanging down his neck! Patrick, may the placing of this mitre upon your head, today and every day, remind you of the source of all your teaching: the words of divine truth spoken by Jesus, he who alone is truth (Jn 14.6) and understood within his Church, which he acquired with his own blood (Acts 20.28) and where he promised to be with us and to guide us always until the end of time (Mt 28.20). Today we ask God to raise up for us a bishop who will always proclaim this Gospel.

This Gospel truth is much needed in our troubled world. Jesus calls us to proclaim fundamental values which have to be found at the heart of the type of society to which we all aspire. These are the values, the principles, of a transcendental humanism. They both underpin and reach beyond the pragmatic values of our age and rest on a hope that we, of ourselves, cannot fulfil. Jesus, God's incarnate Son (Jn 1.14), is the ultimate vision of this humanism, for he is the one human being who, through his sinless life and sacrifice, has reached fulfilment and thereby makes that fulfilment attainable for every human soul. In the face of every threat we encounter, this way of life is our way of salvation. Forgiveness and mercy are at the heart of this Christian humanism. These virtues expose the darkness of the ideologies of death and explain why they are to be rejected by all who believe in the mystery of God at the heart of life.

Dear Patrick, soon in this liturgy you will be newly adorned! Mitre, ring and crozier: may God raise up in you a bishop endowed with wisdom to guide and shepherd all people, a bishop bound so closely to his Son that nothing will ever shake your peace and a bishop who, in the manner of his Master, will speak words of divine truth with unfailing clarity, courtesy, charity and sensitivity.

So let us proceed!

[*This homily was preached in the Cathedral Church of St Barnabas in Nottingham on 3 July 2015, the feast of St Thomas the Apostle, on the occasion of the episcopal ordination of Monsignor Patrick McKinney as the tenth Bishop of Nottingham. The Readings are: Wis 9.1–6; 9–10; Ps 116 (Heb 117); Eph 2.19–22; Jn 20.24–9.*]

## Notes

1. I had the honour of preaching at the service for the reception of the remains of King Richard III into Leicester Cathedral on 22 March 2015. I should like to thank the Bishop, the Dean and the Canons for their kind invitation and warm hospitality. I also celebrated the Requiem Mass for the soul of King Richard at Holy Cross Priory, Leicester, on 23 March 2015. It was a truly uplifting occasion.
2. This event took place near Sousse after the massacre of 38 people by an Islamist gunman on 26 June 2015. The full extent of the horror was revealed at the inquest held in the Royal Courts of Justice; see *The Times*, 1 March 2017.

3  This prayer is based on the personal prayer of Solomon for wisdom found at Wis. 9.4, 10–11.
4  For the metaphor of the building for ministry see the discourse of St Augustine on Ps. 126.2, *DO, III*, p. 294, 'the Lord Jesus Christ builds his own house [...] Who are those building it? All who preach the word of God in the Church, the ministers of God's sacraments.'
5  *The Rites* (1991), Vol. 2. Collegeville, MN, The Liturgical Press, p. 75, n. 30.
6  From a hymn composed by St Thomas Aquinas, *Adoro te devote,* Eng. trans., G. M. Hopkins, 'Godhead here in hiding', found in *Hymns Old and New* (1993), Stowmarket, Kevin Mayhew, 176.

# 13

## *The Presbyterate*[1]

Today we give thanks to God, with great joy, for the gift of eight new priests,[2] and what a gift this is! We also give thanks, in a heartfelt manner, for the parents and families in whose love they have been nurtured, for all those who have contributed to their formation in Allen Hall in Chelsea, in the Beda College, Rome, in neocatechumenal communities and in our parishes and for those across the Diocese of Westminster who pray for our students and contribute generously to the funds we need for this work of priestly formation.

In the first reading Peter and John go to the Temple in Jerusalem together in order to pray (Acts 3.1). Here they are demonstrating the unity of apostolic companionship and practice that should characterize the followers of Jesus. Peter and John meet the crippled beggar at the Beautiful Gate of the Temple and give him the great gift of healing in the name of Jesus (Acts 3.6; see also Lk 7.22 and 14.13–14). Through this priceless gift the apostles, in their poverty, are revealing by their words and actions that the new age of the Father's kingdom has dawned (Lk 12.32–4) and, therefore, the

Father's healing love and grace cannot be bought with 'silver and gold' (Acts 3.6). In your priestly ministry you should follow always this example of poverty and discipleship given by Jesus to his apostles, and remember that we have nothing of our own to bring, except the gifts that are bestowed on us by God. Little is known about this Beautiful Gate into the Temple. We know full well, however, that for this poor crippled beggar it was indeed a beautiful gate, and today it is also beautiful for us. At this Gate the first miracle of healing in the new Spirit-filled era ushered in at Pentecost (Acts 2.4, 16–21, in fulfilment of Joel 2.28–32) took place. At this Gate and with this great deed of healing, the power of the Holy Spirit is shown in action. The onlookers are left astonished (Acts 3.10–11), unable to provide an explanation for all they have seen, for it is truly the work of God.

Immediately after this healing miracle, and of great importance, Peter gives another homily (Acts 3.12–26; the first being at Pentecost, Acts 2.14–36) – on this occasion in the portico of Solomon within the Temple. Here Peter proclaims the Gospel that Jesus is the Christ of God (Acts 3.20) who offers salvation to all people. Peter speaks boldly and unambiguously. 'Why do you wonder at this?', he asks the onlookers, as if the man had been healed 'by our own power' (Acts 3.12). Peter responds to their puzzlement by declaring the apostolic *kerygma* that 'The God of Abraham, and of Isaac and of Jacob, the God of our fathers, glorified his servant Jesus, [...] [but you] killed the Author of life, whom God raised from the dead. To this we are witnesses [...] by faith in his [Jesus'] name, [...] [he] has given the man this perfect health' (Acts 3.13–16). In this declaration we see the love of God in Jesus both in preaching and in action, which provides a mandate for the ministry of the Church and in this celebration is focused on the priesthood, which gives the pastors their authority from God for the proclamation of the Gospel and the offering of its healing power.

The gate by which we enter in order to hear this Good News is indeed a Beautiful Gate, the very *Porta Fidei*, the Gate of Faith; and it is through this Gate that we are invited to enter afresh during this Year of Faith.[3] Announcing the Good News in word and deed is the task of each of us as followers of Jesus. We do so even in the midst of daily tasks, whenever we behave with compassion, with ready forgiveness and with generosity towards those in need. When we are seen to act in the manner of Jesus, then we may well make others wonder, at least a little, why we do so. Like Peter, we should be ready to speak with simplicity and directness the reasons for our behaviour: the truth about whom we know, love and worship.

In the Gospel passage from St John we see the commissioning of the disciples by the Risen Lord Jesus for the ministry of evangelization and the preservation of the unity of the believing community (Jn 21.11). This commission reminds us of the great importance of our love for the Lord. Only when our lives are really rooted in love for him are we on a sound footing in our discipleship (Jn 21.19). Let us now consider St John's account of the commissioning of St Peter for his future ministry after the resurrection (Jn 21.15–19). The Risen Lord asks Peter three times, 'Do you love me?' His positive response here of declaring his love for Jesus three times, 'Yes, Lord; you know that I love you' (Jn 21.15–17), means that his denial, and of all knowledge of Jesus, three times in quick succession before his crucifixion (Jn 18.15–18, 25–7), is reversed. On the basis of Peter's declaration of love, Jesus commissions Peter as his pastor. By this ministry Jesus is making it clear that Peter's love must be expressed in action which will result in his future martyrdom (Jn 21.18–19). In your life as a priest, therefore, you should always follow this sacrificial example of St Peter. As the Risen Lord spoke to him, so the Lord is speaking to us today. As shepherds who profess our deep love for Jesus, we are to 'Feed [his] lambs' (Jn 21.15), 'Tend [his] sheep' (Jn 21.16) and 'Feed [his] sheep' (Jn 21.17). This is our summons from the Risen Lord: to show in daily practice, in love for each other, the love we have for the Lord himself. We are to watch over, nurture and encourage each other: parents towards their children, friends and colleagues towards one another, caring for our neighbours, especially those who are the weakest and most vulnerable. Such love in practice is at the heart of the priest's life, and these men whom we ordain today are bidden to follow this example of love. Everything that you do for your people, in all the years of your priesthood, will be an expression of your love for the Lord. If your ministry is not grounded in him, it will soon become a burden and immensely tiring. Stay rooted in the Lord each day. With St Peter you must answer, 'Yes, Lord; you know that I love you' (Jn 21.15); then the work that you do will be your strength and a joyful offering to God.

Two particular tasks will be at the heart of your ministry as a priest: to help to keep us all grounded in Christ; and to help to keep us all united in Christ.

Through your ministry of word, sacrament and pastoral care, the Lord will enable those whom you serve to become rooted in his life. In the baptisms that you will administer, in the confessions that you will hear, when you anoint the sick and the dying, in the homilies that you will preach, in the marriages that you will prepare and celebrate – even in all those marriage forms – in the pastoral visits that you will make, your every action, every manner, word and gesture, will have the potential to root people more deeply in Christ. Such is the grace and privilege of the priesthood! Remember also that a careless word, a harsh remark, have their own amplified capacity to hurt, to uproot someone from their life in the Lord. We are servants of Jesus, 'the Author of life' (Acts 3.15). May this understanding be clear in all that we say and do for him in the ministry of the Church.

You are also to be visible signs of our unity in the person of Christ. You come from diverse backgrounds and circumstances. Yet today you express that remarkable unity of mind and heart which is the great gift of our faith. For you the tunic of Jesus is not torn (Jn 19.23), nor the net of the Church broken (Jn 21.11). You are as one, like the first apostles of Jesus (Acts 1.14), in the lifelong commitment that you are about to give: a commitment to the people in service; a commitment to the Church in obedience; a commitment to Jesus in love. In the light of this commitment and service in the unity of the Church you know that the imposition of personal preferences has no part in your ministry and the fostering of personal favouritism must be avoided. All is for Christ, not for self;[4] all is within obedience to the mind of the Church.

This ministry of unity finds its true source and power in the celebration of the Mass. The Eucharist, as the unique offering of thanksgiving to God, celebrating his activity of 'creation, redemption and sanctification' (*CCC*, 1328), recreates the Church afresh each day. At this Mass we can sense a new vitality in the Church, and so we should. For today we are receiving a remarkable new gift – your future ministry as priests. Yet at every Mass we are able to know a new vitality. On many occasions we enter the door of the church buffeted and bruised. At the Mass we are healed and restored, formed again into the body of Christ. The porch of every church, the doorway into the Mass, is indeed always a Beautiful Gate.

My brothers and sisters, soon we shall go out from here through this Beautiful Gate of faith with our eight new priests, to confirm in word and deed the wonderful grace that God is bestowing in this ordination Mass. May St Peter, the first to proclaim our faith (Acts 2.14), be with us and confirm our faith. May St Paul, the great adventurer of our faith (2 Tim 4.7), encourage and embolden us. May our own St John Southworth, our saintly patron and martyr, watch over us in every difficulty and by his example and prayers draw us always closer to the Lord Jesus, Amen.

[*This homily was preached in Westminster Cathedral on 29 June 2013, the feast of St Peter and St Paul, on the occasion of the ordination of eight men to the priesthood. The readings are: Acts 3.1–10; Ps 18 (Heb 19).2–5; Gal 1.11–20; Jn 21.15–19, for the Vigil Mass of St Peter and St Paul, apostles.*]

THE PRESBYTERATE

# Notes

1 The term 'Presbyterate' comes from the Greek word *presbyteros*, 'elder' in English, and was related to a man ordained to minister within the local Christian community, which met usually in the houses of its members. 'Presbyterate' indicates a 'council of elders' (1 Tim 4.14) who, as co-workers with the Bishop, preached the Gospel, taught the faith and administered the sacraments. St Cyprian of Carthage (*c.* 210–258; Bishop, 248–58) first used the term 'priests' (Latin *sacerdotes*) to describe the ministry of the presbyters. This change was due to the understanding of the Eucharist in terms of sacrifice and the interpretation of Christian elders as priests in terms of the high priesthood of Christ who fulfilled and transcended the priesthood of Israel (e.g., Ps 110 [Vg 109].4 and Heb 5.5–10). To demonstrate the antiquity of the Christian priestly office (*CCC*, 1564), however, the term *presbyterium* is retained to describe 'a unique sacerdotal college' (*CCC*, 1567) of the priesthood.

2 The men ordained on this occasion were: Oscar Ardila, Jeffrey Downie, Fortunato Pantisano, Giles Pinnock, Martin Plunkett, Jeffrey Steel, Martin Tate and Mark Walker. I pray every day for all the men whom I have ordained.

3 The Year of Faith was promulgated by Pope Benedict in his Apostolic Letter *'Motu Proprio Data', Porta Fidei*, 6 January 2012. The Year of Faith began on 11 October 2012, the 50th anniversary of the opening of the Second Vatican Council and the 20th anniversary of the publication of the *Catechism of the Catholic Church*, and concluded on 24 November 2013, the Solemnity of Christ the King. It proved to be a year in which our faith was deepened and our relationship with our Lord renewed.

4  In this regard I admire greatly the '*Quo vadis*' story when St Peter, fleeing from persecution in Rome, was greeted by Christ on the Appian Way. Peter asked the Lord, '*Domine, quo vadis?*' When Peter received the reply that Christ was returning to Rome to be crucified again, Peter understood that he was to suffer for the sake of Christ and returned to Rome, where he was martyred during the reign of Nero (*c.* AD 64; *HC*, 2. 25). The story, which is a powerful symbol of the spirit of sacrifice that we priests should exhibit, is recounted in *The Acts of Peter,* found in Elliott, J. K. (ed.) (1993), *The Apocryphal New Testament*, Oxford, Oxford University Press, p. 424.

## 14

## The Diaconate

In the exploration of the diaconate we enter first into the heart of the ministry of Jesus (Mt 12.14–21, in fulfilment of the first 'Servant Song' of the prophet Is 42.1–4). As a result, we are able to identify with him, given that to be a deacon (meaning a servant) is to be called to exercise a ministry in the name of Jesus Christ (*CCC*, 1570, nn. 55 and 56) and within the Church: a ministry of proclamation and service. St Luke, in his recording of the passion of Jesus (Lk 22.1–23.56), helps us to enter again into this reality. After describing the institution of the Eucharist by Jesus (Lk 22.14–23), Luke notes that a dispute arose amongst the apostles as to which of them was the greatest (Lk 22.24). Jesus believes that this desire for importance is worldly, the way in which political leaders, emperors, kings and governors exercise civil power. Within the Messianic community formed by Jesus, however, it is often the youngest member who demonstrates the greatest wisdom, and it is imperative, therefore, that the apostolic leader is the one who always serves (Lk 22.26).

Then Jesus asks two fundamental challenging questions: who is the greatest, the one who is served at table, exercising worldly superiority, or the one who serves the meal? Surely it is the one who sits at table. Jesus reverses this established social position (as his mother, Mary, does before his birth, Lk 1.52–3) because always through his ministry he acts as God's servant. Jesus is fulfilling the ancient prophecy of Isaiah relating to the 'Suffering Servant' (the fourth 'Servant Song', Is 52.13–53.12, quoted in Lk 22.37). Jesus is the new servant of God totally obedient to the Father's will. In this light, therefore, although all Christians are called to diaconal service (after the pattern of Mt 6.24), it is the order of Deacons, in particular, who help us to focus on a fundamental aspect of the Church's mission in the name of Jesus: proclamation and service. How are we to fulfil faithfully this mission? My answer is the Greek word used to name the Church's service of charity – *diakonia*.

In his second volume, the Acts of the Apostles, Luke demonstrates the ways in which the infant, Spirit-filled Church conformed to, and identified with, the ministry and mission of Jesus (e.g. Acts 2.43–7). One example of this conformity is seen when the apostolic company of the twelve, chose seven men (Acts 6.3) of 'good repute, full of the Spirit and of wisdom' (Acts 6.3) to ensure that the 'love commandment' of Jesus (Lk 10.27–8, the prelude to the story of the Good Samaritan) was being fulfilled within the Church (Acts 6.1–2). By this appointment it was intended that the diaconal ministry should be seen in action and that any needless arguments about the distribution of charity could be avoided (Acts 6.1). The strict division of the twelve 'preaching the word' and the seven serving 'tables' (Acts

6.2) soon became blurred. Of the seven Luke records that Stephen (the first martyr, Acts 7.54–60) and Philip (Acts 8.4–40) were speakers of great power (Stephen, Acts 6.8; Philip, Acts 8.5–6), and Philip, in particular, is portrayed as a missionary, evangelist and prophet of the Gospel (Acts 21.8–9). We should not think that either the twelve or the seven gave up the ministry of charity but, rather, that in the diaconal ministry of the Church, preaching and service belong together. What Luke records is concerned with emphasis rather than with any rigid distinction. Nor should it be supposed that the seven ignored their fellowship with the twelve; on the contrary, Luke expresses both the unity and variety of the apostolic ministry in the power of the Holy Spirit. From the beginning of the Church, therefore, its ministers were concerned that everyone in the community had what was required for a dignified life. This fact remains an obligation for the Church as she serves the world in love.

Also, from the earliest days of the Church, the Bishops, as the successors to the apostles (*1 Clem.* 42.1–5), had the primary responsibility for ensuring that the offerings presented at the Eucharistic celebration were used to support those in need. This responsibility for overseeing charitable activity remains at the core of the episcopal ministry. Deacons have a privileged vocation in assisting the Bishop with the distribution of charity. We should recall the ancient prayer of the psalmist: 'Lord, do not forget the poor' (Ps 9B [Vg 10].17). Thus, from the earliest days of the Church (Phil 1.1; 1 Tim 3.1–13; *1 Clem.* 42.4; *Did.* 15.1), a special bond has existed between the Deacon and the Bishop, more so than between the Deacon and the local church to which he is appointed.

These relationships today, I believe, need further investigation to ensure that we are all living by the demands of the Gospel. At the diaconate ordination deacons are called to draw strength from the gift of the Holy Spirit to help the Bishop as ministers of the word, the altar and charity. By the consecration which binds you more closely to the altar, Deacons are to perform works of charity in the name of the Bishop after the example of those men who were chosen by the apostles.

The focus for this ministry is to be found in the three liturgical actions that the deacon performs during the Mass: first, in the proclamation of the Holy Gospel. This reading represents 'the high point of the Liturgy of the Word'.[1] It is set apart from the other scriptural readings as it is read by the deacon or, in his absence, by the priest. It is given marks of special honour: the deacon asking the celebrant for a blessing in order that the deacon might prepare himself spiritually for this great liturgical act. By this action it is acknowledged that Christ is truly present through the words of the Gospel, that the deacon is speaking to the whole assembly, who stand in reverence to receive the teaching, company and grace of Christ Jesus our Lord. At their ordination the newly ordained deacons receive this Book of the Gospels. As a result they become Gospel-bearers, echoing Mary, the Child-bearer (Lk 1.31). We pray, likewise, that through their preaching (*CCC*, 1570) and proclamation of the Gospel in their ministry of service, prayer and self-offering they will bring forth Jesus Christ, the King, the ruler of heaven and earth. That is the promise of this sacrament of holy orders: that God will use us as his instruments to do the work of his kingdom after the pattern of Jesus, who proclaimed and lived this new age of 'the gospel of God' (Mk 1.14–15). Through us (Mk 3.13–14) the Father draws people to himself in ways we do not often see (Mk 4.30–32) and more through our weaknesses than through our strengths (2 Cor 12.9).

Second, the deacon assists the priest at the altar. This ministry represents the fulfilment of that offered by the tribe of Levi (Num 1.48–53), who were chosen for service, initially at the Tent of Meeting in the wilderness (Num 3.5–9), and then in the Jerusalem Temple, where they brought gifts for sacrifice. Indeed, the prayer of ordination itself places the priesthood of Aaron (see Num 6.22–6) and the seventy elders (see Num 11.24–5) as forerunners of all those of us who have received the sacrament of holy orders in the Christian era (*CCC*, 1541–3). At the beginning of the liturgy of the Eucharist the deacon prepares the altar and receives the gifts of bread and wine presented by the faithful. In addition their financial offerings and gifts for the poor are included but placed aside from the altar. In this presentation the diaconal ministry of service and sacrifice which follows the pattern set by the Lord (e.g., Mk 10.45) is being made manifest. It also provides the focus for other aspects of the diaconal ministry: the distribution of the Holy Communion at Mass and to the sick, the administration of baptism, the assisting and blessing of marriages, the giving of the Viaticum to the dying and officiation at funeral and burial liturgies, together with other liturgical acts such as the adoration of the Blessed Sacrament (*LG*, 29). The exercise of this ministry highlights the pastoral service at the entry into the fellowship of the Church (baptism), the new step of personal union in marriage, and departure from this world and the journey to heaven. The deacon is responsible for the distribution of charity following the way indicated by St Polycarp: 'the deacons should be [...] free from the love of money [...] compassionate, attentive, and proceeding according to the truth of the Lord, who became a minister (*diakonos*) for everyone.'[2]

Third, this theme is continued by the dismissal proclaimed by the deacon at the end of the Mass, '*ite, missa est*', 'Go forth, the Mass is ended'. This proclamation, however, does not really state that the Mass is ended; rather, it says that the celebration within the Church building has reached its temporal conclusion. The Eucharist is not confined by the walls of any building; rather, the Eucharist is carried 'outside' through the mission given to us all. Our being, which during the Eucharistic celebration, is taken up into the Trinitarian love of the Godhead, is at the same time being turned outwards towards the whole of humanity. Our Eucharistic communion must pass over into the actual practice of love for others, no matter who they are. For the Father not only gives us the Son in the Eucharist but also, in the power of the Holy Spirit, sends us out to walk with the Lord. We are to be a wonderful procession carrying to others the one we have received. Our charitable activity always flows from the Eucharist and makes us radiant manifestations of divine *agape*. For when, by our charity, we live the Eucharistic mystery, others are able to see the work of the Trinity in action on our pilgrimage. Yes, the mission of the incarnate Son continues in and through us. We continue this mission, carry him to others, only because Jesus walks with us, leads us and carries us. The Eucharistic procession reminds us that the Lord is with us every step of the way, renewing our strength. No matter how many obstacles we encounter, we can travel the path of charity because it proceeds out from the Mass itself.

This indissoluble bond between the Eucharist and charitable activity is essential to the nature and mission of the Church. It is as necessary as the proclamation of the Word and the administration of the sacraments. These three elements presuppose each other and are inseparable. The Church cannot neglect her ministry of charity any more than she can neglect the sacraments and the Word. This understanding is focused in the diaconal proclamation, *ite, missa est,* and highlights again the importance of the ministry of deacons within the holy orders of the Church. Pope Francis, in his injunctions to deacons, says that they are to 'be active apostles of the new evangelization. Lead everyone to Christ! Through your efforts, may his kingdom also spread in your family, in your workplace, in the parish, in the diocese, in the whole world!'[3] Through this vision and following the servant ministry of Jesus, the community will be strengthened and the frontiers of our mission enlarged. Deacons are apostles of service, proclamation and charity, working with fellow deacons in close unity with priests and in faithful communion with the Bishop in order to further the work of God's kingdom. It is only when the sacred ministry is seen in the light of this *communio* that the true purposes of God for the Church and her mission to the world will be made manifest and found to be true.

In the Latin Church of the West, within the diaconal ordination rite, the majority of Deacons who have a vocation to the priesthood are asked to embrace the commitment to lifelong celibacy. The words used by the Bishop highlight both the depth and the seriousness of this commitment. It is 'a sign of your [the deacon's] interior dedication to Christ' and undertaken 'for the sake of the kingdom'. As a commitment made freely, celibacy is the language of the heart as well as of the body. It is the language of love and, like all true love, the language of freedom. We rejoice in the sign of hope that the commitment to celibacy gives, both when it is made publicly in the ordination rite and also within our largely uncomprehending society. This vocation, however, ought to be seen against the diverse background and the varied experience from which today's deacons and priests emerge. Also, after ordination they enter different spheres of ministerial life: diocesan, religious and missionary orders. You will find deacons who are celibate and those who are married and, of course, who possess different abilities and personalities. The focus of unity within this diversity is the Bishop, the Pope, the Bishop of Rome, being the supreme pastor and also the servant of the servants of God. In this latter title we see diaconal language highlighted. Once you have been ordained a deacon, you subsequently always remain a deacon, the ministry of *diakonos* being intrinsic to all ordained ministries. In this regard one of my favourite quotations about deacons comes from St Ignatius, Bishop of Antioch (writing *c.* AD 107): 'and the deacons, who are especially dear to me, entrusted with the ministry [*diakonia*] of Jesus Christ, who was with the Father before the ages and in these last days has been made manifest.'[4] Ignatius has already said that the bishop presides 'in the place of God' and 'presbyters in the place of the council of the apostles', so together with the deacons a 'harmony'[5] is formed for proclamation and service which finds its focus in the love and service of the Lord within the family, in the ark of the Church and towards the renewal of the world.

*[This edited version comprises two homilies and an address. The first homily was preached in Westminster Cathedral on 18 June 2011 on the occasion of the ordination of three men to the Diaconate.[6] The readings are 2 Cor 12.1–10 and Mt 6.24–34.*
*The address was given at St Mary's University, on 26 June 2011, on the occasion of a Conference for Deacons.*
*The second homily was preached in Westminster Cathedral on 19 July 2014, on the occasion of the ordination of three men to the Permanent Diaconate (CCC, 1571).[7] The readings are: Num 3.5–9, Ps 9B (Heb 10).17–18 and Mt 12.14–21.]*

# Notes

1. *General Instruction of the Roman Missal*, 60.
2. *Pol.*, 5.2.
3. Audience Address of Pope Francis Saturday, 19 February 2016, to permanent deacons and their families during Jubilee celebration in Rome. Earlier that day a lecture had been given on the life and martyrdom of St Laurence (d. AD 258), the example of whom is important for all of us to follow; see *DO III*, pp. 178*–9*, from sermon 304 of St Augustine.
4. *Ign. Mag.*, 6.1, my rendering.

5   *Ibid.*
6   The men who were ordained to the diaconate on 18 June 2011 were: Kim Addison, Lorenzo Andreini and Ivano Millico.
7   The men who were ordained to the permanent diaconate on 19 July 2014 were: Justin Cross, Ian Edwards and Stephen Khokhar.

## 15

## *The Consecrated Life*

Today I welcome you to this Mass for the celebration of the Year of Consecrated Life which has been proclaimed by Pope Francis for the whole Church.[1] In his Apostolic Letter *To All Consecrated People* he states three aims for the Year, which he believes will encourage all engaged in the religious and consecrated life 'to look to the past with gratitude', 'to live the present with passion' and 'to embrace the future with hope'.[2] We shall do our best! Pope Francis has also, graciously, established that on the occasions of Masses such as ours today a plenary indulgence may be received by those attending the Mass who also spend time in prayer in the Cathedral. This prayer ought to conclude with the Our Father, the Profession of Faith and an approved invocation to the Blessed Virgin Mary, observing the normal conditions of sacramental confession, Eucharistic communion and prayers for the intentions, which surely include his aims for us all in the Year. This observance will ensure that the spiritual and pastoral ideals set before us may be renewed as we embark on a further stage in our pilgrimage of faith, the journey towards God.

With regard to the past, Pope Francis has written that 'it would be appropriate for each charismatic family to reflect on its origins and history',[3] the purpose being that we shall be able to glimpse the providential grace of God through the lives of those who have responded to the call to accept the specific vocation of the consecrated life. I should like to highlight one aspect of this providential grace: to remember and rejoice in those of your brothers and sisters who have made the supreme sacrifice of offering their lives in martyrdom. With great awe and humility I am thinking particularly of St Teresa Benedicta of the Cross (Carmelite), St Maximilian Mary Kolbe (Franciscan) and Fr Engelmar Unzeitig (Mariannhill Missionaries),[4] all of whom perished in the concentration camps of Nazi Germany. What wonderful examples they are for us in our time!

In relation to the injunction of Pope Francis that we should 'live the present with passion' I extend greetings, first, to those celebrating significant jubilees at this time or on this day. Second, I also welcome those who are new to the Diocese of Westminster: in particular, Mother Mary Gregory, the newly elected Mother General of the Adorers of the Sacred Heart of Montmartre and present here in London at Tyburn.[5] I pray for all who are leading religious communities: may they do so 'with passion' and with love. Third, I greet Sister Martina Teresa, who yesterday made her final profession into the Poor Clare community at Arkley.[6] I pray with earnestness for all who have been professed recently as members of your communities and for an increase in vocations to the religious life. As we gather in this Year of Consecrated Life, which we know embraces not only those who profess publicly the evangelical counsels of chastity, poverty and obedience by taking vows as members of religious institutes in all their wonderful variety but also those who do so by other kinds of sacred bond, I rejoice in the richness and strength which your vocations bring to the life of the whole Church. As I pray for you all, I am reminded of some words of St Benedict: 'But as we progress in this way of life and in faith, we shall run on the path of God's commandments, our hearts overflowing with the inexpressible delight of love.'[7]

What, then, unites gratitude for the past, the present passion and the future hope in 'the inexpressible delight of love'? I believe that the answer lies in the fact that we have chosen to place Jesus, the Christ, the Son, the High Priest, at the centre of our lives, both privately and publicly. We have chosen this way of life because Jesus has shared totally the human condition, yet without sin, and, as a result, and through his sacrifice, he is able to atone for our sins (Heb 2.17). Jesus, then, is our choice. Or rather, as we know well with great and enduring thankfulness, we are his choice. Jesus is first in our hearts, our minds and actions. Echoing St Paul, we are able to say 'for me to live is Christ' (Phil 1.21), for we know that Christ entered into time (Phil 2.6–7) but that he is Lord of all time (Phil 2.9–11). This fact is, of course, true for all Christians, yet for those called to the Consecrated Life the acceptance of this vocation is lived in a particular way: in community, with vows and for service. Even though I am not a member of an institute of consecrated life being ordained to the diocesan priesthood, please permit me to dare to offer some reflections on how your particular calling to the religious life is a marvellous gift and an inspiration to us all. I should like to concentrate on three aspects of your love for Jesus (see Jn 21.15–19).

First, the love for Jesus within your community: in exploring this theme, I return to the fact that Jesus is the first in your hearts. Your love is first of all for him. I am reminded of the wonderful words of St Thérèse of Lisieux, which are a source of constant inspiration: 'O Jesus, I know it, love is repaid by love alone.'[8] It is that love which is his gift, and which should shape every other love in your lives. This kind of loving gives new shape and depth to the continuing love within your natural families. It moulds the course of the love of friendship in your lives, your intimacy with those whom you name as your beloved in your life story. As St Aelred of Rievaulx comments: 'The source and origin of friendship is love. Although love can exist without friendship, friendship can never exist without love'.[9] For him, as for us, all friendship begins and ends with Christ. The love of Jesus then fashions and preserves that love in the purity and fruitfulness that you strive to show. The love of Jesus is at the heart of the life of your community. The patterns of human friendship, rich as they may be, are never enough to sustain your community living. It must be centred on the Lord, on the shared desire to serve him; otherwise the community will not last because it has only witnessed to human generosity, and we know how frail that will be. Rather, community life must be focused on Jesus as the source of unity. The contemplation of the holy face of Jesus and action in the name of Jesus are inseparable.

Second, your love for Jesus must be at the forefront of your minds as you struggle to discern the truth within the multitude of the complex circumstances in which you live. Theories abound; the human sciences can enthral and enlighten, yet in all your study and research you must cling to Jesus, who is the fullness of the truth of our human condition. He alone opens the mystery of our humanity, the secrets and designs written into our nature by the Creator. You study, explore and discuss always in his presence. He is surely with you and delights in you. He guides you to contemplate the compassionate light of his face and protects you from allowing intellectual pride and human achievement, no matter how brilliant, to consume your spiritual obligations. Through love we are led into the mystery of the Trinitarian God: Father, Son and Holy Spirit, who renews and sustains us and the whole universe.

Third, the love of Jesus must also shine through your actions. Whatever you do, whatever field you enter, your every engagement is to be shot through with the hallmark of Christ himself. Let the presence of Jesus shape your dedication, fashion your conviction, be visible and unmistakable in all that you do, not simply implicit or barely discernible but evident, radiant and attractive to all who witness your ministry. Your consecrated life is your proclamation of Jesus! This proclamation, both intensely personal and clearly public, forms the basis of your pathway of discipleship. You are public signposts to Christ, proclaiming him by your very way of being. That is why it is right that we celebrate important anniversaries of that act of commitment, that moment when you asked the Lord to take you into this special and enduring relationship with him, a relationship that is ever new and never-ending.

Today, as we renew our love for Jesus and our vocation to serve him, we turn to the event of the Presentation of the Lord in the Temple in Jerusalem, to the themes of holiness and sacrifice, and to the holy people engaged in that wonderful moment when the infant Jesus (for reference to his name, Lk 2.21 and 1.31) is offered to his heavenly Father (Lk 2.22). In this atmosphere of sanctity stand Mary and Joseph, the parents (Lk 2.27), Simeon, the prophet (Lk 2.34–5), and Anna, the prophetess (Lk 2.36), who were expectant that God was doing great things for the salvation of humanity, both for Israel and for the Gentile nations (Lk 2.31–2).[10] They were thankful for God's goodness and were filled with the Holy Spirit. This scene is all-embracing: of gender, age and vocation. Primarily, Simeon and Anna point to the presence of the Saviour, 'the Lord's Christ' (Lk 2.26), the infant Jesus in their midst. In different ways Simeon and Anna proclaim: 'Look, look here. This is the one. This is he for whom your heart longs. Come and see. Come and meet him. Come.'

To engage in this proclamation is also your role: to enable the world, the world of your colleagues, streets, shops, offices, hospitals, schools, universities, residential homes, nurseries and housing estates – as with the Presentation scene, which is all-embracing – to meet Jesus, to look upon him in all his loving compassion, to know that he longs for his Father's will to be fulfilled – for our happiness! Be constantly on the look-out for those emerging places in which the needs of the world are most clearly to be seen. This vision is surely one of the sources of renewal in the consecrated life – here the aged Simeon and Anna act as your guides – to see with fresh eyes the wounds in the flesh of our family, our society, and to discern through the wisdom which the Holy Spirit offers (Is 11.2; Lk 2.26–7) how best we are able to respond to these challenges, even if it means abandoning our old ways.

In order to engage fully in this ministry of renewal you are to be like Mary and Joseph, who offered to the Father the precious gift of the first-born Son, Jesus (Lk 2.22, fulfilling Ex 13.2 and Lev 12.1–3, 12.6). In a similar way you are to offer afresh to God what is most precious in your lives and, in the pattern of your profession or consecration, seek to present Jesus to our world, bearing him wherever you go with joy in your hearts, offering him to all those whom you meet.

Simeon's hymn, *Nunc Dimittis* (Lk 2.29–32), presupposes the ministry of evangelization: to present the light and glory of Christ as revealed in the Gospel. At this time all our parishes are being invited to renew all their activities with a fresh focus on the first and enduring proclamation of the Gospel, the *kerygma*, the heralding of God's love in Christ. How well this quest for a fresh energy for evangelization accompanies this year of Consecrated Life! I make this comment because in the life of each of you, as truly consecrated people, there is an act of evangelization. Your very presence is testimony to the transcendent in the midst of life. Your personal stories and those of your religious family, at their best, give flesh to the invitation of the Lord that all can come to know him, love him and serve him in the world, and to be happy with him for ever in eternity. I hope that during this year you will have many opportunities to tell your stories, to invite others to listen to all that has been experienced and learned during your ministry. These are rich stories, often reaching back to the past, but remain fascinating to young people.

I pray that during this fresh initiative for evangelization you play your full part. I ask earnestly that you bring to this endeavour all the richness of your experience and the deep love that you have of all that is truly human. Our society longs for the word that only Jesus can bring, and with that word the vision offered to the world in the Presentation scene. Jesus is the Word made flesh (Jn 1.14); he is the word which proclaims that love through him endures, that his mercy gives resurrection, that his compassion does not condemn, that his sacrifice does not count the cost and that the hope he offers has its horizons beyond death.

In the spirit of his proclamation, and on this day, let us together entrust ourselves to Our Blessed Lady, the Virgin Mary, the mother of Jesus (Lk 2.19, 2.34), the star of evangelization and the most precious mother of us all, and to Blessed Joseph, her spouse. May they guide our ministry now and always. Amen.

[*This homily was preached in Westminster Cathedral on 2 February 2015, the feast of the Presentation of the Lord, on the occasion of the Solemn Diocesan Celebration of the Year of Consecrated Life. The readings are: Mal 3.1–4, Ps 23 (Heb 24).7–10, Heb 2.14–18 and Lk 2.22–40.*]

## Notes

1. Details to be found in *Keep Watch! Year of Consecrated Life: A Letter to Consecrated Men and Women Journeying in the Footsteps of God from the Congregation for Institutes of Consecrated Life and Societies of Apostolic Life* (2014), London, CTS. What is said about 'a new call to watchfulness' and

'placing the Gospel and what is essentially Christian at the centre of things' (p. 7) is a timely reminder to all of us, and we reflect on the obligations of being Our Lord's disciples. See also Apostolic Letter of His Holiness Pope Francis (2014), *To All Consecrated People on the Occasion of the Year of Consecrated Life*, III.2.

2  *To All Consecrated People*, I.1; I.2; I.3.
3  *To All Consecrated People*, I.1.
4  I refer to Fr Engelmar Unzeitig in more detail in my homily for the closing of the Year of Consecrated Life, 2 February 2016, www.rcdow.org/cardinal/homilies
5  The rich diversity of ministry relating to the various religious communities can be seen, for example, by consulting the *Westminster Year Book*. The Tyburn convent, near Marble Arch, was established in 1903, having been founded in Paris in 1898. This convent is now the mother house of the Benedictine order of nuns of the Adorers of the Sacred Heart of Jesus of Montmartre, and they can trace their origin to St Scholastica (c.480–c.543), the sister of St Benedict. The convent is situated close to the Tyburn Tree, where 105 Catholic martyrs were executed between 1535 and 1681. The particular charism of this order is prayer before the Perpetual Exposition of the Blessed Sacrament.
6  The Poor Clare nuns have been established in Arkley, Hertfordshire, since 1970, having arrived in Notting Hill from Bruges in 1857. As their name implies, they originate with St Clare of Assisi (1193–1253), who was inspired by St Francis and founded a religious community for women in 1212. The particular charism of the Poor Clares is to live by the model of poverty found in the Gospels, to emphasize contemplative prayer and the necessity of preserving the loveliness of God's created order.
7  Rule of St Benedict, Prologue, 49. *RB 1980: The Rule of St Benedict In Latin and English with Notes*. Collegeville, MN, Liturgical Press, 1981, p. 159.
8  *S of S*, MS B, 4r, 1, p. 303.

9 Aelred of Rievaulx (2010), *Spiritual Friendship*, trans. C. Braceland, ed. and intro. by Marsha L. Dutton. Collegeville, MN, Liturgical Press, Book Three, 2, p. 88.

10 Ratzinger, Joseph, Pope Benedict XVI (2012), *The Infancy Narratives: Jesus of Nazareth*. London, Bloomsbury, pp. 80–88.

# 16

## *The People of God*

The Dogmatic Constitution of the Second Vatican Council on the Church, *Lumen Gentium*, opens with the statement that 'the Church, in Christ, is in the nature of sacrament – a sign and instrument, that is, of communion with God and of unity among all' (*LG*, 1). It is my intention to concentrate on this latter idea: the Church in Christ looking outward from herself in love towards the world, given her mandate from the Risen Christ through his apostles to 'make disciples of all nations' (Mt 28.19). The question that needs to be asked is, how are we, as members of the Church, measuring up to this mandate? In some ways it is an old question. Pope St John XXIII believed, for example, that the Second Vatican Council ought to be seen as 'a continuation of our Lord's commandment' from St Matthew 28.19–20 (12 September 1962).[1] This declaration was based on the earlier suggestion of Cardinal Leon-Josef Suenens that in order to respond to the Lord's command 'the whole Church must be put "on a mission footing"'.[2] In 2015 Pope Francis is equally determined that missionary endeavour should be the principal feature of the life of the Church because, 'In virtue of their baptism, all the members of the People of God have become missionary disciples (cf. Mt 28.19). All the baptized, whatever their position in the Church or their level of instruction in the faith, are agents of evangelization', a ministry in which 'every Christian is challenged, here and now, to be actively engaged' (*EG*, 120). The use of words such as 'all' and 'every' remind me, first, of the shared responsibility of the clergy, the religious and laity in the task of mission. Second, I am challenged by the idea of the universality of the People of God, that as Catholics we are members of a worldwide family, one 'in matters of faith and morals' (*LG*, 12) and also one in charity, expressed, for example, in our obligation to assist victims of famine, war and persecution. Our horizons can never be merely local or parochial. As the universal 'one People of God', we seek to serve all people whatever their ethnic origin or religion, given that God created all people 'after his likeness' and that the 'image' (Gen 1.26) of the divine dwells in every person. God did not create us as solitary beings but, by virtue of our humanity, has established a communion between us by which we are capable of demonstrating virtue towards each other as we respond to the light and wisdom 'of the divine mind' (*GS*, 15).

Thus, in order to understand our mission we return to the contemplation of the heart of God, 'the divine mind', found in the mystery of the Holy Trinity, the inner life of God (*CCC*, 234–7). This mystery is expressed in terms of the divine *communio* – the sharing within the mystery of the persons of God, of life, love, truth, goodness and beauty. It is only from that inner heart of God that our vocation as 'missionary disciples' arises. It is only from that inner heart of God that our mission finds its shape, purpose and energy. We are to do something beautiful, something that is of God, something that is for God. Our mission has its origin always in our prayer. Mission flows from prayer and from our daily openness to the great mystery of the life of God; mission cannot begin from any other source. From this source the numerous rivers of Catholic spirituality flow, the celebration of Mass being our central act of worship: that is why we say that the Eucharist makes the Church. That is why our pondering and reading of the Scriptures are crucial, why our gazing on Our Lord present in the Blessed Sacrament is our silent centre. From this devotion, both public and private, and from our study of the Catholic spiritual tradition in all its rich diversity we encounter primarily the *communio* of God but also the fellowship, the *communion*, of all the faithful in life and love (e.g., 1 Jn 1.3 and 7).

During this Year of Mercy I should like to express the evangelizing mission of the people of God in terms of the unbounded mercy of God towards the world, humanity and the Church.[3] In order to understand this expression of divine mercy we need to perceive that Jesus is the face of his Father's mercy and that to look at Jesus is to see how the Eternal Father looks on us. In the face of Jesus we see that our Father is prepared to do anything, everything, to draw us into the love for which we have been made. God's mercy is the shape taken by the love of God when it comes face to face with broken human reality. God weeps and pours out his heart in Jesus that we may know how much he longs for us to be with him for ever. It would be a grave mistake, however, to believe that the propagation of this mercy is either 'a soft option' or lacking 'the costly grace' of the Gospel.[4] We are called to confront both ourselves and humanity first in terms of our sinfulness in all its aspects: selfishness, greed and violence. We know that all too often we have presented the world with messages and actions that lack the identity of the Gospel and the morality of faith and life. Mercy becomes a useless idea 'when it no longer has a trace of trembling before God, who is holy, and trembling before his justice and his judgment'.[5] Yet these failures of ours to bring a balanced perspective to the exercise of mercy must never dissuade us that we are the hands, voices and actions of that mercy in the flesh of our world today. God's mercy is not an idea; it is a reality, the fullness of love offered to us in Jesus. In other words, the only way in which we learn the truth about mercy is by experiencing it in our own lives, the mercy which we receive from Jesus and from the saving events of his ministry: his preaching, teaching, death and resurrection. We know that when confronted by these events in the deepest part of our being we are able to acknowledge that we too are broken and marked by sin; it is at this point that we are caressed by mercy and become filled with God's grace. Then mercy and grace flowing from our hearts can be offered to others, and so we shall find in that mercy the source of all that we are and all that we do as the People of God.

Today we are asked to consider our actions: the formulation of concrete proposals for the evangelizing mission by you, the People of God, which the clergy and lay faithful are being asked to put into practice. Before we embark on any plans, however, we must return again to three great acts of God by which our proposals are given framework and meaning. First, the mercy of God as demonstrated by his act of creation (Gen 1.1–2.4a). His Spirit hovers over the darkness, and the light of an ordered universe emerges (Gen 1.1–5). Thus we live within a cosmos, an ordered world, and not in chaos. The ordering of creation is designed for its ultimate fulfilment and not for annihilation. This creative and renewing act of God is a great mercy; it is an enormous blessing and is fundamental to our mission (Gen 1.31). Second, God's mercy is revealed through his calling into existence of each person (Gen 1.26–30), who is given a 'design', a destiny, a purpose. God's purpose for every human being is that we come to share in God's eternal life. We are not called into being in order to live an existential moment and then be extinguished. We are not created for futility. We are given the gift of life for this great destiny: to dwell with God in fulfilment and joy for ever! Third, in Jesus we see the fullest manifestation of the loving design of the Father, his mercy providing us with a vision of the world and ourselves in a way that makes it possible for us to achieve righteousness. Through the ministry of 'Christ Jesus' (Rom 8.31–9) all of creation will emerge from its 'groaning in travail' (Rom 8.22) and be raised to its fulfilment: the redemption of the world and humanity (Rom 8.18–27). In union with 'Christ Jesus' through baptism (Rom 6.3–11) we have been brought into the very heart of the life of the Blessed Trinity; our lives will be totally identified with this life at the time of the final resurrection (Rom 6.5b; 1 Cor 15.51–7). Through the power and intercession of the Holy Spirit (Rom 8.26–7) we are not only able to live each day in the hope and anticipation of that joy, but also, in our daily efforts, we are able to serve its realization, its heralding.

How, then, can these ideas find their realization in practice? Or, to frame the question another way, what does the activity of demonstrating mercy imply in concrete terms? At this point we need to examine ways in which the activity of mercy, the corporal and spiritual works of mercy (*CCC*, 2447), might be exercised now in a way that provides a loving face to the presence of divine mercy. I suggest that we think of the matter in this way: God has created for us an ordered world in which to live. Yet this divine order is not always visible or experienced. The corporal works of mercy are practical, Gospel-inspired ways, through which, day by day, we re-establish and regenerate the mercy of God's ordered creation. When we give food to the hungry we are re-establishing, through Jesus, the Son of man (Mt 25.31, 34–40) the proper sense of divine order. When we give drink to the thirsty, clothe the naked, welcome the stranger, heal the sick, visit the imprisoned and bury the dead, we are performing the divine mission (Mt 28.20) of restoring, in the name of God, the proper order to life; for no one should be left thirsty, naked, lost in sickness, isolated in jail, unwelcomed in need, left abandoned, unburied in death. When these things happen, as they do every day and on a grand scale, any sense that we are living in an ordered world is rendered implausible and the judgement of God upon our failure is forthcoming (Mt 25.32–3, 41–6). The corporal works of mercy, therefore, are ways in which in our neighbourhood, in our streets or in our communities we can help to restore that sense of place and belonging, of respect and acceptance, that our cosmic home, as created by God, should embody.

With regard to the spiritual works of mercy I suggest that we reflect on the way in which God has created each person to dwell in the glory of his presence for ever, which is the ultimate vocation of every human being. The spiritual works of mercy serve the fulfilment of this ideal: to offer counsel to the lost and confused is to help them redirect their lives to their true purpose. To instruct the ignorant, to admonish those who are heading in an erroneous direction, to comfort the lost and the bereaved, to forgive those who have offended us, to be patient with those who truly test us and to pray always for the living and the dead are precisely the ways in which we serve the great mercy of God, who has created us for this high destiny of honouring him through this ministry of love. The spiritual works of mercy are characterized by all the nudges and encouragement that we give to each other on our pilgrimage to God.

The ministry of the People of God in terms of mission and evangelization should be seen and practised in the light of our understanding of the ways in which we live these works of mercy. This ministry is enhanced not necessarily through superior planning, great efficiency or high-class management but as a result of the quiet, often hidden, work of the faithful as they bring the light of Jesus to humanity (e.g., Lk 10.1–2, 8; 2 Thess 2.13–17) through their pastoral tasks of praying, caring and loving. Every action of mercy is performed because we shall be blessed and caressed ourselves by mercy (Mt 5.7). Any of these works of mercy can become the vehicle for our ministry of evangelization as every work of evangelization can be related to these works of mercy and, if they are conceived rightly and practised sincerely, can display clearly the divine mercy at work in the world. Thus, our efforts will serve to proclaim again that God's work of creation is purposeful and that it represents the divine call to every person to discern the deepest meaning of our life, the foundation of our dignity. This work manifests the continual outpouring of God's salvation in Jesus, the fountain of all mercy (Lk 23.34), the Saviour who 'always leads us in triumph, and through us spreads the fragrance of the knowledge of him everywhere' (2 Cor 2.14). The restoration of this horizon, step by step through our actions, reveals a true proclamation of the Gospel and a clear invitation to know Christ Jesus more clearly, to love him more dearly and to follow him more nearly, day by day. This prayer of St Richard of Chichester (1197–1253) reveals clearly that Christ alone is the vision of this truth and that he alone is the one in whom it is attainable.[6] It also provides the mandate for the ministry and mission of the People of God.

[*This is an edited version of an address given at the Proclaim Westminster Conference in the Royal Horticultural Halls, Westminster, on 14 November 2015. I also make reference to the address that I gave at the National Proclaim '15 Conference held in Birmingham on 11 July 2015.*]

## Notes

1 Suenens, Cardinal Leon-Josef (1986), 'A Plan for the Whole Council', *Vatican II Revisited by Those Who Were*

   *There*, ed. Alberic Stacpoole. Minneapolis, MN, Winston Press, p. 90.
2  *Ibid.*, p. 98.
3  The Year of Mercy was from 8 December 2015 until 20 November 2016. It was a time of great blessing.
4  The idea of the radical difference between 'cheap' and 'costly grace' is taken from Bonhoeffer, Dietrich (1959 [6th edn]), *The Cost of Discipleship*, trans. R. H. Fuller, London, SCM Press, pp. 35–47.
5  Kasper, Walter (2014), *Mercy: The Essence of the Gospel and the Key to Christian Life*, trans. William Madges. New York and Mahwah, NJ, Pauline Press, p. 10.
6  St Richard's prayer:

Thanks be to thee my Lord Jesus Christ,
For all the benefits which thou hast given me,
For all the pains and insults which thou hast borne for me,
O most merciful Redeemer, Friend and Brother.
May I know thee more clearly,
Love thee more dearly,
And follow thee more nearly,
Day by Day.

# References and Abbreviations

## Scripture

The Revised Standard Version (RSV), An Ecumenical Edition (London, Collins, 1973), has been used except where stated. Abbreviations to Biblical books are as found on pp. xv and xvi).

| | |
|---|---|
| JB | Jerusalem Bible |
| NJB | New Jerusalem Bible |
| NRSV | New Revised Standard Version |

The text of Scripture used at the Mass can be found in *The Roman Missal: Lectionary in Three Volumes*, London, Collins, 1973. Numerous other editions are available.

For the explanation of the variable numbering of the Psalms (9–147) between the Greek Septuagint, followed by the Latin Vulgate, and the original Hebrew, see *DO*, I, 640★.

| | |
|---|---|
| Vg | Vulgate version (Latin) |

## Apostolic Fathers

*The Apostolic Fathers,* Vols 1 and 2, ed. and trans. Bart D. Ehrman, Cambridge, MA, Harvard University Press, 2003 (Loeb Classical Library)

REFERENCES AND ABBREVIATIONS

| | |
|---|---|
| *1 Clem.* | The First Epistle of Clement to the Corinthians |
| *Ign. Mag.* | The Epistle of Ignatius to the Magnesians |
| *Pol.* | The Epistle of Polycarp to the Philippians |
| *Did.* | The Didache or Teaching of the Twelve Apostles |

## Church Fathers

*Justin (c. 100–165)*

*1 Apol., 2 Apol.*     Barnard, L. W. (trans.) (1997), *St Justin Martyr, The First and Second Apologies*, vol. 56 of *Ancient Christian Writers: The Works of the Fathers in Translation*, ed. W. J. Burghardt, J. J. Dillon, D. D. McManus. New York/Mahweh, NJ, Paulist Press

*Jerome (c.345–420)*

*Comm. Isa.*     Scheck, T. P. (trans.) (2015), *St Jerome, Commentary on Isaiah*, Ancient Christian Writers, 68. New York/Mahweh, NJ, Newman Press

*Augustine (354–430)*

*Conf.*     Chadwick, H. (trans.) ([1991] 2008), *Saint Augustine Confessions*,

|  |  |
|---|---|
|  | Oxford World Classics. Oxford, Oxford University Press |
| Trin. | McKenna, S. (trans.) (1963) *Saint Augustine The Trinity*, The Fathers of the Church: A New Translation. Washington, DC, The Catholic University of America Press |
| CD | Bettenson, H. (trans.) (2003 [rev. edn]), *Saint Augustine Concerning the City of God against the Pagans*, with a new introduction by G. R. Evans. London, Penguin |

*Gregory (c.540–604)*

|  |  |
|---|---|
| PR | Demacopoulos, George E. (trans.) (2007), *St Gregory the Great, The Book of Pastoral Rule*. Crestwood, NY, St Vladimir's Seminary Press |
| DO | *The Divine Office: The Liturgy of the Hours according to the Roman Rite* (1973–4), vols I, II, III, London, Collins, contains a rich treasury of Scriptural and Ecclesial texts indicated, for example, as *DO*, I, 148★–150★ |

## Church Teachers

*Eusebius of Caesarea (c. 260–340)*

|  |  |
|---|---|
| HC | Williamson, G.A (trans.) (1989 [rev. edn]), *Eusebius: The History of* |

*the Church*, rev, A. Louth. London, Penguin Books

*Bede the Venerable (c. 673–735)*

EH — Sherley-Price, L. (trans.) (1990 [rev. edn]), *Bede Ecclesiastical History of the English People*, rev. R. E. Lathan, trans. of the minor works, D. H. Farmer. London, Penguin Books

*Francis of Assisi (1181/2–1226)*

FA I, FA II, FA III — Armstrong, R. J., J. A. W. Hellman and W. J. Short (eds) (1999–2001), *Francis of Assisi: Early Documents*: Vol. I (1999), *The Saint*; Vol. II (2000), *The Founder*; Vol. III (2001), *The Prophet*. New York, London and Manila, New City Press

*Thomas Aquinas (c. 1225–1274)*

ST — Fathers of the English Dominican Province (trans.) ([1911] 1981), *St Thomas Aquinas Summa Theologiae Complete English Edition in Five Volumes,* London, Sheed & Ward. The referencing to this great work is not easy to follow. It consists of three parts, the second part being divided into two sub-parts: I, II-I; II-II, III. Each unit is called an article, which takes the form of a debate containing the question at issue, opposing views, researching of previous answers, answering the question, response to opposing views. For example, whether the union of the Incarnate Word took place in nature? *ST* III, q 1 a 1.

## *Thérèse of Lisieux (1873–97)*

*S of S* — Clarke, J. (trans.) (2005), *St Thérèse of Lisieux, Story of a Soul,* study edition, M. Foley. Washington, DC, ICS Publications. For the referencing of the text, p. viii: Ms. A, B or C, 'recto' or 'verso' for the front or back of the page and the line number.

# Church Documents

## *The Catechism*

*CCC* — *Catechism of the Catholic Church* ([rev. edn] 1999). London, Bloomsbury.

*Second Vatican Council* — Flannery, Austin, OP (gen. ed.) ([new rev. edn] 1992), *Vatican Council II: The Conciliar and Post Conciliar Documents.* Dublin, Dominican Publications and E. J. Dwyer PTY

Church documents are referenced by the initial words of the original Latin text.

## REFERENCES AND ABBREVIATIONS

| | |
|---|---|
| LG | *Lumen gentium*, Dogmatic Constitution on the Church (21 November 1964) |
| NA | *Nostra aetate*, Declaration on the relation of the Church to non-Christian religions (28 October 1965) |
| DV | *Dei verbum*, Dogmatic Constitution on Divine Revelation (18 November 1965) |
| AG | *Ad gentes divinitus*, Decree on the Church's Missionary Activity (7 December 1965) |
| GS | *Gaudium et spes*, Pastoral Constitution on the Church in the Modern World (7 December 1965) |
| DH | *Dignitatis humanae*, Declaration on Religious Liberty (7 December 1965) |
| PO | *Presbyterorum ordinis*, Decree on the Ministry and Life of Priests (7 December 1965) |

*The Encyclicals of Pope Benedict XVI*

| | |
|---|---|
| DCE | *Deus Caritas Est*, On Christian Love (25 December 2005) |
| SS | *Spe Salvi*, On Christian Hope (30 November 2007) |
| CV | *Caritas in Veritate*, On Integral Human Development in Charity and Truth (29 June 2009). Published |

individually (2006, 2007, 2009), or in one volume (2013), London, Catholic Truth Society (CTS)

*The State Visit of Pope Benedict XVI to the United Kingdom, 16–19 September 2010*

SVJennings, P. (ed.) (2010), *Benedict XVI and Blessed John Henry Newman: The State Visit 2010*, The Official Record. London, CTS.

*Documents of Pope Francis*

EG*Evangelii Gaudium, The Joy of the Gospel*, Apostolic Exhortation on the Proclamation of the Gospel in Today's World. London, CTS, 2013

LS*Laudato Si'*, Encyclical Letter on Care for our Common Home. London, CTS, 2015

AL*Amoris Laetitia, The Joy of Love*, Apostolic Exhortation on Love in the Family. London, CTS, 2016

*Documents of the Catholic Bishops' Conference of England and Wales*

CCG*Choosing the Common Good.* Stoke, Alive Publishing, 2010

FS*Meeting God in Friend and Stranger: Fostering Respect and Mutual Understanding between the Religions.* London, CTS, 2010

## Acknowledgements

This book began as a simple reassessment of the essays, speeches, articles and homilies which I have given during my time as the Archbishop of Birmingham and of Westminster. This reassessment quickly developed into a fresh exploration of the wonder and beauty of our faith. This faith is the source and rock of my life so I should first like to thank all those who have formed my faith and who have supported and guided me throughout my life and ministry within the Church.

During the preparation of *Faith Finding a Voice* I have received valuable assistance from my brother priests and the staff in Archbishop's House, Westminster, the Sisters of the Poor Handmaids of Jesus Christ, St Joseph's Convent, Hendon and the personnel of the British Library and the National Gallery, London.

I thank Sean Ryan who has given generous assistance by reading the first draft of the manuscript, the proofs and has helped with the preparation of the index. I am grateful to Robin Baird-Smith, Jamie Birkett and the staff at Bloomsbury Publishing for their patience and creativity.

I should like to thank especially Fr Richard and Elaine Parsons for their untiring and irresistible enthusiasm for

## ACKNOWLEDGEMENTS

this project. During the process we have engaged in interesting and lively discussions in relation to literary criticism, theology and history – especially concerning the Orioli altarpiece. They have also edited the material and typed the manuscript. They have checked numerous source references, read the proofs and prepared the index. I am so grateful for their indefatigable energy by which this book has been brought to completion. I thank them and acknowledge that any mistakes which remain are mine.

+*Vincent Nichols*
Our Lady of the Rosary
7 October 2017

# Further Reading

It is my hope that by the inclusion of the Further Reading section and the notes at the end of each chapter, philosophical, historical and theological research will be encouraged.

## I. God Revealed

Benedict XVI (2007), *Christ and His Church: Seeing the Face of Jesus in the Church of the Apostles*. London, CTS
Benedict XVI (2009), *The Fathers of the Church: From Clement of Rome to Augustine of Hippo*. Grand Rapids, MI, Eerdmans
Benedict XVI (2010), *Church Fathers and Teachers: From Saint Leo the Great to Peter Lombard*. San Francisco, CA, Ignatius Press
Cantalamessa, Raniero (2005), *Sober Intoxication of the Spirit: Filled with Fullness of God*. Cincinnati, OH, Servant Books
Cantalamessa, Raniero (2012), *Sober Intoxication of the Spirit: Part Two: Born Again of the Water and the Spirit*. Cincinnati, OH, Servant Books
Kerr, Fergus (2007), *Twentieth-Century Catholic Theologians*. Oxford, Blackwell

Kreeft, Peter (1990), *Summa of the Summa*. San Francisco, CA, Ignatius Press
Norman, Diana (2003/2009), *Painting in Late Medieval and Renaissance Siena*. New Haven, CT, and London, Yale University Press
Rausch, Thomas P. (2003), *Who is Jesus? An Introduction to Christology*. Collegeville, MN, Liturgical Press
Rowland, Tracey (2017), *Catholic Theology*. London, Bloomsbury, T & T Clark

## II. Education for Life

DeGregorio, Scott (ed.) (2010), *The Cambridge Companion to Bede*. Cambridge, Cambridge University Press
Jones, David Albert, and Barrie Stephen (2015), *Thinking Christian Ethos: The Meaning of Catholic Education*. London, CTS
Ker, Ian, and Merrigan Terrence (ed.) (2009), *The Cambridge Companion to John Henry Newman*. Cambridge, Cambridge University Press
Little, Tony (2015), *An Intelligent Person's Guide to Education*. London, Bloomsbury

## III. Religious Dialogue and the Hope for Humanity

Borden, Sarah (2003), *Edith Stein*. London/New York, Continuum
Democopoulos, George E. (2015), *Gregory the Great: Ascetic, Pastor, and First Man of Rome*. Notre Dame, IN, University of Notre Dame Press
Doyle, Dominic (2011), *The Promise of Christian Humanism: Thomas Aquinas on Hope*. New York, Crossroad Publishing
Hamas, Paul (2008), *Edith Stein and Companions on the Way to Auschwitz*. San Francisco, CA, Ignatius Press (also important for Part IV, below)

Hillesum, Etty (2002), *Etty: The Letters and Diaries of Etty Hillesum, 1941–1943*. Grand Rapids, MI, Eerdmans

Sacks, Jonathan (2005), *To Heal a Fractured World: The Ethics of Responsibility*. London/New York, Continuum

## IV. Ministry: Treasure in Earthenware Vessels

St John Paul II, Karol Wojtyła (2017), *In God's Hands: The Spiritual Diaries, 1962–2003*. London, Collins

O'Donnell, Christopher (1997), *Love in the Heart of the Church: The Mission of Thérèse of Lisieux*. Dublin, Veritas

O'Meara, Thomas F. ([2nd rev. edn] 1999), *Theology of Ministry: Completely Revised Edition*. New York, Paulist Press

Robson, Michael J. P. (ed.) (2011), *The Cambridge Companion to Francis of Assisi*. Cambridge, Cambridge University Press

I should like to thank Fr Eugene Duffy, Fr Eamonn Mulcahy CSSp, Canon John O'Leary, Elaine Parsons, Fr Richard Parsons and Bishop John Sherrington for assisting me with the compilation of this further reading list.

# Index of Biblical References

OLD TESTAMENT

*Genesis*

| | |
|---|---|
| 1-2 | 187 |
| 1.1-2.4a | 291 |
| 1.1-5 | 291 |
| 1.2 | 80, 82 |
| 1.26-30 | 291 |
| 1.26 | 6, 8, 11, 19, 32, 95, 288 |
| 1.31 | 117, 291 |
| 2.8 | 39, 50 |
| 3.13 | 39 |
| 3.14-19 | 81 |
| 3.24 | 39 |
| 5.1-2 | 11 |
| 5.1 | 8 |
| 9.1-17 | 187 |
| 12-24 | 187 |
| 12.3 | 162 |
| 17.7 | 189 |
| 25-50 | 187 |

*Exodus*

| | |
|---|---|
| 1-15 | 187 |
| 13.2 | 283 |
| 13.21-22 | 187 |
| 16.9-36 | 187 |
| 17.1-7 | 187 |
| 17.5-6 | 44 |
| 19.3-20.17 | 187 |
| 32.1-6 | 187 |
| 32.7-14 | 246 |
| 32.8 | 244 |
| 32.14 | 245 |
| 34.6-7 | 187 |

*Leviticus*

| | |
|---|---|
| 12.1-3 | 283 |
| 12.6 | 283 |
| 19.2 | 234 |
| 19.18 | 188, 206 |

*Numbers*

| | |
|---|---|
| 1.48-53 | 271 |
| 3.5-9 | 271, 275 |
| 6.22-26 | 271 |
| 6.24-26 | 47, 60 |
| 11.24-25 | 271 |

*Deuteronomy*

| | |
|---|---|
| 5.1-22 | 187 |
| 6.4-5 | 187 |
| 6.4 | 105 |
| 9.13-21 | 187 |

# INDEX OF BIBLICAL REFERENCES

*1 Samuel*
10.9-10          85

*1 Kings*
3.9              143
19.12            5

*1 Chronicles*
29.11            190

*Psalms*
2.7              4
8.4-5            47
10.17-18         275
10.17            269
16.8-11          49
18.2             179
19.2-5           264
19.4             65, 199
23               240
23.1             10
24.7-10          284
30.4             189
33.4             11
33.6             22
34.1             190
34.3             190
42.7             19
85.10-11         146
91.4             75
104              82
104.30           73, 80, 195
106.19-23        246
110.4            226, 265
113-118          189
117              235, 256
127.1            257
139.1-3          207
150.1            59
150.6            59

*Proverbs*
1.2-3            85

*Song of Solomon (Song of Songs)*
2.12             110, 111

*Isaiah*
1.27             199
7.14             31
11.2             79, 85, 282
11.6-9           84, 184
35.8             189
42.1-4           267
42.1             4
52.13-53.12      268
53.4-6           43
53.9b            42
56.5             190-1
59.20-21         150
61.1-2           74
61.1             85, 243
66.18-19         153

*Jeremiah*
31.31-34         189
32.40            217

*Ezekiel*
13.4             211
36.35            50

*Hosea*
6.6              189

*Joel*
2.28-32          66, 73, 260

*Malachi*
3.1-4            284

# INDEX OF BIBLICAL REFERENCES

## DEUTEROCANONICAL BOOKS

*Wisdom*
| | |
|---|---|
| 3.1a | 176 |
| 3.4 | 213, 220 |
| 6.17-20 | 252 |
| 7.16 | 135 |
| 8.1 | 160 |
| 9.1-6 | 256 |
| 9.4 | 253, 257 |
| 9.5 | 251 |
| 9.6 | 251-2 |
| 9.9-10 | 256 |
| 9.10-11 | 253, 257 |
| 18.14 | 25 |

*Sirach (Ecclesiasticus)*
| | |
|---|---|
| 6.32-3 | 91 |

## NEW TESTAMENT

*Matthew*
| | |
|---|---|
| 1.18-25 | 31 |
| 1.23 | 31, 35 |
| 1.24 | 31 |
| 2.1 | 27 |
| 3.17 | 4 |
| 5.3-12 | 28 |
| 5.3 | 3, 218 |
| 5.7 | 293 |
| 6.21 | 202 |
| 6.24-34 | 275 |
| 6.24 | 268 |
| 6.33 | 3 |
| 7.24-27 | 207 |
| 10.1 | 79 |
| 10.20 | 79 |
| 12.14-21 | 267, 275 |
| 13.44-46 | 67 |
| 16.13-20 | 225 |
| 16.13-19 | 240 |
| 16.16-19 | 57 |
| 16.17-19 | 246 |
| 17.5 | 4 |
| 19.21 | 228 |
| 22.21 | 201 |
| 22.37-40 | 59, 206 |
| 25.31 | 292 |
| 25.32 | 292 |
| 25.34-40 | 292 |
| 25.40 | 59 |
| 25.41-46 | 292 |
| 26.14-16 | 40 |
| 26.36-46 | 38 |
| 26.47-56 | 39 |
| 26.47 | 40 |
| 26.49 | 40 |
| 27.32-54 | 41 |
| 27.57-61 | 44 |
| 27.57 | 45 |
| 27.60 | 46 |
| 28.1-8 | 48 |
| 28.11-15 | 50 |
| 28.11 | 51 |
| 28.13 | 46, 51 |
| 28.16-20 | 76, 228 |
| 28.19-20 | 287 |
| 28.19 | 51, 76, 228, 287, 288 |
| 28.19a | 76 |
| 28.19b | 77 |
| 28.20 | 255, 292 |

*Mark*
| | |
|---|---|
| 1.4-8 | 34 |
| 1.11 | 4 |
| 1.14-15 | 3, 271 |
| 1.15 | 3, 28, 232 |
| 1.20 | 41 |

## INDEX OF BIBLICAL REFERENCES

| | | | |
|---|---|---|---|
| 1.21-28 | 28 | 1.28 | 75 |
| 2.1 | 27 | 1.30-35 | 49 |
| 3.13-19 | 41 | 1.30 | 232 |
| 3.13-14 | 271 | 1.31-33 | 31 |
| 3.18 | 251 | 1.31 | 270, 282 |
| 3.19 | 40 | 1.32 | 75 |
| 4.30-32 | 271 | 1.35 | 75 |
| 6.7 | 109 | 1.38 | 15, |
| 6.14-29 | 34 | | 45, 64, 75 |
| 9.7 | 4 | 1.52-53 | 268 |
| 10.35-44 | 227 | 2.7 | 31 |
| 10.45 | 227, | 2.9 | 38 |
| | 228, 271 | 2.11 | 56 |
| 12.13-17 | 165 | 2.16-19 | 30 |
| 12.17 | 201 | 2.19 | 284 |
| 12.26-27 | 244 | 2.21 | 282 |
| 12.29-31 | 206 | 2.22-40 | 284 |
| 14.24 | 189 | 2.22 | 282, 283 |
| 14.26 | 189 | 2.26-27 | 282 |
| 14.32-42 | 38 | 2.26 | 282 |
| 14.35-36 | 38 | 2.27 | 282 |
| 14.36 | 36 | 2.29-32 | 283 |
| 14.36a | 38 | 2.31-32 | 282 |
| 14.36b | 39 | 2.33-35 | 210 |
| 14.37 | 36, 38 | 2.34-5 | 282 |
| 14.43-52 | 39 | 2.34 | 211, 284 |
| 14.45 | 36, 40 | 2.36 | 282 |
| 14.48-49 | 40 | 3.1-3 | 28 |
| 14.50 | 41 | 3.22 | 4 |
| 14.51-52 | 41 | 4.18-19 | 74 |
| 15.1-15 | 28 | 4.18 | 243 |
| 15.27ff | 28 | 4.20 | 56, 244 |
| 15.21-39 | 41 | 6.15 | 254 |
| 15.42-47 | 44 | 7.22 | 259 |
| 15.43 | 45, 46 | 7.36-50 | 43 |
| 16.1-8 | 48 | 7.37 | 43 |
| | | 7.38 | 43 |
| *Luke* | | 7.48 | 43 |
| 1.26-38 | 31, 75 | 7.50 | 43 |
| 1.26 | 64 | 9.1-6 | 224 |

314

## INDEX OF BIBLICAL REFERENCES

| | | | |
|---|---|---|---|
| 9.35 | 4 | 1.14 | 21, 23, 52, 60, 255, 284 |
| 10.1-2 | 293 | | |
| 10.8 | 293 | 1.18 | 60 |
| 10.25-37 | 128 | 1.29 | 43, 55, 64 |
| 10.27-28 | 268 | 2.5 | 42 |
| 10.37 | 206 | 3.3 | 223 |
| 12.32-34 | 259 | 3.16 | 27 |
| 12.34 | 202 | 5.25-26 | 4 |
| 14.13-14 | 259 | 5.31-47 | 246 |
| 20.25 | 201 | 5.36b-37a | 246 |
| 22.1-23.56 | 267 | 5.43 | 244 |
| 22.14-23 | 267 | 6.52-59 | 235 |
| 22.24 | 267 | 6.54 | 234 |
| 22.26 | 267 | 10.3 | 4 |
| 22.37 | 268 | 10.4 | 4 |
| 22.39-46 | 38 | 12.28 | 4 |
| 22.42 | 38 | 12.32 | 207 |
| 22.43-44 | 38 | 13.5 | 207 |
| 22.43 | 38 | 13.34 | 40 |
| 22.44 | 38 | 14.5 | 254 |
| 22.47-53 | 39 | 14.6 | 159, 255 |
| 22.51 | 41 | 14.11 | 60 |
| 22.52-53 | 41 | 14.25-27 | 244 |
| 22.54 | 41 | 14.26 | 77 |
| 23.26 | 41 | 16.13 | 160 |
| 23.32-49 | 41 | 17.18 | 77 |
| 23.34 | 43, 58, 294 | 17.24 | 244 |
| | | 18.1-19.42 | 96 |
| 23.50-56 | 44 | 18.2-11 | 39 |
| 23.50 | 45 | 18.3 | 40 |
| 23.51 | 45 | 18.10 | 41 |
| 23.53 | 46 | 18.15-18 | 262 |
| 24.1-12 | 48 | 18.25-27 | 262 |
| 24.25-26 | 5 | 18.36 | 45, 51 |
| 24.34 | 48 | 18.37 | 96 |
| | | 18.38 | 96 |
| *John* | | 19.17-30 | 41 |
| 1.1 | 21, 23 | 19.23 | 41, 263 |
| 1.12-14 | 31 | 19.25 | 41, 43 |
| 1.12-13 | 21 | 19.26-27 | 36, 42, 55 |

315

| | | | |
|---|---|---|---|
| 19.27 | 42 | 2.3 | 255 |
| 19.30 | 44 | 2.4 | 260 |
| 19.34 | 41, 44, 207 | 2.14-36 | 260 |
| 19.35 | 42 | 2.14 | 74, 264 |
| 19.38-42 | 44 | 2.16-21 | 73, 260 |
| 19.38 | 36, 45 | 2.17-21 | 66 |
| 19.41 | 36, 50 | 2.32 | 46, 49 |
| 19.42 | 36 | 2.36 | 73 |
| 20.1-10 | 48 | 2.37-39 | 75 |
| 20.11-18 | 48 | 2.38 | 74 |
| 20.21-22 | 224 | 2.42 | 74 |
| 20.22 | 207 | 2.43-47 | 268 |
| 20.24-29 | 251, 256 | 2.44-45 | 74 |
| 20.25 | 254 | 3.1-10 | 264 |
| 20.28 | 244, 254 | 3.1 | 259 |
| 20.29 | 254 | 3.6 | 259, 260 |
| 21.7-8 | 48 | 3.10-11 | 260 |
| 21.11 | 261, 263 | 3.12-26 | 260 |
| 21.15-19 | 225, 261, 264, 280 | 3.12 | 260 |
| | | 3.13-16 | 260 |
| 21.15-17 | 243, 261 | 3.13-15 | 244 |
| 21.15 | 262 | 3.15 | 263 |
| 21.16 | 262 | 3.20 | 260 |
| 21.17 | 262 | 5.35-37 | 28 |
| 21.18-19 | 262 | 6.1-2 | 268 |
| 21.19 | 261 | 6.1 | 268 |
| 21.24 | 42 | 6.2 | 58, 268-9 |
| | | 6.3-6 | 33, 65 |
| *Acts of the Apostles* | | 6.3 | 268 |
| 1.4-5 | 49 | 6.6-7 | 58 |
| 1.8 | 5, 224, 228 | 6.8 | 57, 269 |
| 1.12-14 | 74 | 7.2-53 | 125 |
| 1.13 | 254 | 7.51-53 | 125 |
| 1.14 | 49, 263 | 7.54-8.1 | 33 |
| 1.15 | 241 | 7.54-60 | 125, 269 |
| 1.21-26 | 241 | 7.55 | 125 |
| 1.26 | 74 | 7.56 | 125 |
| 2.1-4 | 12, 73 | 7.58 | 58 |
| 2.1 | 74 | 7.59 | 58, 126 |
| 2.2-3 | 74 | 7.60 | 58, 126 |

# INDEX OF BIBLICAL REFERENCES

| | | | |
|---|---|---|---|
| 8.4-40 | 269 | 8.22-23 | 81 |
| 8.5-6 | 269 | 8.22 | 82, 291 |
| 8.31 | 114 | 8.23 | 81, 82, 215 |
| 8.38 | 115 | 8.24-25 | 81 |
| 9.1-20 | 235 | 8.24 | 215, 221 |
| 9.1-3 | 49 | 8.25 | 221 |
| 9.3 | 232 | 8.26-27 | 82, 291 |
| 9.5 | 49 | 8.26 | 82, 222 |
| 9.15 | 49 | 8.27 | 219 |
| 9.31 | 67, 229 | 8.28 | 219 |
| 10.34-35 | 183 | 8.31-39 | 291 |
| 13.52 | 67 | 8.31 | 120 |
| 14.17 | 160 | 8.32 | 60 |
| 14.27 | 93 | 8.34 | 221, 222 |
| 17.26 | 160 | 8.37-39 | 151 |
| 20.28 | 253, 255 | 8.39 | 150, 215, 221 |
| 21.8-9 | 269 | 9-11 | 150 |
| | | 10.17-18 | 3 |
| *Romans* | | 10.18 | 65 |
| 1.1 | 63 | 11.17 | 161 |
| 1.8 | 150 | 11.25-26 | 150 |
| 2.6-7 | 160 | 11.26-27 | 150 |
| 2.11 | 209 | 12.1-2 | 215 |
| 5.1-5 | 81 | 12.1 | 239 |
| 5.2 | 213 | 12.9 | 199 |
| 5.5 | 114 | 13.8-10 | 150, 206 |
| 6.3-11 | 291 | 14.17 | 207 |
| 6.5 | 79 | 15.5-6 | 220 |
| 6.5b | 291 | 15.15-17 | 64 |
| 6.11 | 63 | 15.16-17 | 150 |
| 8 | 8, 150, 221 | | |
| 8.11-29 | 87 | *1 Corinthians* | |
| 8.11 | 82 | 1.30 | 70 |
| 8.18-27 | 291 | 2.2 | 49 |
| 8.18-25 | 34, 81 | 2.15-16 | 110 |
| 8.18 | 214, 221 | 2.16 | 58, 70 |
| 8.18a | 220 | 11.26 | 235 |
| 8.18b | 219 | 12.4-13 | 9 |
| 8.19 | 221 | 12.4ff | 79 |
| 8.21 | 221 | | |

| | | | |
|---|---|---|---|
| 12.12–13 | 74, 79 | *Ephesians* | |
| 13.1–3 | 209 | 2.19–22 | 256 |
| 13.13 | 215 | 2.19–20 | 253 |
| 15.3–11 | 28 | 2.22 | 253 |
| 15.4 | 37 | 4.4–6 | 9 |
| 15.20–28 | 50 | 4.5 | 224 |
| 15.20–24 | 37 | 4.11–13 | 9 |
| 15.20 | 49, 52 | 4.11 | 224 |
| 15.23 | 2 | | |
| 15.26 | 42, 47, 56 | *Philippians* | |
| | | 1.1 | 227, 269 |
| 15.45–50 | 52 | 1.21 | 279 |
| 15.51–57 | 291 | 1.27 | 66 |
| 15.54–55 | 56 | 2.1–5 | 58 |
| 15.57 | 56 | 2.1 | 70 |
| | | 2.3 | 70 |
| *2 Corinthians* | | 2.5–6 | 58 |
| 2.14 | 294 | 2.5 | 70 |
| 4.1 | 253 | 2.6–8 | 58 |
| 4.4 | 8 | 2.6–7 | 279 |
| 4.5 | 8 | 2.9–11 | 279 |
| 4.7 | 62, 226 | 2.11 | 60 |
| 5.18–19 | 159 | 3.20 | 219 |
| 5.20 | 109 | 4.4–7 | 75 |
| 8.7 | 32 | | |
| 8.9 | 32 | *Colossians* | |
| 12.1–10 | 275 | 1.11–14 | 3 |
| 12.9 | 271 | 1.19–20 | 44 |
| 13.14 | 78, 83 | 3.16 | 189 |
| | | | |
| *Galatians* | | *1 Thessalonians* | |
| 1.11–20 | 264 | 1.9 | 244 |
| 1.15–16 | 109, 224 | 2.1–8 | 253 |
| 4.1–7 | 105 | | |
| 4.4–6 | 60, 78 | *2 Thessalonians* | |
| 5.1 | 79, 114 | 2.13–17 | 293 |
| 5.16–17 | 79 | | |
| 5.22–24 | 58 | *1 Timothy* | |
| 5.22–23 | 79, 84 | 1.3 | 225 |

## INDEX OF BIBLICAL REFERENCES

| | | | |
|---|---|---|---|
| 2.4 | 160 | 9.11 | 63 |
| 2.5-6 | 63 | 11.1 | 213, 219 |
| 2.5 | 159 | 13.20 | 47 |
| 3.1-13 | 269 | | |
| 3.1 | 225, 251 | *James* | |
| 4.7-8 | 6 | 2.17 | 118 |
| 4.14 | 265 | | |
| | | *1 Peter* | |
| *2 Timothy* | | 2.2-3 | 223 |
| 1.10 | 52 | 5.1-4 | 240 |
| 4.7 | 264 | | |
| | | *2 Peter* | |
| *Titus* | | 1.11 | 52 |
| 1.5 | 225 | | |
| 3.4-7 | 76 | *1 John* | |
| | | 1.3 | 289 |
| *Hebrews* | | 1.7 | 289 |
| 1.1-2 | 23 | | |
| 2.14-18 | 284 | *Revelation (Apocalypse)* | |
| 2.17 | 279 | 2.28 | 129 |
| 4.14-16 | 251 | 21.5 | 44 |
| 5.5-10 | 251, 265 | 21.23ff | 150 |
| 5.6 | 226 | 22.1-2 | 50 |
| 7.25 | 63 | | |

# Index of Proper Names and Subjects

Aaron 271
*Abba*, See God
Abraham 162, 187, 188, 244, 260
Adam 39, 52
Aelred of Rievaulx, Saint 280, 286n9
*Agape* 272
Aid agency workers 220, 221
Allen Hall Seminary, Chelsea 259
Altar 53, 66, 270, 271
Altarpiece 7, 30–71, 74, 306
   centre piece 30–35, 47, 48, 54, 56, 59
   predella 36–53, 54, 55, 60
Amsterdam 170, 172, 192
Angels 31, 38, 47, 48, 49, 56, 64, 170, 232
Anna (prophetess) 282
Annunciation, See Mary, Blessed Virgin.
Anointing of the sick 224, 263
Antony, Saint (of Egypt) 227, 229n2
Apostle 49, 63, 225, 240, 254–6
Apostolic age 63

Apostolic commission 70n11, 109, 151
Aquinas, Saint Thomas 17, 54, 61, 70n14, 96, 214, 219, 254, 257n6, 300, 308
   *Summa Theologiae* 70nn15&17, 222nn2&5, 300–1
Aristotle 166
Art (religious) 29, 35, 67n1, 68nn4&8, 117, 216
   exhibitions 117, 127n7
Ascension, *See* Jesus Christ
Assumption, *See* Mary, Blessed Virgin
Augustine of Hippo, Saint, 15, 25n4, 95, 105, 112, 127n4, 169, 181n62, 200–3, 211n1, 257n4, 275n3, 298–9, 307
   *City of God* 200–3, 211nn1–7&9–10, 299
   *Confessions* 95, 107n3, 169, 178n30, 298–9
   *The Trinity* 105, 206, 211n11, 299
Augustus, Caesar 27
Auschwitz 169, 170, 174, 179n32, 192, 308

# INDEX OF PROPER NAMES AND SUBJECTS

Baha'is 163
Baptism 4, 5, 12, 51, 66, 74, 76,
  77, 78, 79, 115, 223, 224,
  228, 252, 263, 271, 288, 291
Beatification 134, 147n4, 232,
  233, 235, 247nn6&8
Beautiful Gate, *See* Temple
  (Jerusalem),
Beauty
  pathway of 116–7
Beda College, Rome 259
Bede the Venerable, Saint 6, 8,
  109–29, 300, 308
  *Ecclesiastical History* 122,
    126–7, 127n1,
    128nn17–20, 300
  *Letter to Egbert* 110, 127n1
  *Commentary on the Song of
    Songs* 111, 127n2
  *Commentary on the Acts of the
    Apostles* 125–6
  *Commentary on the Revelation
    of St John* 129n21
Benedict, Saint 229n2, 279,
  285nn5&7
  *The Rule of St Benedict*
    229n2, 285n7
Benedict XVI, Pope (Emeritus)
  70n18, 96–7, 102, 105,
  107n4, 116, 118, 121, 124,
  128nn12&15, 134–5, 136, 141,
  143–5, 148nn28–30, 162,
  164–9, 178n20, 206, 222n1,
  233, 235–40, 241, 242, 244,
  247nn6–13, 248nn14–17,
  265n3, 286n10, 302–3, 307
  Apostolic visit to the
    UK, 116, 134–6, 141–2,
    147nn4–6, 148nn26–7, 164,
    165–9, 178nn24–5&28–9,
    248n16, 303
  *Caritas in Veritate* 102,
    108n11, 302
  *Deus caritas est* 105, 118,
    128n9, 202, 203, 205, 206,
    208, 209, 247n4, 302
  *Jesus of Nazareth* 96, 97,
    107nn4–6, 286n10
  *Spe salvi* 222n3, 302
Bentham, Jeremy 138–9
Bereaved
  comfort of 293
Berechurch 185, 197nn2–3
Bethlehem 34, 56, 63
Bible 143, 165, 181n62, 211n1,
  217, 297
  *See also* Scripture, Sacred.
Bishop, *See* Episcopate.
Blessedness 28, 61, 65, 214, 218
Blessed Virgin Mary
  *See* Mary, Blessed Virgin.
Body of Christ 36, 37, 39, 45,
  46, 47, 51, 54, 79, 160, 208,
  237, 239, 264
Bonhoeffer, Dietrich 295n4
Boord, Mother Mary Angela
  100–2, 107, 107n9, 108n10
Bread
  and wine 54, 63, 271
  of heaven 234
  *See also* Eucharist and Mass.
Brougham, Henry 138–9
Buddhism 162–3

Caedmon 126–7, 128nn17–20
CAFOD (Catholic
  Agency for Overseas
  Development) 118

## INDEX OF PROPER NAMES AND SUBJECTS

Calling 4–5, 60, 87, 97–8, 161,
    226–7, 279, 291
  baptismal 5
  priestly 5, 60, 224, 226, 228
  prophetic 5, 87n2, 224
  royal 5, 224
*Caritas* (*See* also Love) 5,
    59, 102, 105, 118, 150,
    199–212, 302
*Catechism of the Catholic Church*
    (*CCC*) 265n3, 301
Catherine of Siena, Saint
    6, 10n1
  *The Dialogue on Divine*
    *Revelation* 10n1
Catholic
  Catholic Church 8, 108n13,
    127n6, 132, 145, 150, 153,
    158–9, 162, 164, 197n2,
    209, 223, 265n3, 301
  Catholic schools 7, 8, 80,
    89–108, 131, 134–5, 145,
    146, 194, 282
  Catholic higher education
    7, 89, 90, 93, 104, 110, 111,
    127n3, 131–148, 164, 169,
    275, 282
  Catholic Bishops' Conference
    of England & Wales
    90, 104, 177n10, 183,
    212n13, 303
  *Choosing the Common Good*
    108n12, 303
  *Meeting God in Friend*
    *and Stranger* 127n6,
    177nn10&19, 183,
    212n13, 303
Catholicism 108n15, 110,
    157–164, 167

Catholic Social Teaching 99,
    203, 204, 205, 210
Cerreto Ciampoli, Siena 53, 57
Charity 8, 32, 118, 125, 164, 195,
    201, 206–8, 210, 216,
    220–1, 226–7, 244, 256,
    268–70, 272–3, 288, 302
Chastity 227, 279
Christ, *See* Jesus Christ.
Christmas 25n4, 28, 29, 30, 32,
    35, 212n14, 247n10
Cicero 211n1
Classical education
    137–8, 211n1
  classical civilization 137
  classical languages 138
Clement of Rome 213, 222,
    269, 298, 307
Collegiality 237
Common Good 3, 84, 90, 93,
    98, 99, 102, 103, 140, 141,
    146, 150, 168, 184, 201, 203,
    221, 229, 303
*Communio* 77–8, 273, 288, 289
Communion 21, 54, 64, 106,
    223, 234, 244, 271–3, 277,
    287, 288–9
  *See* also Eucharist and Mass.
Community 76–9, 193–7
Compassion 5, 6, 7, 45, 51, 60,
    69n10, 90, 92, 132, 146,
    163, 170, 174, 187, 189,
    196, 204, 208, 216, 221,
    227, 245, 261, 272, 281,
    282, 284
Confession (Sacrament of) 93,
    224, 263, 277
Confirmation (Sacrament
    of) 223

## INDEX OF PROPER NAMES AND SUBJECTS

Conscience 83, 84, 96, 102, 143, 160, 203
Consecrated Life (Religious Orders) 9, 124, 227, 228, 277–86
Contemplation 40, 43, 54, 59, 60, 67, 85, 142–3, 170–2, 176, 280–1, 285n6, 288
Cornelius 183
Cosmos 21, 50, 228, 291
Covenant 150, 161, 187, 189, 217–8, 222n4, 224
Creation
 divine creation 11, 39, 61, 81, 85, 126, 187, 291, 294
 ecological conversion 84
 groaning of 81, 82, 86, 87n5, 291
 relationship with 7, 34, 83, 86, 144
 restoration of divine will for 37, 47, 50, 61, 82, 224, 291
Crucifixion, *See* Jesus Christ.
Couve de Murville, Archbishop Maurice 186

Darkness 3, 4, 9, 24, 192, 213, 233, 248n22, 255, 291
Darwin, Charles 138
David, King of Israel 190
Davis, Fr Francis (Frank) 185–6, 197n3
Death, *See* Jesus Christ, death of.
 the last enemy 47, 56
 victory over 42, 44, 47, 52, 56, 126
de Montfort, Saint Louis Marie Grignion 232, 246n1
Desert, Silent 18, 19, 22, 26n5

Devotion 18, 27, 28, 45, 53, 57, 67, 93, 127n7, 202, 246n1, 289
Diaconate (Deacons) 9, 33, 57, 58, 65, 151, 224, 225, 226, 227, 267–76
*Diakonia* 226, 227, 268, 274
Dialogue
 Inter-religious Dialogue, 1, 149–50, 153, 157–164, 165, 169, 176n1, 177nn10–11&17, 183–197, 209–210, 221
 principles of dialogue 157–161, 238
Dickens, Charles 155
*Didache* 269, 298
Disciples 1, 3, 5, 15, 36, 38, 40, 41, 42, 45, 46, 48, 49, 51, 67, 76, 77, 79, 207, 261, 285n1, 287
 missionary disciples 1, 3, 4, 66, 67, 76, 228, 288
Discipleship 3, 29, 42, 260, 261, 281, 295
*Divine Office (DO)* (*Liturgy of the Hours*) 299
dos Santos, Lúcia de Jesus Rosa, (Lúcia of Fatima) 231
Dublin University (now University College Dublin) 136
Dunn, Bishop Kevin 109, 111, 127n3
Durham University
 Bede Chair of Catholic Theology 110, 111, 127n3
 Centre for Catholic Studies 104

## INDEX OF PROPER NAMES AND SUBJECTS

Easter 28, 29, 74, 197n3
   Maundy Thursday 26n9
   Good Friday 28, 43, 180n42
   Easter Vigil 66, 223
   Easter Sunday 68n8
Eckhart, Meister 14–22, 25, 25nn2&4, 26n9, 181n62
Ecology, *See* Creation.
Eden, Garden of 39, 50
Education 91–151
   and formation of character 99–103
   and the human person 92, 95, 106, 135
   deficiencies of utilitarian philosophy 99, 135, 138–140, 157
   lifelong learning 7
   partnerships 92–3
   school 91–108
   university 131–151
Edward the Confessor, Saint 26n7
Elijah 5
Engelmar Unzeitig, Fr 278, 285n4
Environment, *See* Creation.
Episcopate 57, 65, 211n8, 224, 225, 251–7, 269
Erbil 220, 222n6
Eternal Life 4, 29, 32, 214, 218, 234, 247n7, 291
Eternity 15, 21, 62, 77, 112, 203, 234, 283
Ethics (Morals)
   ethical formation 34, 37, 91, 102, 103, 104, 119, 136, 202, 222n4
   ethical principles 4, 84, 104, 117, 119, 131, 135, 141, 142, 153, 163, 165, 166, 167, 168, 197n3, 200, 204, 288, 290, 309
Eucharist 54, 57, 59, 60, 67, 208, 224, 234, 235, 238, 264, 265n1, 267, 269, 271, 272, 273, 277, 289
   *See* also Communion and Mass.
Eusebius 299
   *History of the Church* 49, 266n4
Evangelists 269 *See* also Gospels.
Evangelization 58, 62, 64, 66, 76, 79, 93, 109, 128n12, 133, 136, 140, 145, 146, 177n17, 227, 228, 261, 273, 283, 284, 288, 289, 290, 293
Eve 39
Evil
   goodness in the midst of 174, 192
   overcoming of 58, 213
   *See* also Darkness and Sin.
Exodus 10n2, 187, 244

Faith
   contemplative faith 142
   faith, hope and love (theological virtues) 105–7, 151, 248n22, 253
   gate of faith (*porta fidei*) 261, 265n3
   journey of faith 11, 169–70, 219
   mystery of faith 11–12, 75, 113, 238

## INDEX OF PROPER NAMES AND SUBJECTS

voice of faith 109–129,
  131–148
Family 29, 32, 33, 52, 56, 89, 97,
  98, 120, 123, 133, 154, 162,
  169, 170, 189, 192, 194, 205,
  217, 220, 226, 245, 249n25,
  252, 259, 273, 275, 278,
  280, 282, 283, 288, 303
Fathers of the Church 6,
  128n15, 297–9, 307
Fatima
  Our Lady of Fatima
    231–2, 235
  See also Mary, Blessed Virgin
First-fruits 2
Fisher, Saint John 89
Forgiveness 43, 51, 69n10, 74,
  77, 126, 187, 188, 190, 255,
  261, 293
Formation 79, 92, 98, 99, 132,
  136, 216, 237, 259
Francis de Sales, Saint
  245, 249n26
  *Treatise on the Love of
    God*, 249n26
Francis of Assisi, Saint 14, 25n1,
  64, 80, 87n4, 118, 128n10,
  176n2, 242–3, 248n22,
  285n6, 300, 309
  *Canticle of the Creatures*
    80, 87n4
Francis, Pope 2, 7, 39, 67, 76, 80,
  83, 85, 86, 87nn3&6, 228,
  240–49, 273, 275n3, 277,
  278, 285n1, 287, 303
  *Amoris Laetitia* 249n25, 303
  *Apostolic Letter to all
    Consecrated People* 277,
    285nn1–3

*Evangelii Gaudium* 2, 3, 7,
  9, 39, 66, 67, 76, 93, 228,
  249n24, 288, 303
*Laudato Si'* 7, 80–87,
  248n21, 303
Francis Xavier, Saint
  243, 248n23
Freedom 4, 20, 32–4, 35, 47, 63,
  79, 82, 85, 96, 98, 101, 102,
  114, 144, 160, 165, 166, 170,
  172, 202, 239, 244, 274
Friendship 1, 85, 98, 133, 135,
  164, 209, 235, 280, 286n9
Friends of the Holy
  Land 194–5
Frost, Robert 35–6, 68n3

Gabriel (Archangel) 31, 48, 49, 64
Gaza 8, 193–7
Generosity 32–3, 35, 61, 69, 196,
  207, 215–16, 261, 280
Genre 53
Germany 15, 26n4, 143, 145,
  173, 185, 186, 278
Gethsemane, Garden of 37
Ghudwara 154
Glorification, *See* Jesus Christ.
Glory 5, 8, 11, 21, 32, 57, 60, 81,
  84, 93, 126, 150, 153, 190,
  202, 203, 213, 214, 219, 221,
  224, 235, 238, 246, 253,
  283, 293
God
  *abba* 36, 38, 105
  blessings of 3, 29, 45, 47, 54,
    60, 67, 75, 79, 82, 125–6,
    189, 190, 209, 235, 240,
    241, 243, 270, 271, 291,
    293, 295n3

## INDEX OF PROPER NAMES AND SUBJECTS

Creator 10, 82, 83, 113, 126, 135, 145, 149, 159, 162, 201, 204, 205, 219, 281
  depths of 13–26, 34
  forgiveness of 43, 51, 69, 74, 77, 126, 187, 188, 255
  gifts of 3, 9, 12, 22, 28, 32, 33, 47, 67, 74, 79, 81, 82, 85, 87n2, 96, 103, 114, 119, 123, 126, 128n17, 160, 188, 189, 215, 219, 224, 245, 251, 259, 260, 263, 264, 270, 279, 280, 283, 291
  goodness of 77, 113, 116–19, 124, 126, 160, 170, 173, 204, 218, 226, 282, 288
  journey to 1, 8, 11, 18, 25, 29, 42, 52, 53, 56, 75, 79, 93, 123, 153–181, 187, 210, 215, 219, 223, 233, 247n12, 271, 277, 284n1
  knowledge of 12, 25, 91, 135, 167, 204, 243, 248n22, 294
  love of 25, 37, 54, 64, 69n10, 105, 118, 150, 187, 189, 194, 208, 209, 241, 249n26, 261, 283, 289
  lure of 6, 13–26, 66, 181n62
  manifestation of 1, 11, 54, 77, 82, 85, 105, 118, 126–7, 146, 151, 181n60, 199–212, 213, 271, 272–3, 274, 291, 294
  *See* also Theophany.
  mercy of 9, 51, 64, 77, 85, 87n7, 194, 206, 207, 220, 228, 245, 247n6, 249n27, 253, 255, 284, 289–94, 295nn3, 5&6
  mystery of 11, 12, 16, 17, 18, 20–1, 23, 55, 60, 77, 78, 80, 113, 218, 223, 237, 256, 281, 288–9
  presence of 1, 7, 15, 31, 54, 78, 85, 95, 119, 123, 160–1, 174, 194, 208, 218, 234, 240, 252, 281, 282, 292, 293
  relationship with 1, 6, 55, 74, 77, 95, 97–8, 103, 123, 137–8, 161–2, 172, 215, 239, 265n3, 281
  revelation of, *See* Revelation.
  transcendence of 16–18, 22, 47, 62, 92, 117, 132, 180n55, 283
  the Father 2, 4, 11, 21, 27–30, 32, 36, 38, 39, 40, 43–47, 51, 53–56, 60–2, 65, 74–9, 83, 86, 105–6, 125, 160, 185, 207, 225, 233, 237, 239, 244, 251, 259–60, 268, 271–2, 274, 277, 281–3, 289, 291
  the Son, *See* Jesus Christ.
  the Holy Spirit, *See*, Holy Spirit.
  *See* also Trinity, Blessed.
  voice of 4–5, 127
  will of 22, 27, 37, 38–9, 40, 47, 53, 65, 79, 83, 175, 180n58, 268, 282
Goodness
  of God, *See* God, goodness of.
  pathway of 117–9
Good News 28, 49, 85, 197n10, 243, 261
  *See* also Gospel.

# INDEX OF PROPER NAMES AND SUBJECTS

Good Shepherd, *See* Jesus Christ.
Gospel 2, 3, 8, 9, 33, 35, 41, 48, 49, 50, 51, 57, 58, 59, 63, 65, 66, 67, 70n10, 76, 81, 83, 87n2, 109, 114, 118, 150, 181n62, 204, 205, 206, 210, 225, 228, 232, 240, 243, 246, 249n24, 254, 255, 260, 261, 265n1, 269, 270, 271, 283, 285nn1&6, 290, 292, 294, 295n5, 303
  Book of the Gospels 48, 57, 254, 255, 270
  Gospel-bearers 270
Grace 4, 15, 22, 24, 28, 32, 42, 54, 57, 66, 67, 75, 79, 85, 110, 114, 150, 160, 173, 176, 204, 205, 209, 213, 219, 226, 234, 241, 260, 263, 264, 270, 278, 290
  costly grace 290, 295n4
Greek 186, 226, 265n1, 268, 297
Gregory the Great, Pope Saint 201, 211n8, 299, 308
  *Pastoral Rule* 199, 211n8, 299

Handel, George Frideric 113
Happiness 94, 103, 214, 218–9, 234, 282
  *See* also Blessedness.
Harmony
  of the created world 34, 35, 37, 66, 163
  of the faithful within the Church 56–7, 228, 275
  with others 29, 90–1, 117, 132, 149, 162–3, 183, 202, 204, 210, 216–7
  with God 15, 37, 66, 207

Hawkins, Edward 136
Heart,
  listening heart 143–5, 148n28
Hebrew 186, 297
Heaven 2, 5, 23, 38, 47–8, 51, 54, 55, 56, 59, 64, 93, 117, 124, 125–6, 127n7, 146, 187, 190, 202, 203, 207, 218, 219, 222, 223, 228, 232, 233, 234–5, 243, 251, 253, 270, 271, 282
  heavenly city 202–3
Herod (the Great) 27
Hillesum, Etty (Esther) 169–181, 193, 197n8, 309
Hinduism 162
Holocaust, *See Shoah.*
Holiness 65, 70n11, 150, 159, 161, 173, 215, 234, 239, 245, 282
Holy Communion 54, 223, 271
  *See* also Eucharist and Mass.
Holy Family (Jesus, Mary, Joseph) 56
Holy Orders 224, 226, 228, 270, 271, 273
Holy Spirit
  and baptism 12, 49, 51, 76–9, 223, 224
  and creation 7, 80–6, 145, 291
  and faith 12, 219, 244
  and mission 7, 76–9, 244
  and prayer 82, 222, 291–2
  and prophecy 5, 85, 282
  descent of 49, 66, 73–5, 83, 126, 251, 255
  fruits of 79, 84
  gifts of 79, 215, 224, 270
  mighty wind 74

## INDEX OF PROPER NAMES AND SUBJECTS

power of 5, 27, 31, 61, 75, 78, 84, 210, 215, 269, 272, 291–2
tongues of fire 74, 255
wisdom of 7, 12, 54, 79, 85, 145, 223, 282
Holy Week 107n4
Homily 224, 231–95
Hope 105–7, 124–7, 149–51, 193–7, 213–222
fragments of hope 215–7
hope of heavenly glory 5, 93, 124–5, 214–5, 218–9, 221–2
Hopkins, Gerard Manley 257n6
Humanism 95, 220, 255, 308
Christian humanism 220, 255
Human person 21–2, 92, 95, 106, 135, 203
dignity of 80, 83, 85, 95, 97, 99, 103, 125, 149, 160, 168, 203, 245, 294, 302
Hume, Cardinal Basil 15, 25n3, 129n21
Humility 24, 39, 55, 58, 69n10, 70n11, 164, 183, 189, 203, 227, 241, 243, 278
Hymn of Simeon (*Nunc dimittis*) 210–11, 212n15, 283

Iconography 37, 41, 48, 50, 67, 68n4
Identity
in relationship with God 97
in relationship with others 98, 218
priestly 225–6
Idolatry 16, 132, 175, 244

Ignatius Loyola, Saint 243, 248n23
Ignatius of Antioch, Saint 274–5, 298
*Epistle to the Magnesians*, 275n4, 276n5
Imagination 6, 24, 30, 74, 157, 215, 255
Image of God 6, 9, 11, 19, 20, 32, 95, 160, 221, 288
Incarnation, *See* Jesus Christ.
Inter-religious dialogue, *See* Dialogue.
Isaac 244, 260
Islam 162, 176n1
Israel 187–190, 192, 193, 244–5, 265n1, 282

Jacob 244, 260
Jains 163
Jerome, Saint 34, 58, 65, 298
*Commentary on Isaiah* 71n19, 298
Jerusalem 8, 37, 46, 48, 49, 51, 74, 107n4, 188, 190–3, 259, 271, 282, 297
Jesus Christ 27–71
ascension of 5, 49, 57
baptism of 4
birth of 7, 15, 22, 23, 25n4, 28, 30, 31–2, 35, 38, 54–7, 60, 62, 69n9, 75, 122, 268
crucifixion of 28, 36, 41, 45, 49, 55, 60, 106, 125, 239, 248n22, 262, 266n4
death of 28, 30, 37, 38, 39, 42–6, 47, 49, 52, 53, 54, 56, 57, 60, 61, 62, 63, 76, 81, 125, 175, 181n60, 213, 290

divinity of 39, 52, 60, 61, 75, 106
Emmanuel 31, 35
faith in 106, 221
glorification of 2, 49, 63, 74, 109, 235, 260
Good Shepherd 4, 10, 171
High Priest 63, 239, 251, 265n1, 279
humanity of 39, 51–2
incarnation of 2, 16, 23, 31, 34–5, 52, 54–7, 60, 61, 63, 65, 69n9, 76, 105, 106, 119, 122, 159, 175, 180n59, 211, 255, 272, 301
Lamb of God 43, 55
Lord 5, 8, 15, 28, 32, 45, 56, 58, 60, 61, 66, 69n9, 70n10, 73, 74, 75, 80, 110, 112, 123, 124, 126, 208, 213, 224, 226, 227, 234, 236, 238, 240, 251, 253, 254, 257n4, 261–4, 265n3, 266n4, 270, 271–2, 275, 279, 280, 281–2, 283, 284, 285n1, 287, 289, 295n6
Mediator 63, 159
ministry of 2, 9, 23, 28, 31, 40, 53, 57, 59, 60, 74, 76, 82, 85, 126, 220, 221, 224–8, 267–8, 273, 290–1
mystery of 7, 27–71, 159
person of 1, 22, 52, 60–2, 112, 113, 132, 224, 244, 263
prayer of 77, 239, 277
Precious Blood 238–9
Redeemer 4, 10, 233–4, 247n2, 295n6
resurrection of 2, 5, 7, 28, 30, 37, 46–53, 54, 56, 57, 60, 61, 62, 63, 76, 81, 107n4, 125, 175, 181n61, 213, 221, 261, 290
Sacred Heart of 44, 278, 285n5
Saviour 52, 60, 282, 294
Son 4, 11, 23, 27, 28, 30, 41, 42, 44, 51, 53, 55, 60, 61, 65, 74, 75, 76, 77, 78, 105, 106, 160, 181n60, 207, 209, 225, 232, 233, 234, 237, 244, 251, 254, 255, 256, 272, 279, 281, 283
Son of God 15, 32, 38, 45, 47, 49, 159, 232, 254
Son of Man 125, 227, 292
suffering of 2, 38, 41, 44, 58, 69n10
Suffering Servant 268
teaching of 3, 14, 35, 40, 96, 202, 205, 206, 227, 255, 270, 290
transfiguration of 4, 5
Word of God 21–5, 27, 28, 31, 52, 60, 65, 112–4, 119, 124, 159, 206, 211, 238, 255, 273, 284, 301
John Paul II, Pope Saint 68n8, 70n16, 140–1, 148n25, 158, 160, 161, 163, 176n2, 177nn11, 18&19, 178n22, 179n32, 188, 210–11, 212n15, 231–235, 242, 245, 246n1, 247nn2–3, 6&8, 309
  *Ex Corde Ecclesia* 141, 148n25
  *Redemptoris Mater* 233, 247nn2–3
John XXIII, Pope Saint 76, 287
John, Saint (Evangelist) 38, 41, 45, 129n21, 259, 261

## INDEX OF PROPER NAMES AND SUBJECTS

John Southworth, Saint 264
John the Baptist, Saint 28, 34, 55, 64, 112, 127n4
Joseph of Arimathea 36, 45–6
Joseph, Saint (Spouse of the Blessed Virgin Mary) 30, 31, 56, 65, 282–4
Joy
   of the Gospel 2, 58, 67, 249n24, 303
   See also *Evangelii Gaudium*.
Judaism 104, 108n15, 161, 162, 187
Judgement (Eschatological) 56, 69n10, 110, 213, 224, 246, 290, 292
Julian of Norwich
   *Revelations of Divine Love* 65, 71n20
Justice 3, 5, 34, 40, 83, 91, 103, 132, 143, 145, 158, 163, 166, 199–205, 208–9, 211n8, 214, 243, 245, 290
   See also Law and Peace.
Justin, Saint 298
   *The First Apology* 71n21

Kerygma 260, 283
Kingdom of God (God's Kingdom) 3, 45, 51–3, 67, 105, 109–10, 124, 125, 126, 190, 210, 218, 227, 234, 259, 270, 273, 274
Kneeling 43, 57, 58, 117, 171–3
Knowledge (Wisdom) 12, 25, 91, 135, 138–40, 145, 146, 147n11, 167, 184, 204, 243, 248n22, 294
Kolbe, Saint Maximilian Mary 278

Latin 74, 139, 186, 265n1, 273, 297, 301
Law 80, 131, 143–5, 148nn28–30, 150, 165, 167, 178, 187, 199–206, 211n1, 220
   See also Covenant, Justice, Natural Law, Peace and Torah.
Lay faithful 53, 68n7, 124, 228, 288, 290
Levi 271
Life
   Catholic/Christian life 3, 8, 12, 56, 79, 84, 109, 202, 206, 225, 233, 237, 288, 295n5
   divine life 4, 77, 105, 107, 218, 234, 288–9, 291
   faith and life 12, 29, 35, 59, 93, 240, 279, 290
   from conception to natural death 158, 245
   source of life 21, 27, 61, 103, 189, 260, 263
   See also Consecrated Life, Eternal Life, and Spiritual Life.
Light
   of eternity 44, 60, 62, 64, 74, 129n21, 232, 234, 291
   of Christ (Light of the world) 2, 4, 59, 67, 129n21, 232, 233, 283, 293
   of the Church 42
   of the Father 59, 60, 62, 64, 74, 248n22, 281, 288
   of the Holy Spirit 86
Liturgy 18, 29, 53, 63, 66, 117, 124, 178n23, 185, 228, 234, 237, 254, 256, 270, 271, 299

## INDEX OF PROPER NAMES AND SUBJECTS

Liturgy of the Word 66, 270
 Liturgy of the Eucharist 271
Locke, John 138–9
Love, *See* also *Caritas*
 of creation 243
 of God, *See* God, love of.
 of Jesus Christ 63, 93, 200–1, 205, 280–1, 290
 of neighbour 105, 187, 208
 of the things of God 25
 of the Trinity 105, 272
 voice of 6
Lucy, Saint 64
Luke, Saint (Evangelist) 27, 31, 43, 49, 73, 74, 125, 183, 267, 268, 269

*Magisterium* (teaching office of the Church) 105, 113–4
Marriage 17, 119, 205, 224, 245, 263, 271
Martyrs 33, 34, 49, 57, 64, 69n10, 125–6, 262, 264, 266n4, 269, 275n3, 278, 285n5, 298
Mary Magdalene 43, 45
Mary, Blessed Virgin
 Annunciation 45, 49, 64, 74, 75
 Assumption 235
 Blessed Virgin 52, 75, 232, 246, 246n1, 247n2, 277, 284
 Madonna of humility 55
 Mother of Jesus 31, 49, 55, 233, 284
 Mother of the Church 41–2, 55, 233, 246
 Mother of Sorrows 44, 55

Our Lady 48, 55, 64, 231–2, 235, 284
Our Lady of the Rosary 231–2, 306
*Theotokos* 49, 55, 68n9
Mass 28, 54, 57, 62–6, 78, 93, 147n4, 194–195, 199, 206, 212n14, 225, 232–5, 239, 240, 246, 247n6, 256n1, 264, 270–3, 277, 289, 297
 *See* also Communion and Eucharist.
Matthew, Saint (Evangelist) 27, 31, 50, 76, 181n62, 287
McKinney, Bishop Patrick 256
Meditation 5, 53, 58, 61
Mercy
 *See* God, mercy of.
 corporal works of mercy 228, 292–3
 spiritual works of mercy 228, 292–3
*Metanoia* 3 *See* also Repentance.
Michael, Saint 155
Michelangelo 113
*Midrash Rabbah, Song of Songs* 184, 196n1
Mill, James 138
Mill, John Stuart 138
Ministry 223–95
 holy orders, *See* Holy Orders.
Mission 2, 5, 7, 11–12, 24, 57–9, 66, 69n10, 70n11, 76–79, 83, 105, 109–110, 140, 177nn17–18, 203–4, 206, 211, 212n13, 226–8, 238, 243–5, 268, 272–3, 287–95, 302

# INDEX OF PROPER NAMES AND SUBJECTS

Missionary disciples, *See* Disciples.
Moral Theology (Morality), *See* Ethics.
Moses 187, 245
Mosque 154
Motherhood 27–8, 31, 44–45, 53, 89, 233, 240
Mozart, Wolfgang Amadeus 113
Muamba, Fabrice 119–20, 128n11
Music 18, 113, 117
Muslim, *See* Islam.
Mystery
  *See* God, mystery of and Jesus Christ, mystery of.
Mysticism 15, 26n4, 30, 33, 239

National Gallery, London 30, 68n8, 117, 127n7, 305
Nativity 30–35, 38, 56, 67, 67n1, 68nn4&8, 74, 75
  *The Nativity with Saints Altarpiece*,
  *See* Pietro Orioli.
Natural law 143, 167, 178n26, 203–5
Nature, *See* Creation.
Newman, Blessed John Henry 8, 131–51, 185, 303, 308
  *The Idea of a University* 133, 137, 146n1, 147nn2, 9–13, 148nn16–25
Nicholas, Saint 31–32, 53, 56–7, 65

Obedience 47, 77, 227, 241, 248n17, 263, 279

Ordination 89, 151, 202, 225–6, 251, 253–6, 264, 270–1, 273, 274, 275
Origen 9, 10n2
  *Homilies on Genesis and Exodus,* 10n2
Orioli, Pietro 7, 30–71, 74, 306
  *The Nativity with Saints Altarpiece* 7, 30–71, 74, 306
Oscott, St Mary's College 184–6, 197n7
Oxford University
  Oriel College 136
Our Lady, *See* Mary, Blessed Virgin.

Palestine 27
Palmer, Martin 154–6, 176nn3–6, 177nn7–9
Papacy 225, 231–49
Paradise 39, 50
Passover 46, 74, 189
Pastoral care 59, 60, 62, 63, 136, 146, 185, 200, 229n1, 263, 271, 277, 293, 299, 302
Patience 84, 150, 194
Patriarchs and Matriarchs 187
Paul, Saint, (Saul) 2, 8, 31, 48–9, 64, 70n11, 81–2, 84, 105, 109, 150, 199, 213–5, 221, 232, 264, 279
Paul VI, Pope 233, 247n5
Peace 3, 5, 43, 47, 75, 84, 126, 133, 145, 146, 158, 162–4, 185, 188, 190, 201, 203, 204, 205, 209, 214, 244, 256
Pentecost 12, 46, 48, 49, 73, 74, 77, 87n6, 126, 255, 260

# INDEX OF PROPER NAMES AND SUBJECTS

People of God 67, 76, 228, 237, 247n5, 287–95
Peter, Saint (Simon) 38, 41, 48–9, 57, 64, 183, 199, 238, 240, 241, 243, 259–62, 264, 266n4
Philip, the evangelist 114–5, 269
Philosophy
   of education 92, 100, 138–40
   of virtue 201
Pilgrim 46, 56, 74, 215, 219
   pilgrim Church 59, 247n2
Pilgrimage (Journey of Faith) 7, 52, 56, 59, 64, 78, 87n7, 169, 175, 193, 203, 219, 232, 238, 272, 277, 293
Plato 166, 211n1
Poetry 35, 68n3, 126, 128n17, 172
Polycarp, Saint 272, 298
   *Epistle to the Philippians* 275n2, 298
Poor, the 2, 31, 32, 39, 64, 86, 208, 227, 228, 243, 260, 269, 271
Pope (successor of St Peter) *See* Papacy.
   Bishop of Rome 238, 241, 274
Poverty 32, 193, 205, 211, 216, 219, 227, 243, 259, 260, 279, 285
Praise 45, 59, 64, 75, 80, 86, 126, 190
Prayer
   and the Holy Spirit 86, 195, 222, 241
   before the Blessed Sacrament 208, 239–40, 271, 285n5, 289
   contemplative 13–25, 170–6, 228, 285n6
   liturgical 54, 64, 208, 228, 235, 277
   of the Psalms 189–90, 269
   of the rosary 233
   silent 5, 25, 120, 239–40
   unceasing prayer 124, 242
   *See* also *Divine Office.*
Preaching 3, 9, 26n7, 28, 49, 58, 73, 74, 109, 110–11, 126, 128n10, 150, 210, 212n14, 232, 235, 236, 238, 239, 240, 243, 246, 247n6, 256, 256n1, 257n4, 261, 263, 264, 265n1, 268–9, 270, 275, 284, 290
Presbyterate (Priests) 59–65, 259–66
Presentation of the Lord 281–4
Priesthood, *See* Presbyterate.
   (High-)priesthood of Christ 239, 265n1
   priesthood of all believers 223, 224
Proclamation (of the Gospel) 2–4, 8, 34, 49, 51, 58, 59, 63, 66, 70n10, 73, 74–9, 85, 105, 109–14, 118, 120, 145, 157, 160, 204, 206, 209, 210, 220, 227, 228, 237, 241, 243, 249n24, 255, 260, 261, 264, 267, 268–75, 277, 281–4, 294, 303

Ratzinger, Cardinal Joseph, *See* Benedict XVI, Pope (Emeritus).
Reason 97, 142–4, 146, 155, 157, 166–8, 171, 200, 203–5
   rationality 17, 91, 145

## INDEX OF PROPER NAMES AND SUBJECTS

Reconciliation 150, 159
Redemption 43, 46, 48, 49, 53, 59–61, 105, 205, 235, 245, 264, 291
Refugees 220–1
Reign, of God, *See* Kingdom of God.
Relativism
  deficiencies of 119–24, 159–61, 216–7
Religion
  other religions 157–64
Religious freedom 160, 202 *See* also Freedom.
Religious heritage 154–7, 175, 176
Religious imagery 18 *See* also Symbol.
Religious leadership 28, 42, 46, 50, 109, 149, 163, 178n22, 199, 201–3, 209, 236, 252, 267
Religious Orders, *See* Consecrated Life.
Religious Studies 103–5, 108nn14–15, 131
Repentance 28, 43, 74, 199, 232
Resurrection, *See* Jesus Christ.
  final resurrection 213, 234, 284, 291
Revelation (God revealed) 11–87
Richard III, King 252, 256n1
Richard of Chichester, Saint 294, 295n6
Righteousness 41, 45, 146, 176n1, 185, 192, 199, 204, 220, 291
Roman Empire 27, 50, 155, 214
  Caesar 27, 165, 201

Roman authorities 28, 50, 183
  *Pax Romana* 50
Ryder, Sue 69n10

Sacks, Rabbi Jonathan 217, 222n4, 309
Sacraments 17, 60, 63, 77, 78, 194, 206, 208, 223–4, 257n4, 263, 265n1, 270, 271, 273, 277, 287
  sacraments of initiation 223
SACRE (Standing Advisory Council on Religious Education) 90
Sacredness 154–7
Sacrifice 34, 39, 43–4, 54, 57, 60–2, 64, 67, 106, 124, 193, 215, 224, 227, 234, 238–9, 244, 255, 262, 265n1, 266n4, 271, 278, 279, 282, 284
Saints 7, 12, 30, 31, 33, 53, 55, 64, 67, 67n1, 68nn4&8, 74, 118, 122, 127n7, 128n15, 129n21, 135, 147n7, 155, 203, 208, 233, 234, 248n22, 264, 297–301
Salvation 2, 4, 7, 22, 28, 29, 32, 38, 40, 45–7, 49–57, 60–2, 64–6, 69n9, 75, 77, 117, 126–7, 127n7, 150, 159–60, 177n12, 207, 215, 221, 224, 228, 233, 254–5, 260, 282, 294
Santa Maria Maggiore (Basilica) 246
Schilling, Alfred 185–6, 197n7

# INDEX OF PROPER NAMES AND SUBJECTS

School
   *See* Catholic schools and Education.
Sciences 133, 137–8, 140, 142, 144–5, 281
Scripture, Sacred 6, 48, 65, 105, 113, 186, 237, 270, 289, 297, 299
Second Vatican Council (Vatican II)
   *See* Vatican Council, Second.
Septuagint 297
Servant Songs 267–8
   Suffering Servant 268
Service
   of God 27, 59, 84, 113, 146, 195, 206, 224, 226–8, 267–76, 279
   of others 8, 59, 84, 98, 132, 145, 195, 224, 226–8, 263, 267–76, 279
   of the common good 98, 146
   of the Gospel/Word of God 63, 65, 66, 114
   to Christ 61
*Shema* 187
*Shoah* 190–3
Siena 6, 10n1, 30, 53, 67n1, 68n4, 308
Sign of the Cross 27
Sikhism 162
Silence 5, 18, 20, 21, 23, 25, 26n7, 120, 121, 128n12, 170–1, 199, 202, 239, 241, 252, 255, 289
   *See also* Desert, Silent.
Simeon (prophet) 210–11, 282–3
   *See also* Hymn of Simeon (*Nunc dimittis*)

Sin 2, 4, 8, 39, 43–6, 51, 52, 56, 58, 61, 64, 74, 81, 126, 181n60, 187, 192, 203, 205, 213, 224, 231, 243, 245, 255, 279, 290
   forgiveness of, *See* Forgiveness.
   repentance of, *See* Repentance.
   social sin 243
Sisters, Religious 71n18, 86n1, 89, 108n9, 179n32, 194, 220, 227, 229n3, 278, 285n5, 305
   *See also* Consecrated Life.
Sinai, Mount 187
Smith, Fr Cyprian 14, 20–1, 25nn2&4, 26nn5–6&9
Solomon, King 143, 145, 251, 252, 257n3
Son of God, *See* Jesus Christ.
Sons and Daughters of God 4, 5, 63, 82, 190–1, 219
Soul 15, 19–22, 23, 25nn1&4, 26n7, 29, 44, 45, 47, 132, 149, 171, 176n1, 187, 191, 200, 202, 213, 214, 222, 237, 255, 256n1, 301
   Ground of the Soul 19–22
Spirit, *See* Holy Spirit.
Spirituality 7, 8, 23, 114, 181n62, 185, 208, 289
Spiritual Life 14–16, 22–5, 25n2, 171, 172, 212n12, 309
Spiritual quest 153, 156, 169–81
State, the 200–3, 206, 209, 214, 303
Stephen, Saint 33, 53, 57–8, 64, 125–6, 269

## INDEX OF PROPER NAMES AND SUBJECTS

St Mary's University, Twickenham 89, 90, 104, 108n15, 131, 134, 164, 169, 275
Suenens, Cardinal Leon-Josef 287, 294n1
Suffering 5, 24, 39, 43, 44, 64, 69n10, 119, 125, 128n11, 170, 172, 174, 188, 190, 197n10, 216, 220–1, 235, 239, 266n4
   *See* also Jesus Christ, suffering of.
Symbol/Symbolism 18, 38, 40, 43, 45, 49, 50, 53, 55–58, 60–3, 73–4, 87n3, 189, 207, 254–5, 266n4
Synagogue 154, 177n19, 184–90
   *Singers Hill Synagogue*, Birmingham 184–90


Tann, Rabbi 184
Teaching
   Art as teacher 29, 61, 63, 65
   Church teaching 3, 6, 8, 10, 23, 56–7, 61, 74, 86n2, 99, 103, 105, 110, 113, 126, 127n6, 128n15, 159–60, 177nn10&14, 183, 187, 203–5, 210, 232–3, 236–8, 297–303
   teaching of Jesus, *See* Jesus Christ
   teaching of the Holy Spirit 77, 244
   *See* also Catholic Social Teaching and Education.
Temple (Jerusalem) 40, 188, 259–60, 271, 282
   Beautiful Gate 259–61, 264

Tent of Meeting 271
   Western Wall 188
Teresa Benedicta of the Cross, Saint, (Edith Stein) 179n32, 278
Teresa of Avila, Saint 218
Teresa of Calcutta, Saint Mother 78, 208, 212n12
Thanksgiving (Mass of) 45, 232, 233, 235, 240, 246, 264
Theology 6, 7, 20, 23, 31, 35, 59, 69n9, 70nn14&18, 86nn1–2, 87n5, 89, 104, 105, 110, 111, 117, 127n3, 131, 137, 138, 140, 145, 185–6, 197n3, 200, 206, 214, 235–8, 242, 247nn9&12, 300, 306–9
Theophany 1
*Theotokos*, *See* Mary, Blessed Virgin.
Thérèse of Lisieux, Saint 23–25, 26n7, 280, 301, 309
   *Story of a Soul* 24, 26nn7–8, 280, 285n8, 301
   the little way 24
Thomas, Saint 251, 254, 256
Thomas à Kempis 58
Tomb (of Jesus) 36, 46, 48, 51
Torah (*Sepher Torah*) 184, 186–9
Trinity, Blessed 6, 11–12, 20–21, 27, 54, 74, 77–9, 105–6, 206, 225; 234, 237, 272, 281, 288, 291, 299
   *See* also God, the Father; Jesus Christ, the Son; Holy Spirit; *Communio*.
Triune God, *See* Trinity.
Truth
   Holy Spirit as guide to all Truth 160

Jesus Christ/Word, the Truth
112–13, 159, 239, 254–5,
261, 272, 280–1, 294
of Church teaching 19, 34,
65, 95, 223
of faith 3, 11, 113, 119–24, 127,
132, 233
of God 16–18, 21, 35, 77, 95,
96–7, 105, 106, 113, 159–60,
194, 201, 256, 288, 290
of love 36–7, 39, 105, 146, 194
of ourselves 20, 35, 95,
97, 106
of the Gospel 118, 254–5
pathway of 119–24

Unity 49, 56–7, 70n11, 74, 93,
150, 159–60, 162, 164, 185,
225, 238, 259, 261, 263–4,
269, 273–4, 280, 287
Universities 7, 89, 93, 104,
110–11, 131–48
curriculum 131, 137, 138–40
role in the modern
world 140–2
See also Education.
University College London 139

Vatican Council, Second 76, 83,
105, 108n13, 109, 177n18,
201, 236, 247nn9&12,
265n3, 287, 294n1, 301–2
*Dei Verbum* 71n19, 302
*Lumen Gentium* 67, 177n17,
223–4, 247n2, 271,
287–8, 302
*Gaudium et Spes* 67, 83, 178n27,
201, 204, 205, 210, 288, 302
*Nostra Aetate* 108n13, 150,
177nn13&15, 178n21, 302

*Ad Gentes* 109, 110, 177n18,
302
Viaticum (ministry to the
dying) 271
Virtue 4, 6, 7, 41, 54, 58, 84,
87n2, 99, 102–3, 106–7,
110, 124, 126, 157, 176n1,
201, 210, 214, 219–22,
222n1, 255, 288
cardinal virtues 103
theological virtues 105–7,
124, 210, 214, 219–22
See also Faith, Hope & Love,
and *Caritas*.
Vocation 4, 24, 38, 39, 45, 61, 64,
66, 101, 109, 173, 174, 225,
226–7, 269, 273–4, 278–9,
281, 282, 288, 293
See also Calling.
Vulgate 297

Waugh, Evelyn 13
Westerbork 170,
179n32, 180n55
Westminster Cathedral 29, 206,
212n14, 223, 235, 239, 240,
246, 264, 275, 284
Will (Volition),
divine will, See God, will of.
human will 6, 69n10, 75, 91,
101, 144, 214, 215
Williams, Archbishop
Rowan 178n31
Wisdom (Knowledge) 7, 12,
52, 54, 57, 70n11, 79, 82,
103, 105, 114, 126, 135,
143, 145, 166, 168, 202,
204, 223, 238, 242, 251–3,
256, 257n3, 267, 268,
282, 288

Witness 5, 23, 24, 31, 42, 47–50, 96, 97, 118, 146, 157, 162, 164, 175, 196, 209, 221, 222n6, 231, 232, 239, 244, 260, 280, 281
Wonder 30, 126, 132, 187, 223, 305
Word of God, *See* Jesus Christ.
Worship 8, 16, 53–6, 58, 59, 61, 69n9, 74, 78, 82, 90, 105, 106, 132, 155, 160, 162, 202, 225, 237, 244, 261, 289
*See* also Prayer.

*Yad Vashem Memorial*, Jerusalem 190–3
Year of Faith 237, 261, 265n3
Year of Mercy 87n7, 206, 249n27, 289, 295n3

Zoroastrians 163, 178n23

*A Note on the Author*

**His Eminence Cardinal Vincent Nichols**
Born Crosby, Liverpool 8 November 1945. Ordained Priest in Rome on 21 December 1969 for the Archdiocese of Liverpool. Appointed assistant priest in St Mary's Parish, Wigan and chaplain to the Sixth Form College and St Peter's High School in 1971. Ordained Bishop of the titular see of Othona and Auxiliary Bishop of Westminster on 24 January 1992. Translated to Birmingham as Archbishop on 29 March 2000, and to Westminster on 21 May 2009. Created Cardinal Priest of the Most Holy Redeemer and St Alphonsus Liguori on 22 February 2014. He is the President of the Bishops' Conference of England and Wales and Vice President of the Council of the Bishops' Conference of Europe (CCEE).

*A Note on the Type*

The text of this book is set in Bembo, which was first used in 1495 by the Venetian printer Aldus Manutius for Cardinal Bembo's *De Aetna*. The original types were cut for Manutius by Francesco Griffo. Bembo was one of the types used by Claude Garamond (1480–1561) as a model for his Romain de l'Université, and so it was a forerunner of what became the standard European type for the following two centuries. Its modern form follows the original types and was designed for Monotype in 1929.